Fighter Operations in Europe & North Africa 1939–1945

Fighter Operations in Europe & North Africa 1939–1945

David Wragg

Pen & Sword
AVIATION

First published in Great Britain in 2012 by
PEN & SWORD AVIATION
An imprint of
Pen & Sword Books Ltd
47 Church Street
Barnsley
South Yorkshire
S70 2AS

ISBN 978-1-84884-481-0

A CIP catalogue record for this book is available from the British Library.

Typeset by Concept, Huddersfield, West Yorkshire.
Printed and bound in England by CPI Group (UK) Ltd, Croydon, CRO 4YY.

Pen & Sword Books Ltd incorporates the imprints of Pen & Sword Aviation,
Pen & Sword Maritime, Pen & Sword Military, Wharncliffe Local History,
Pen & Sword Select, Pen & Sword Military Classics, Leo Cooper,
Remember When, Seaforth Publishing and Frontline Publishing

For a complete list of Pen & Sword titles please contact
PEN & SWORD BOOKS LIMITED
47 Church Street, Barnsley, South Yorkshire, S70 2AS England
E-mail: enquiries@pen-and-sword.co.uk
Website: www.pen-and-sword.co.uk

Contents

List of Plates

10. The main opposition, not just during the Battle of Britain, was the Messerschmitt Bf109, which appeared in many guises, each usually more formidable than the one it replaced. Although not available on early versions, the fitting of a cannon firing through the propeller hub made the aircraft even more effective.

11. When the Germans struck east in Operation Barbarossa, invading the Soviet Union, one of the more modern Russian aircraft encountered was the Yakovlev Yak-1, but for the most part the *Luftwaffe* encountered obsolete types.

12. In Malta, aerial bombardment was so heavy, especially over airfields, that stone 'sangers' were built to protect aircraft on three sides whilst on the ground. Army and Navy personnel often helped in the work of construction as there were few RAF ground personnel on the island.

13. When Italy entered the war, the only fighter defence available for Malta was the Gloster Sea Gladiator, three of which became the famous trio of *Faith*, *Hope* and *Charity*.

14. A typical wartime shot, with a mobile AA gun to protect this Spitfire as it is serviced between sorties.

15. Fighter pilots of No. 213 Hurricane Squadron being debriefed after a sortie at a base in the Western Desert.

16. Supermarine Spitfire wearing desert markings. Aircraft camouflage had to be changed as the theatre of operations changed.

17. A more effective fighter than the Bf109 was the Focke-Wulf Fw190, seen here lined up. It was not available in time for the Battle of Britain or for the invasion of the USSR.

18. Not all fighters had a base to return to or even an aircraft carrier, such as this Sea Hurricane, which belonged to the RAF's Merchant Service Fighter Unit, whose aircraft were catapulted off CAM-ships (catapult-armed merchant ships). They made a single sortie and the pilot then had to bale out and hope to be picked up.

19. The solution to the heavy night bombing was the night fighter, once airborne radar could be provided – first on the Bristol Beaufighter and then later on the de Havilland Mosquito, one of which is seen here.

20. The Messerschmitt Me110 was originally used at the outset of the Battle of Britain as a long-range escort fighter, but it was no match for the Spitfire and was soon switched to other duties. Later, it did become an effective night fighter.

21. The USAAF's arrival in Britain soon brought long-range escort fighters to the skies over occupied Europe. One of these was the North American P-51 (later F-51) Mustang, seen here with 'invasion stripes'. These are early versions without the later bubble canopy and licence-built Merlin engine.

22. The Mustang as most people recall it, as a much more handsome aircraft with a bubble canopy.

23. The twin-boom fuselage of the Lockheed P-38 (later F-38) was distinctive. This was one of the most successful long-range escorts.

24. Despite its rotund appearance, the Republic P-47 (later F-47) Thunderbolt was an effective fighter, albeit one that seems to have been prone to burst into flames, if Heinz Knoke's accounts are typical of aerial combat with this aircraft.

25. The cockpit of a Thunderbolt – roomier than that of a Spitfire.

26. A Mosquito night fighter lands after a sortie. The steel strip used for runways and taxiways can be clearly seen.

27. Experience in North Africa had shown that cannon and rocket-armed fighters were highly effective against ground targets, even including armour. This was one role for the Hawker Typhoon, one of which is seen here at Gatwick. Another role was disposing of the V-1 missiles, or 'Doodlebugs'.

28. Despite almost five years of war before the Allied landings in Normandy, aircraft recognition remained poor, hence the use of black and white 'invasion' stripes on aircraft, while this was another attempt to draw attention to the distinguishing features of the Typhoon.

29. The Messerschmitt Me262 should have been the world's first jet fighter, but Hitler insisted that it be used as a bomber until Adolph Galland insisted to Goering that the policy be changed.

30. An Me262 on the ground. Once used as a fighter, the aircraft had a devastating effect on USAAF day bomber formations, and might have prolonged the conflict for a short period had it been deployed earlier to fighter squadrons.

Acknowledgements

In researching and compiling any such book as this, an author is heavily dependent on the help and assistance of many others. In particular, I am grateful to the Sound Archive and Photographic Archive teams at the Imperial War Museum.

This book looks at just one aspect of the Second World War in the air so cannot cover every inch of ground, and for those whose appetite is whetted by this book, I would draw their attention to the bibliography at the back. There are accounts of the war in the air from every perspective, including the all-important personal accounts, as well as volumes of sheer factual matter.

David Wragg
Edinburgh
June 2011

Glossary

AA – Anti-aircraft fire

AA Co-operation – Exercising with AA units, providing target tugs, simulated attacks etc.

AAEE – Aircraft and Armaments Experimental Establishment

AASF – Advanced Air Striking Force

ACM – Air Chief Marshal

ADGB – Air Defence of Great Britain (a name used until the command structure was introduced in 1936, but adopted by RAF Fighter Command later in the war)

AEAF – Allied Expeditionary Air Force

AI – Airborne Interception (radar)

Air Cdre – Air Commodore

Angels – Altitude, with 'Angels 20' meaning 20,000 feet

AOC – Air Officer Commanding

AOP – Air Observation Post – artillery spotting for the Army

ABC – Airborne Cigar – radio-jamming device

AM – Air Marshal

ASR – Air-Sea Rescue, now known as SAR, search and rescue

ASV – Air-to-Surface Vessel radar

Army Co-operation – AOP duties, tactical reconnaissance and close support

AuxAF – Auxiliary Air Force (not 'Royal' until 1947)

AVM – Air Vice-Marshal

BEF – British Expeditionary Force

Boozer – Anti-fighter radar warning device used on bombers

CAS – Chief of the Air Staff

Circus – Fighter escort for daylight bombers

Clarion – US plan to disrupt German communications

Corona – False orders broadcast to German fighters by aircraft of the RAF's 100 Group

Crossbow – 'V'-weapon countermeasures

DAF – Desert Air Force

DR – Dead Reckoning navigation

Erk – Airman below the rank of corporal

ETA – Estimated Time of Arrival

FAA – Fleet Air Arm

1st TAF – Allied First Tactical Air Force

Fishpond – Bomber anti-fighter radar warning device

Flak – AA fire (*Fliegerabwehrkanonen*)

Flt Lt – Flight Lieutenant

Flt Sgt – Flight Sergeant

F/O – Flying Officer

Gardening – Aerial mine-laying operations in coastal waters and in German ports, rivers and canals

Gee – British radar navigating device

G-H – British blind bombing device using signals transmitted from ground stations

Glycol – Aircraft engine coolant

Grand Slam – 22,000-lb 'earthquake' bomb

Grp Capt – Group Captain

HCU – Heavy Conversion Unit

H2S – RAF radar navigation and blind-bombing aid

Husky – Allied invasion of Sicily

IFF – Identification Friend or Foe – transmission to British radar screens

Mandrel – Swamping of German radar by 100 Group

Monica – Fighter warning device fitted to RAF bombers

Newhaven – Pathfinder codename for H2S combined with visual support

Nickel – Name for RAF propaganda leaflet-dropping operations over Germany

Oboe – British blind-bombing device fitted to Pathfinders

OTU – Operational Training Unit

Overlord – Normandy landings

Paramatta – Pathfinder codename for target fixing using Oboe

P/O – Pilot Officer

Pointblank – June 1943 directive from the Allied Combined Chiefs of Staff for a Combined Bomber Offensive

PRU – Photographic Reconnaissance Unit

RAAF – Royal Australian Air Force

Ramrod – Strafing fighter patrol

Razzles – Incendiary bomb for igniting forests and crops

RCAF – Royal Canadian Air Force

Rhubarb Fighter-bomber mission

RNZAF – Royal New Zealand Air Force

R/T – Radio/Telephone, i.e. voice rather than Morse

SAAF – South African Air Force

SASO – Senior Air Staff Officer

SBA – Standard Blind Approach
SCU – RAF Servicing Commando Unit
2nd TAF – Allied Second Tactical Air Force
SHAEF – Supreme Headquarters Allied Expeditionary Force
Sqn Ldr – Squadron Leader
Tallboy – 12,000lb 'earthquake' bomb
Thunderclap – Allied plan to deliver overwhelming assault on major German cities
Tinsel – Jamming of German fighter communications by radio operators on RAF bombers
Torch – Allied invasion of Vichy French North Africa
USAAF – United States Army Air Force
VCAS – Vice-Chief of the Air Staff
Wg Cdr – Wing Commander
Window – Tinfoil strips used by British bombers to confuse German radar
Wingco – Wing Commander (slang)
W-Mines – Air-dropped mines for use against locks and canal traffic
W/T – Wireless Transmission using Morse rather than voice

Introduction

There was no such thing as a phoney war for airmen, with early reconnaissance, mining and bomber missions by both sides in the months that preceded the German invasion of first Denmark and Norway and then the Low Countries and France. Nevertheless, there were distinct phases to the war in the air, as elsewhere. The early aerial combats as fighter pilots struggled to contain the German raids on the Home Fleet at Roysth and over France were as nothing compared to the Battle of Britain, when the *Luftwaffe* set out to destroy the Royal Air Force.

The phoney war was a British concept, something the Germans more aptly described as the '*Sitzkrieg*' or 'sitting war'. For the Luftwaffe, of course, the war had started a couple of days earlier with the invasion of Poland, and for them it was a burst of activity in the east followed by a relative lull in the west until the invasion of first Denmark and Norway, and then a month later of the Low Countries and then France.

That first winter of war was also far from peaceful. It marked the Winter War between the Soviet Union and Finland as the Russians sought to regain a country that had achieved independence during the Russian Civil War. Soviet might faced Finnish resistance, and while some territorial concessions were made by Finland to ensure peace, there could be no doubt that the Soviet military had failed in its objectives. Stalin's purges of senior officers in the armed services during the late 1930s were to haunt him and impair the ability of the Soviet armed forces in the severe challenges that lay ahead as the Second World War developed.

In *Fighter Operations in Europe & North Africa 1939–1945*, the story is confined to Allied and German fighter pilots in Europe, over the Mediterranean and in North Africa during the Second World War. The book starts with preparations for war as it became increasingly obvious that this was inevitable, followed by the early skirmishes as each side tested the other's defences both in the British Isles and over France with the British Expeditionary Force. It then moves through the Battle of Britain and the Blitz, when the emphasis switched from single-engined day fighters to twin-engined night fighters, while as the war progressed fighters were used to sweep over enemy airfields and lines of communication in occupied France. This overlapped with the need to provide air cover for the besieged island fortress of Malta by day and by night, as well as defensive operations against Axis forces in Crete and North Africa, but, as the balance of power changed in North Africa, the Desert Air Force was formed incorporating elements from many Allied air forces, and the emphasis moved to offensive operations in support of ground forces. The invasions of Italy and the South of France also called for fighter cover, initially by carrier-based aircraft. The lessons learnt in North Africa were put to good use by the 2nd Allied Tactical Air Force, which accompanied the advancing Allied armies towards, and eventually into, Germany.

Chapter 1

Britain Prepares for War

'The bomber will always get through!' This was the widely held and often quoted belief between the two world wars, a period of just twenty-one years from the end of hostilities and their resumption. If anything, the belief became more fixed as the years advanced and the 1920s gave way to the 1930s. After all, cinema audiences and newspaper readers were fed on accounts of Japanese atrocities in China, then Italian attacks on the tribesmen of Abyssinia (present-day Ethiopia), and the Spanish Civil War, which became a testing ground for the equipment and training ground for aircrew of the *Luftwaffe* and the *Regia Aeronautica* on the one hand, supporting the Nationalists, and the Red Air Forces on the other, supporting the Republicans.

Much of the fighter combat in the First World War had been over the Western Front and usually between fighters or fighters and scouting or reconnaissance aircraft. Although the First Lord of the Admiralty, the then Winston Churchill, had volunteered the Royal Naval Air Service for the air defence of the United Kingdom, the early fighters were still primitive. Faced with a fighter, a German Zeppelin airship simply had to dump its water ballast to out-climb most fighters of the day. The performance of the fighter was in any case often hampered by many seaplanes, or floatplanes, as they were usually known at the time, being burdened by the weight and drag of their floats. Of the others, many were burdened by being two-seaters. A rear-gunner was seen as being indispensable. When the Allies were slow to introduce aircraft with machine guns synchronised to fire through the propeller ring and went for aircraft with pusher-propellers, these too were manned by two men, whose extra weight affected performance.

Aircraft performance, or the lack of it, was not the only great weakness suffered by the fighter and anti-aircraft artillery defences of the First World War. Detection of attacking enemy aircraft of whatever kind was restricted to what many in aviation call the 'Mark One Eyeball', aided by the telephone and telegraph. The defenders had to see it coming, or perhaps hear, before they could react. Standing fighter patrols were mounted, mainly

1

over the front line, but even these struggled to engage the enemy as closely as they wished.

DETECTING THE ENEMY
Not surprisingly, between the two world wars much effort was put into systems that would provide advance warning of aerial attack. At first, radar was an unknown technology, let alone unproven. The most obvious means of detection to many scientists was sound.

The first means of detecting an attacking bomber force before it could be seen was developed in the United Kingdom and consisted of large concrete sound detectors, known as sound mirrors, most of which were located on the south coast. This process, known as sound location, was derived from an artillery technique, sound ranging, developed during the First World War. It was found that by using moveable microphones and using two sound mirrors, the source of the sound could be fixed using triangulation. Smaller, mobile sound locators were often used with anti-aircraft artillery to help locate the position of approaching enemy bombers, useful as the sound reverberating off buildings could confuse the ear.

Nevertheless, as aircraft speeds rose, sound ranging provided very little advance warning of an attack, and by the late 1930s this was just a few minutes, and insufficient for fighters to be scrambled and climb to a position from which they could attack an incoming bomber force and its fighter escort.

Fortunately, radar was to provide the answer.

Although no less than eight countries, all of them involved in the Second World War, were involved in radar research during the 1930s, the approaches differed. The most dynamic approaches were those of the United States and United Kingdom. In Japan, competition between the Imperial Japanese Navy and Imperial Japanese Army wasted much effort and progress was inefficient. In France and the Netherlands, prototype sets were in use, but work was ended by invasion. As in the US and UK, the Germans developed marine radar for naval gunnery, and anti-aircraft radar for air defence, but progress was fragmented and slow with the *Luftwaffe* and the *Kriegsmarine* fighting for resources.

The United Kingdom considered radar for a wide range of purposes, including early warning of aerial attack and ground control of interception, gun laying and both air and sea search from warships, as well as airborne detection of surface vessels and airborne interception, necessary for successful night fighter development.

Much of the credit for the use of radar in Britain's air defences goes to one A.P. Rowe, who in 1934 was an assistant to the director of scientific research at the Air Ministry, the government department that oversaw the Royal Air Force. He was shocked by the lack of preparedness against any aerial attack, and pressed for this to be given urgent treatment. At this time, the state of Britain's defences was generally poor, and the Royal Air Force, created on 1 April 1918 from the merger of the Royal Flying Corps and Royal Naval Air Service, had seen its strength drop after the end of the First World War from more than 200 squadrons to just twelve. By the early 1930s, it was on the road to recovery, but the poor state of the economy meant that progress was slow. Despite this lack of urgency and poor attention to defence, by 31 May 1935, a prototype transmitter and receiver was on trial at Orford Ness in Suffolk, on the east coast of England. The name used by the British at this time was RDF (radio direction finding), and it was not until the middle years of the Second World War that the American term 'radar' was adopted by them.

The trials were successful, and that summer a chain of early warning radar stations was planned, to become known as the Chain Home (CH) network, so that on the outbreak of war in Europe in September 1939, no less than eighteen CH stations were operational and connected to the Stanmore filter room in North London. Another two were open in Scotland, but these operated independently of the network, and so in effect were hardly part of the 'chain'. This was an astonishing achievement and involved numerous exercises involving operational units. Information went via the filter room so that it could be evaluated before being passed to the operations room. The value of the system lay not just in providing an early warning but in enabling fighters to be directed in an appropriate force to counter an enemy raid. It meant that standing patrols of fighters were not needed, and that reinforcements could be called upon as and when necessary. Each fighter group in RAF Fighter Command had its own area, but could be moved forward as and when necessary to an adjoining area.

The development of the Chain Home network also involved the British inventor of radar, Robert Watson-Watt, who made his discovery while superintendent of the radio department of the National Physical Laboratory at Teddington, just outside London. With official backing, he set up the Air Ministry's research station at Bawdsey in 1936, and in 1938 became the ministry's director of communications development.

Meanwhile, in 1937 the British Government allocated the then massive sum of £1.5 billion for defence over the ensuing five years, and changed the emphasis from bombers to an integrated air defence system.

The question arises as to why such resources were made available before the UK embarked on an all-out emergency programme of rearmament, and indeed why radar was favoured when service chiefs were demanding ships and aircraft and other armaments. Some credit this to Lord Swinton, who was Secretary of State for Air from 1935 to 1938, but according to a letter written in 1988 by the late Lord Douglas Hamilton, it also seems that British Prime Minister Neville Chamberlain was also very keen that defensive measures be pursued. This is interesting as history has dealt harshly with Chamberlain for his policy of appeasement, even though many now recognise that this bought vital time that was put to good use by the British armed forces and industry. It was also the case that not only did Chamberlain view the prospect of war with horror, with the memories of the First World War still vivid and an appreciation of just how much aircraft performance had improved, but his rejection of war was also found by the surveys of Mass Observation to be in tune with the feelings of the bulk of the population.

There was another element to the defensive preparations put in hand before the outbreak of war. Industrial production was to be as much part of the war effort as military might, and without it there would be no military might. British industry was to be switched from consumer goods and even many capital goods to war production. The peacetime output of the defence equipment industry would be inadequate for wartime demands and in any case the shipyards, aircraft, tank and gun factories would all be prime targets. There was some relocation of industry, but the main emphasis was on what became known as the 'shadow factory' system. Under this, factories that had produced cars or other inessential items found themselves earmarked to shadow the output of a defence equipment factory. For example, the Ford factory near Manchester started to produce Rolls-Royce Merlin engines, while railway workshops were turned over to producing guns and other equipment, even though this brought about a steady deterioration in the standard of service that could be provided so that the railways struggled to cope with wartime demands.

CREATING AN AIR FORCE

As already mentioned, the Royal Air Force shrank to just twelve squadrons after the First World War. In 1924, it was recognised that the new service needed reserves just as much as the two older services and the Auxiliary Air Force (AuxAF) was founded. For many years seen as an exclusive club for well-educated young men who were known as the 'weekend fliers', during the 1930s it was expanded, initially with obsolete aircraft so that flying hours could be built up, and then its role expanded to provide manpower for the barrage balloon squadrons that would be necessary to help counter a bomber offensive.

From just twelve squadrons, it was eventually planned that the RAF would consist of seventy-four squadrons, of which fifteen fighter and thirty-seven bomber squadrons would be based in the UK. Another twenty-two squadrons would be based abroad. The UK-based fighter and bomber squadrons were formed into a single command, the Air Defence of Great Britain (ADGB), although in 1936, Fighter, Bomber, Coastal and Maintenance Commands were established. A combination of the poor economy during the years of the Great Depression and the largely Treasury-inspired Ten Year Rule, which stipulated that the country would have ten years in which to prepare for a major war, meant that the planned strength was not achieved until 1936. Even this understates the situation, as many aircraft were obsolescent, and it was not unknown for squadrons to have two or more different types of aircraft. Even when new aircraft were obtained, they were sometimes simply sufficient to equip one squadron.

There was also innate conservatism even in this, the youngest of the British armed services. As late as 1932, a monoplane design for a fighter was rejected in favour of a biplane with a fixed undercarriage, the Gloster Gladiator, although at least this was the first British fighter to have an enclosed cockpit. The most charitable view one can take of this decision was that the RAF also had in mind an aircraft that could operate from aircraft carriers as the Fleet Air Arm was at the time part of the Royal Air Force until it was eventually returned to the Royal Navy. In fact, as we will see later, on Italy's entry into the war in June 1940, the air defence of Malta was in the hands of three Sea Gladiators, 'borrowed' from the Royal Navy. The Hawker Hurricane, which bore the brunt of the Battle of Britain, was the RAF's first monoplane fighter and also entered service that year, but as many senior naval officers refused to believe that high performance aircraft would operate from aircraft carriers, it was not until the pressures of war taught them differently that a Sea Hurricane appeared.

A new auxiliary creation as war loomed was the Women's Auxiliary Air Force (WAAF). Initially this was intended to free manpower for front-line duties, especially in administration and catering, but, even before the outbreak of war, they assumed many technical functions such as plotters in the operational control rooms, radar plotters, and also worked in the Y-service, which eavesdropped on *Luftwaffe* communications.

The WAAF had its origins in the Emergency Service, formed in October 1936 by Dame Helen Gwynne-Vaughan, who had been Commandant of the Women's Royal Air Force from its formation in 1918 until it disbanded in 1920. Its members committed themselves to training at least one evening a week and to attending annual summer camps, for which they received an annual fee of just ten shillings! They were treated with some disdain and described as a 'blouse and shorts army'. With the Munich Crisis of September 1938, they were absorbed into the new Auxiliary Territorial Service (ATS), with every county throughout the UK committed to raising several ATS companies that would be affiliated to a Territorial Army unit, but in each county an ATS company was to be affiliated to an AuxAF unit. The WAAF was formed from these companies on 28 June 1939, initially with 1,734 personnel spread through 47 companies, each supposed to have 67 women, and commanded by Katherine Trefusis-Forbes.

At first, women substituted for men on a ratio of three men to one woman, but later, in some trades it was a case of one for one. Apart from the obvious example of the WAAF police, no less than eighteen trades were completely served by women, including dental hygienists and wireless telegraphy slip readers. The RAF Signals Branch, which included radar, had nearly 32,000 WAAF by September 1944.

Sir Robert Watson-Watt, the pioneer of radar, believed that women would make better radar operators in the Chain Home network than men because of what he described as their 'anti-hamfistedness', and these were amongst the earliest WAAF trade recruits, but for reasons of secrecy, they, and the plotters, were simply known as Special Duties Clerks (or in British service terminology, 'clks sd').

The expansion plans were soon to be proved necessary, but this was not the widespread view at the time. For every person who saw the emerging threat from Germany, and even from Italy and Japan, both of which had been First World War allies, there were another nine who could not imagine another war, and even those for whom peace at almost any price seemed reasonable.

When war did come, the RAF had just an eighth of the manpower of the *Luftwaffe* and two-sevenths of its equipment. For many this disparity was all too clear and German success, especially in Poland, led many to believe that the enemy was invincible. Frederick Gash was a sergeant in the RAF at the time. He recalls: 'We felt we had to stop the Germans if they tried to invade. I did talk to several of my [No.] 264 [Squadron] friends and comrades about that. "What are we going to do if the Germans do get here?" And most of them said, "We have got to stop them from getting here ... We've just got to stop them."'

THE ROYAL AIR FORCE

In common with the British Army, but unlike the Royal Navy,[1] the headquarters for the Royal Air Force was completely separate from the operational commands. From its creation until the 1960s, the RAF had its own department of state, the Air Ministry, with a minister of Cabinet rank, the Secretary of State for Air. Nevertheless, there were points in common between all three services, with each run by a board or council comprised of senior officers, politicians and civil servants.

In the case of the RAF, the ruling body was the Air Council, presided over by the Secretary of State for Air, while the head uniformed member was the Chief of the Air Staff (CAS). The Chief of the Air Staff was commander-in-chief of the Royal Air Force, as well as having intelligence, planning and operations under his control. Two other uniformed members were the Deputy Chief of the Air Staff (DCAS), who concentrated on planning, and the Assistant Chief of the Air Staff (ACAS), who was the link between the Air Ministry and the operational commands. The other uniformed members were the Air Member for Personnel (AMP); Air Member for Supply and Organisation (AMSO); Air Member for Training (AMT); and the Vice Chief of the Air Staff (VCAS), who was the deputy to the Chief of the Air Staff. A civilian member was the Air Member for Development and Production. This post disappeared in May 1940, with the creation of the Ministry of Aircraft Production under Lord Beaverbrook, but under the guise of the Controller of Research and Development, this post re-emerged in 1941, while also performing the vital role of representing the Ministry of Aircraft Production on the Air Council.

The Air Council in 1939 was chaired by the Rt. Hon. Kingsley Wood, MP, as President of the Council, with Captain H.H. Balfour as Parliamentary Under-Secretary of State for Air; Air Chief Marshal Sir Cyril Newall as Chief of the Air Staff; Air Vice-Marshal C.F.A. Portal as Air Member for Personnel; Air Marshal Sir Wilfred Freeman as Air Member for Development and Production; Air Vice-Marshal W.L. Welsh as Air Member for Supply and Organisation; E.J.H. Lemon as Director-General of Production; and Sir Arthur Street as Permanent Under-Secretary of State for Air. Deputy Chief of the Air Staff was Air Vice-Marshal R.E.C. Peirse.

The 1936 re-organisation had split the RAF into Bomber, Fighter, Coastal, Reserve and Training Commands, but Reserve Command was absorbed by Training Command, which in turn split into Flying Training and Technical Training Commands early in the war. Wartime demands meant that new commands were established, including Army Co-operation, Balloon, Maintenance and Ferry Commands, with the last-named and the Air Transport Auxiliary together responsible for the delivery of aircraft from factories to operational units. Ferry Command was absorbed into Transport Command when that was established in 1943. Army Co-operation Command dated from 1940 to coordinate and direct air operations that were in direct support of ground forces, but disappeared in June 1943, into the Second Tactical Air Force as preparations for the Normandy landings began in earnest. The Army's Anti-Aircraft Command was under the operational control of Fighter Command for the air defence of the UK. The fact that Balloon Command belonged entirely to the RAF reflected the thinking that had led to the creation of the RAF in the first place, which was that if it flew it belonged to them, and this was only starting to undo with the return of the Fleet Air Arm to the Admiralty.

Essentially, Fighter Command had Nos. 10–13 Groups; Balloon Command, 30–33 Groups; and Army Co-operation Command, 70 and 71 Groups.

This was very much the UK headquarters structure, with another set of organisations, the overseas air forces, responsible for day-to-day operating matters. The overseas commands included RAF Middle East, based on Cairo; RAF Mediterranean, based on Valletta; RAF Far East, based on Singapore; and the Royal Air Force in Palestine and Trans-Jordan, based on Jerusalem; British Forces in Iraq, based on Habbaniya; and Air Forces in India (covering both RAF units and Royal Indian Air Force units), based on Simla, as well as British Forces in Aden. These differed from the home commands in that they were all-embracing, having their own fighter, bomber, army co-operation and maritime-reconnaissance elements, and air transport as well, which had been an important function from the earliest days of the RAF, although for many years hybrid 'bomber-transports' were the mainstay.[2]

Each command had its own air officer commanding-in-chief, or AOC, who applied the policies and priorities laid down by the Air Ministry, but was free to use his resources as he saw fit to achieve the desired results. Below him came the operational groups, usually spread over a number of stations, each with its own commanding officer, and each station had its squadrons. In Fighter Command, wings were usually interposed between the group and the squadron, usually with three squadrons to a wing and two wings to a group. Fighter Command also had a sector structure.

There were some blurred edges. In addition to the above, there was an Air Ministry Directorate of Air-Sea Rescue within Fighter Command, but in August 1941, such operations in open waters passed to Coastal Command, while Fighter Command retained control of operations around the coast. Initially the Army had responsibility for airfield security, but an RAF Regiment was formed in February 1942, although for the first two years of its existence its members wore khaki uniforms rather than Air Force blue. At first, they were also looked down upon by the air and ground crews who saw themselves as technical specialists and so 'true RAF'. The formation of the RAF Regiment was largely prompted by the loss of Crete, with the invasion led by German paratroops and glider-landed troops. The new organisation expanded rapidly so that by the end of the war there were more than 220 RAF Regiment squadrons, although the armoured car squadrons remained with the Army until 1946.

Notes

1. The British Army was run by the War Office and the Royal Navy by the Admiralty. Uniquely, the Admiralty was an operational headquarters as well as a strategic and political headquarters. This meant that it could, and often did, bypass local commanders and go straight to subordinate commanders, including the commanding officers of individual warships, with direct orders.
2. This was a marked difference to the *Luftwaffe* practice, in which there were no dedicated transport pilots. Instead, whenever a major airlift was needed, instructors were taken from the flying training schools, which interrupted pilot training, and obviously could do so dramatically if heavy losses were incurred. Flying transport aircraft over a hostile battlefield was never the soft option that it might seem.

Chapter 2

The Fighter Forces

While the United Kingdom, France, Germany and Italy were all expecting war sooner or later, not every country was expecting to have to fight. Amongst the exceptions was Belgium, which had been involved in the First World War and, except for a small area around Ostend, almost completely overrun. The Belgians knew that they would be dependent once again on Britain and France even as the threat of war in Europe became real, but defence was accorded a low priority between the wars and there were no joint exercises with the country's putative allies.

By contrast, Germany needed armed forces for its plans, which were presented to many of the German people and those concerned at German expansionism as simply regaining territory lost after the First World War, or of reuniting their fellow ethnic Germans scattered across much of Europe. The real cause was, of course, the need for *Lebensraum* (living space).

Italian plans were different to the extent that the country wanted the prestige of a colonial empire and saw Africa and the Balkans as the natural places for expansion. While there had been an arms race with France during the 1930s, it is doubtful whether either country wished to take the other on in warfare, and, indeed, France had passed up the chance when Italy invaded Abyssinia, in 1935, when Italian ambitions could have been curbed simply by closing the Suez Canal to Italian shipping. This would have left metropolitan France on the front line with a border with Italy, but there would have been British support, mainly from its main Mediterranean naval base in Malta, but with other bases at Gibraltar and Alexandria.

Like Germany, the Soviet Union felt that it had a right to influence the surrounding states and wanted to regain those areas lost during the Russian Civil War. Some, such as the Ukraine, had been recovered quickly, but both Finland and Poland had managed to retain their independence.

There was mutual suspicion between Germany and the Soviet Union, but there was also much inter-dependence. The USSR had been a successful bolt hole for German aircraft designers during the period when their activities were banned by the Treaty of Versailles. Germany needed

9

food and fuel from the USSR, and the latter needed the hard currency and access to technology.

The Netherlands, Denmark and Norway had not been involved during the First World War and saw their salvation in any future conflict as lying in neutrality once again. The Germans did not see it this way, as their failure to control the Skagerrak and Kattegat had enabled British submarines to penetrate into the Baltic during the First World War, only leaving when the spread of the Bolshevik Revolution denied them suitable bases. There was another problem. With few natural resources other than coal, German industry was heavily reliant on Swedish iron ore. The direct route was through the Gulf of Bothnia and the Baltic, but the Gulf of Bothnia became icebound in winter leaving a railway journey to a Norwegian port and coastal shipping as the only viable all-year alternative. The fear was that the Allies might seize Norway and even Denmark as well, with the latter marking a second front in the land war for both sides.

The United States was hoping that war could be avoided in Europe, and, if it did happen, that the US could maintain its policy of isolation. This was the official view and not shared by many Americans, especially those with Jewish connections who were all too aware of what was happening inside Germany.

It is worth looking at the state of the major air forces during the immediate pre-war years and at the outset of the conflict. The air forces are taken in the order in which they first encountered combat, and while Hungary, Romania and Yugoslavia were involved, these were relatively minor players during the air war. It is also worth remembering that Finland endured a Winter War with the Soviet Union during the first winter of war, 1939–1940.

THE *LUFTWAFFE*

Although its history was not quite as long as that of the United Kingdom, German military air power dated from the purchase of a Zeppelin dirigible in 1907. By the start of the First World War a Military Air Service (MAS) was in existence, and during the war years tactical developments included the introduction of large fighter formations – known as 'flying circuses'. All this came to an end with the signing of the Treaty of Versailles in June 1919, disbanding the MAS in 1920, prohibiting the manufacture of military aircraft and even, until 1926, restricting the size of civil aircraft that Germany could build. The Treaty conditions were circumvented through training pilots in so-called civil gliding schools and at a centre established in the USSR in 1928, while aircraft factories were established in Russia, Sweden and Turkey. A nucleus of wartime pilots was also secretly retained.

After Adolf Hitler came to power in 1933, the *Luftwaffe* was established in March 1935, as an autonomous air force taking absolute control over all German service aviation. The new *Luftwaffe*'s initial aircrew and other key personnel were based on a core of wartime veterans, boosted by graduates from the flying schools. Aircraft design and development was achieved through bomber types being developed in the guise of airliners for Deutsche Luft Hansa, the national airline and predecessor of today's Lufthansa. The *Luftwaffe* was soon equipped with Heinkel He51 fighters, He45 and HE46 reconnaissance aircraft, Junkers Ju52/3M transports, Dornier Do11 and Do23 bombers and Focke-Wulf Fw44 Stieglitz and Arado Ar66 trainers. A research centre was established by the *Luftwaffe* to evaluate new aircraft, many of which were to play an important part in the Second World War. Within a short time, the young *Luftwaffe* had 2,000 aircraft.

New aircraft designs were soon feeding into the *Luftwaffe*'s operational units, including the Messerschmitt Bf109 and Me110 fighters, Junkers Ju87 Stuka dive-bombers, and Dornier Do17 and Heinkel He111 bombers. Invaluable operational experience came when the Spanish Civil War broke out, and Germany allied herself with the Nationalists, with aircraft flown by the 'volunteers' of the German Condor Legion. More up-to-date aircraft followed to counter new Soviet fighters also finding their way to Spain on the Republican side. In 1937, Messerschmitt Bf109B/C fighters replaced the He51s. The Condor Legion returned to Germany in 1939 when the war ended. The conflict had tested aircraft and tactics, and given personnel invaluable combat experience.

The annexation of Austria and the Czech Sudetenland in 1938 and the occupation of Bohemia and Moldavia in 1939 were all assisted by a massive show of *Luftwaffe* air power that made resistance pointless. The Austrian Air Force was merged into the *Luftwaffe*. This was followed by a reorganisation, replacing the original *Gruppenkommandos* (area groups) with *Luftflotten* (air fleets), one of which was commanded by an Austrian officer. *Luftflotten* were divided into *Luftgou* (air districts), and these were further divided into *Gruppe* (groups), and *Staffelnen* (squadrons). At the outbreak of the Second World War in Europe in September 1939, the *Luftwaffe* had a front-line strength of almost 4,000 aircraft, including 1,300 Bf109 series fighters, 350 Ju87 Stuka dive-bombers and 1,300 Do17 and He111 bombers.

POLISH AIR FORCE
Poland gained independence from Russia in 1918, during the chaos of the Russian Civil War. During the Great War, Polish personnel had served as aviators in the Russian, German and Austrian armed forces. In 1938, the Polish Air Force (PAF – *Polskie Lotnictwo Wojskowe*) became a separate air service following army reorganisation. It had fifty-five fighters and

seventy-six bombers, as well as transport, liaison and training aircraft. More than 250 aircraft were attached to the army for AOP and liaison duties. Ambitious plans for expansion of the PAF recognised that many of its aircraft were obsolete. Yet, of the many modern aircraft planned, only the PZL P-37 bomber was in service when German forces invaded on 1 September.

The overwhelming strength of the *Luftwaffe*, with its modern aircraft, gave the Germans aerial superiority, aided by the rapid advance of the Panzer divisions and invasion by Soviet forces on 17 September, although Poland did not finally surrender until 27 September. Polish personnel took the few surviving aircraft to Rumania, where they abandoned them, and continued to France, arriving in time to provide a pool of experienced pilots for the *Armée de l'Air*. As German forces advanced westwards, Polish personnel flew Morane-Saulnier MS40C and Caudron C714 fighters before the fall of France, when they fled to the UK. Polish squadrons were formed in the RAF, initially being equipped with Hawker Hurricane fighters and Fairey Battle bombers, later replaced by Supermarine Spitfires and Vickers Wellingtons respectively. One squadron flew Boulton-Paul Defiant night fighters, later replacing these with Bristol Beaufighters and then with de Havilland Mosquitoes.

THE ROYAL AIR FORCE

Nevertheless, it was in 1936 that it was decided that the RAF needed to increase in size still further, and a target was set of 134 regular squadrons and 138 AuxAF squadrons. As bombers and maritime reconnaissance aircraft were becoming more complex, it was decided that the part-time fliers of the AuxAF would be confined to single-engined aircraft, but, in 1938, as industrial capacity rather than finance became the limiting factor in expansion, many modern aircraft types were allocated to AuxAF squadrons by the time war broke out.

In the immediate pre-war period, many new aircraft types joined the RAF. Some of these were to become classics, with a good reputation, such as the Hawker Hurricane and Supermarine Spitfire, or the Vickers Wellington bomber and the Short Sunderland maritime reconnaissance aircraft, but others, far too many, were outclassed from the start. The Fairy Battle was supposed to be a single-engined light bomber with the performance of a fighter, but it hadn't. Amongst fighters, the Boulton-Paul Defiant had a rear turret, supposedly to defend the aircraft from attack from behind, but German fighters soon learned to attack from below, and with the weight of an extra crew member and extra guns and ammunition, it was hopelessly outclassed in a dogfight and also struggled to catch even German bombers. This was not to stop Winston Churchill trying to persuade the RAF that all fighters should have a rear turret.

The outbreak of war in 1939 found Fighter Command with twenty-two squadrons of Hawker Hurricanes and Supermarine Spitfires, and another thirteen of the obsolete Gloster Gladiator biplanes. Initially, twenty-seven squadrons were deployed to France, including the light bombers of the Advanced Air Striking Force (AASF), which accompanied the British Expeditionary Force (BEF), which also had its own air component. Just 600 British and French aircraft faced more than 3,000 *Luftwaffe* aircraft. The RAF could only provide token support for the battle for Norway, partly because of the limited number of suitable airfields, but did manage to send a small number of Hawker Hurricane fighters.

At home, the headquarters of RAF Fighter Command was located at RAF Bentley Priory, near Stanmore, in Middlesex, where Air Chief Marshal Sir Hugh 'Stuffy' Dowding, the AOC of Fighter Command, had an operations room that gave a complete picture of developments. Fighter Command was divided into four regional groups. South Wales and the west of England, from Land's End to Middle Wallop, in Hampshire, was covered by 10 Group based on RAF Box in Wiltshire, under AVM Sir Quintin Brand. The south and south-east of England, as well as London, was covered by 11 Group at RAF Uxbridge, to the west of London, under AVM Keith Park. North and mid-Wales, and the Midlands as far south as Duxford, in Cambridgeshire, were covered by 12 Group at RAF Watnall, in Nottinghamshire, under AVM Trafford Leigh-Mallory. The north of England and Scotland was covered by 13 Group at RAF Kenton Bar, near Newcastle-upon-Tyne, under AVM Richard Saul.

Each group was divided into a number of sectors. The largest number of these belonged to 11 Group, closest to France, which had sector stations at Biggin Hill, Debden, Hornchurch, Kenley, Northolt, North Weald and Tangmere. Filton and Middle Wallop were the only two sectors in 10 Group, while 12 Group had sector stations at Church Fenton, Digby, Duxford, Kirton-in-Lindsey and Wittering, and 13 Group at Acklington, Dyce, Turnhouse, Usworth and Wick. Each sector station would have a number of operational fighter stations under its command, and many of the fighter stations had satellite stations in turn, sometimes because the number of aircraft movements were more than a single station could manage, but mainly as a reserve or alternate station if the main station was badly damaged in an attack.

THE *ARMEE DE L'AIR*

The origins of the French *Armée de l'Air* dated from 1910 with the formation of the *Aviation Militaire* (AM), which was involved in early experiments in aerial photography and radio transmission. In 1912, the squadron (*l'escadrille*) was created.

On the outbreak of the First World War, the AM had twenty-one squadrons in France and another four squadrons in the colonies. Rapid

13

expansion under wartime conditions saw the AM suffer sixty per cent casualties, the highest of any Allied service, in the air or otherwise. The return of peace found it with 3,480 combat aircraft in 255 squadrons. Peace saw a reduction to 180 squadrons spread across France, Germany, and in the colonies, including Algeria and Tunisia, and elsewhere in Africa. In 1920, a squadron was formed in French Indo-China with Breguet Br14 bombers. New aircraft started to appear, including Breguet Br16 bombers and Nieuport 29C fighters.

Post-war, the AM had grown into the 'fifth arm' of the French Army, behind the infantry, cavalry, artillery and engineers. In 1928, it became an autonomous air force, the *Armée de l'Air*. The new service soon suffered neglect, as the uncertain French political situation aggravated the problems already experienced during the Depression, and the lower priority accorded defence expenditure in peacetime. In 1935, events in neighbouring Germany and Italy forced an urgent modernisation and expansion programme, with deliveries of Dewoitine D501 and D520 fighters, Morane-Saulnier MS406 and Bloch MB151 fighters, Farman F221, Bloch MB210 and Liore-et-Oliver LeO 45 bombers, plus Potez and Bloch general-purpose aircraft. The programme soon fell behind, aggravated by the decision to nationalise the French aircraft industry in 1936 and 1937. As the threat of war loomed, aircraft were ordered from the USA.

THE RED AIR FORCES

Dating from 1924, the Soviet Military Aviation Forces (*Sovietskaya Voenno-Vozdushnye Sily* – SV-VS) absorbed the post-revolution Red Air Fleet. During the 1930s there was a growing emphasis on heavy bombers, despite which, Soviet military doctrine was similar to that of the Germans, with air power used in close support of ground forces rather than strategically, as with British and American forces.

In 1936, SV-VS personnel and aircraft were sent to Spain to fight on the Republican side during the Spanish Civil War, with some 1,400 of the latest Soviet fighter and bomber aircraft deployed in Spain, many of them flown by Spanish pilots. Their performance has since been claimed to have been as good as that of the German and Italian opposition flying with the Nationalist side, although the Republicans lost the war! The explanation could be that the first generation of German aircraft deployed in Spain were soon shown to be inferior, but the second generation proved to be far more effective. This period was also marked by the Soviet dictator Stalin's purges, with Andrei Tupolev imprisoned and his ANT-42 heavy bomber design, which entered service as the TB-7, later passing to Petlyakov and becoming the Pe-8, while Tupolev's light bomber design, the SB-2, became the Pe-2.

Warfare flared up in 1938 and 1939, fighting Japanese forces and eventually pushing them out of Mongolia with heavy Soviet casualties. This conflict used the same aircraft sent to Spain. In addition, from 1937 onwards, large numbers of Soviet aircraft were provided for Chinese Communist forces, often with 'volunteer' pilots and ground crew. The SV-VS had by this time grown to 6,000 aircraft, but its efficiency was affected, in line with the rest of the Soviet forces, by the regular purging of senior officers on political grounds, with subsequent imprisonment and often execution. In common with the rest of the Soviet forces, during the Communist period each unit had a political commissar as well as the more usual commanding officer. Examples of US and German aircraft were obtained during this period to gain an insight into rapidly changing aviation technology, and this was aided further in 1938 by a Russo-German agreement, which provided a number of Messerschmitt, Dornier and Heinkel aircraft. The Polikarpov I-17 fighter was being introduced in limited numbers when war started in 1939, and was accompanied by ground-attack and dive-bombing aircraft, including the Polikarpov VIT-1 and VIT-2, the Ilyushin Il-2, the Archangelski Ar-2, and the Tupolev R-10 reconnaissance-bomber.

The Russo-German pact allowed Soviet forces to invade eastern Poland in September, 1939, after German forces had all but crushed Polish resistance. Later that year, Soviet forces invaded Finland, which had seized its independence during the revolution and civil war. Determined Finnish resistance and poor Soviet planning meant that the war ended in 1940 with Finland making territorial concessions but retaining her independence, despite the fact that 2,000 Soviet aircraft had been deployed against Finland's numerically inferior forces. New aircraft types continued to enter service, including Lavochkin I-22 and Yakovlev I-26 (which became the Yak-1 shortly afterwards when designations were changed to reflect the design bureau rather than the aircraft's role), Yatsenko I-28, Mikoyan I-61 (MiG-1) and I-200 (MiG-3) fighters; Sukhoi Su-1 strike aircraft; Ilyushin DB-3 (Il-4), Petlyakov Pe-2 and Pe-8, and Yermolaev Yer-2 and Yer-6 bombers; Antonov A-7 transport and SS-2 liaison aircraft.

The number of aircraft actually entering service remained small. By 1941, the Soviet armed forces had some 18,000 aircraft, but just a fifth of these could be regarded as modern. Attempts to boost production were hampered both by the Soviet system and by the very necessary movement of the key factories eastwards, out of the range of German medium bombers, in anticipation of a possible war with Germany. In June 1941, Germany launched the invasion of the Soviet Union, Operation Barbarossa, using the well-tried *blitzkrieg* strategy of combining air power with fast-moving armoured formations. Half of the USSR's aircraft were deployed in the west, in anticipation of a German attack, and against these 9,000 aircraft, the *Luftwaffe* had 1,945 aircraft, joined by another 1,000 aircraft from Germany's allies, mainly Italy, Hungary and Romania, as well as some from Finland and Croatia. The *Luftwaffe* caught most of the Soviet airfields by surprise, striking at the sixty-six airfields that accommodated seventy per cent of Soviet air power in the West, although as many as fifty per cent of the Soviet aircraft are believed to have been non-operational. One Soviet commander committed suicide after losing 600 aircraft without making any impact on the invading German forces. Individual pilots tried desperate measures, even ramming German bombers by inserting their fighter's propeller into the elevators, although it seems that most survived this form of attack, which was not comparable to the kamikaze attacks on high flying Boeing B-29 Superfortress bombers over Japan.

FINNISH AIR FORCE (*ILMAVOIMAT*)
Finland seized her independence from Russia during the Russian Revolution, but as with Poland across the Baltic, the USSR did not accept Finnish independence. Between the two world wars the USSR demanded the use of Finnish bases, and the continuing tension ensured that a steady stream of new aircraft was introduced. Germany detained thirty-five Fiat G50 fighters en route to Finland before the Second World War broke out in 1939, but eighteen Bristol Blenheim bombers were delivered from the UK. The Soviet Union invaded Finland on 30 October, 1939, amassing vastly superior forces both on land and in the air. At first, the *Ilmavoimat* held its own against some 900 obsolescent Soviet aircraft, but the USSR transferred additional aircraft to the Finnish front and the numbers reached 2,000 by 1940. Despite deliveries of additional Blenheims, Gloster Gladiator, Hawker Hurricane, Brewster 239 and Curtiss Hawk 75A and A-4 fighters, and Westland Lysander AOP aircraft, Finland was forced to cede territory to the USSR, in 1940. The following year, when the Russo-German alliance collapsed, Finland allied herself with Germany.

ROYAL DANISH AIR FORCE
Danish military aviation dated from 1912, when the Army and the Navy received their first aircraft. The country remained neutral during the First World War. In 1932, a reorganisation created an Army Aviation Corps (*Havaens Flyvertropper*), with five squadrons (*eskadrille*). Bristol Bulldog fighters equipped No. 1 Eskadrille until replaced by Gloster Gladiators in 1935; Fokker CV reconnaissance aircraft equipped No. 2 *Eskadrille*, and No. 3 when its Fokker CIs were replaced in 1934, as well as No. 5 when it formed in 1935. Defence cuts meant that No. 4 was never formed.

Denmark hoped to remain neutral again during the Second World War, but the country was overrun by German forces in spring, 1940. Having lost most of their aircraft on the ground, a number of pilots managed to reach the UK to join the RAF.

ROYAL NORWEGIAN AIR FORCE

After early experience with aircraft provided by wealthy well-wishers, official support followed in 1915, when the Naval Air Service (*Marinens Flyvevaesen* – MF), and Army Air Force (*Haerens Flyvapen* – HF), were formed. Norway remained neutral during the First World War, and afterwards, the peacetime strength of the two services was established at thirty-six fighters and thirty-six bombers for the HF, with twenty fighters, twenty torpedo-bombers and twenty-four reconnaissance aircraft for the MF. Additional aircraft were provided for both services, with the HF receiving thirty Curtiss Hawk 75A and Gloster Gladiator fighters, Caproni Ca310 and Ca312 bombers, Douglas DB-8A attack aircraft, and Fokker CV and CVD reconnaissance bombers. The small size of the two services, and their elderly aircraft, meant that the spirited resistance mounted against the German invasion of April 1940, was to no avail, despite the support of the RAF and the Fleet Air Arm. Aircraft and personnel escaped to the UK. HF personnel in the UK were formed into two fighter squadrons, initially flying Hawker Hurricanes, but these were later replaced by Supermarine Spitfires, with one of the squadrons becoming the highest scoring Allied unit during the war, and also having the lowest accident rate.

ROYAL NETHERLANDS AIR FORCE

Dutch military interest in air matters started with an artillery observation balloon operated for a brief period in 1886, but, in contrast to the UK, this early interest was not sustained. Between the two world wars, neglect of Dutch air defences was founded on a policy of neutrality, which had seemed to serve the country well during the Great War. No plans were made for co-operation with Belgium, the UK or France, the most likely allies.

A last-minute attempt to rearm came in 1938. Reorganisation turned the Aviation Division into the Army Air Service (AAS). Aircraft were ordered from Fokker and US manufacturers, but there was insufficient time. On 10 May 1940, German forces rushed into the Netherlands, using paratroops and air-landed troops, but the AAS had too few aircraft. It had thirty Fokker DXXI, some DXVII and twenty G1 fighters, sixteen Fokker TV bombers, eleven Douglas DB-8A attack aircraft, forty Fokker CV and CX reconnaissance aircraft, and a few Koolhaven trainers on AOP duties. Overwhelmed by the *Luftwaffe*, this small force fought valiantly for five days, after which the survivors and the flying school escaped to England.

FORCE AERIENNE BELGE

Belgian military aviation originated in the creation of an army flying corps in 1911, using Farman HF3 and F20 biplanes manufactured under licence in Belgium. During the First World War, a new title, *Aviation*

Militaire, was adopted in 1915, but a shortage of pilots and the lack of a training organisation inhibited expansion as Belgium was almost overrun by German forces, with only a small area in the vicinity of Ostend left unoccupied.

During the mid-1930s, Gloster Gladiator fighters entered service, with Fokker FVII transports, Stampe SU-5 general-purpose biplanes and Koolhaven FK56 trainers. By the time the Second World War had started in September 1939, Belgium was producing Hawker Hurricane and Fiat CR42 fighters and Fairey Battle light bombers under licence, but most aircraft were obsolescent and destroyed on the ground when German forces invaded on 10 May 1940. Those that did get into the air fought against overwhelming odds. As Belgian resistance collapsed, the flying school squadrons escaped to French Morocco and other personnel managed to reach Britain from Belgium and from Africa, to be absorbed into the RAF, which eventually had 1,200 Belgian personnel. Personnel serving in the Belgian Congo joined the South African Air Force, many seeing service in North Africa. Later, two Belgian fighter squadrons were formed within the RAF, scoring 161 victories, 37 probables and 61 damaged enemy aircraft.

THE *REGIA AERONAUTICA*

The Italian Army formed an aeroplane company during the Italo-Turkish War in 1911, buying Bleriot XIs, Etrich Taubes, Maurice Farman S-11s and Nieuports for reconnaissance duties. In 1912, the Aviation Battalion (*Battagliore Aviatori*) was formed, being renamed the Military Aviation Service by the end of the year, but in 1914 it changed its name to the Military Aviation Corps (*Corpo Aeronautico Militare*).

Italy was one of the Allies in the First World War. The CAM rose from 70 aircraft at the outbreak of the war to 1,800 at the end. As elsewhere, postwar, the CAM's strength dropped sharply, with little new equipment.

Benito Mussolini's assumption of power in 1923 marked a revival for Italian military aviation. The CAM became the autonomous *Regia Aeronautica* (RA). Steps were taken to increase its strength, and in 1933 the RA reached a strength of 1,200 aircraft, including 37 fighters. The RA was involved in Italy's invasion of Abyssinia in 1935, and was accused of bombing attacks against lightly-armed Ethiopian tribesmen while there was no Ethiopian air defence of any consequence. In 1936, the Spanish Civil War started, and the RA sent a strong contingent to fight alongside German and Nationalist forces.

Italy entered the Second World War in June 1940, shortly before the fall of France, as an ally of Germany. At the outset, the RA had some 3,000 aircraft, of which some 400 were obsolete or obsolescent types based in the African colonies.

ROYAL HELLENIC AIR FORCE

The Royal Hellenic Army established an air squadron in 1912 using four Farman biplanes, deploying these during the Balkan Wars of 1912–13. During the First World War, army and naval aviation arms were merged into the Hellenic Air Service in 1916, operating against German and Turkish bases in Bulgaria before re-dividing into separate air arms in 1917. The two air arms were unified once again in 1931 into an autonomous Hellenic Air Force, becoming the Royal Hellenic Air Force with the restoration of the monarchy in 1935.

Before the outbreak of the Second World War in Europe in 1939, new aircraft included PZL P-24 and Bloch MB151 fighters, Bristol Blenheim, Fairey Battle and Potez 63 bombers, Henschel Hs126 AOP aircraft, Avro Anson reconnaissance bombers, and Dornier Do22 and Fairey IIIF seaplanes. Many of these types – including the Battle and Blenheim, and in the offensive role, the Anson – were to prove poor performers elsewhere. Even so, the RHAF managed to repel an Italian invasion in 1940, but Greece was overrun by German forces in 1941. Some personnel managed to escape to Egypt, where fighter squadrons were formed with the help of the RAF using Hawker Hurricanes, and a bomber squadron was equipped with Blenheims. Later, these were replaced with Supermarine Spitfire fighters and Martin Baltimore bombers.

UNITED STATES ARMY AIR FORCE

Although part of the United States Army, and in fact only renamed the United States Army Air Force in 1941 having been the United States Army Air Corps since 1926, the United States Army Air Force (USAAF) had a similar strategy to the Royal Air Force, seeing itself as an instrument of strategic air power rather than a tactical force providing air support for ground forces, which was the role adopted by both the *Luftwaffe* and the Soviet air forces.

Although the United States did not enter the Second World War until 7 December 1941 and the Japanese surprise attack on the US Pacific Fleet at Pearl Harbor in Hawaii, preparations had been in hand from much earlier following the Munich crisis of 1938. Very large orders were placed, especially after war finally broke out in Europe in September 1939. Aircraft ordered included additional Boeing P-26, Seversky P-35 and Curtiss P-36 fighters and Northrop A-17 and Curtiss A-12 and A-18 ground-attack aircraft, as well as bombers, amphibians and transports.

Amongst the bombers, many types benefited considerably from experience gained with service with the British and French armed forces before full-scale entry into US service.

Within the United States, the USAAF consisted of four main constituent air forces, the 1st and 2nd in the north, and the 3rd and 4th in the south, deployed primarily for the defence of the United States. When the Japanese attacked Pearl Harbor on 7 December 1941, there were some 2,500 aircraft in service. The latest were the Bell P-39, Curtiss P-40, Republic P-43 and P-47 (later changed to F-47 when classifications were changed from P-pursuit to F-fighter) Thunderbolt, and North American F-51 Mustang fighters, as well as Douglas A-20 Boston and A-24, and Curtiss A-25 attack aircraft. Most aircraft were still based in the continental United States, while many in Hawaii and the Philippines were destroyed on the ground by air attack. There were no USAAF units in Europe at the time, although sufficient American volunteers were serving with the RAF at the time to man three fighter squadrons.

While US entry into the war was provoked by the Japanese attack, the US was doing almost everything short of an open declaration of war. Debate raged over whether the war against Japan should be given priority, defeating that country first before settling the war in Europe. In the end, the US decided to wage war on two fronts. This decision helped to shorten the war. The USAAF would have had great difficulty in taking the offensive against Japan until bases had been secured within range of the Japanese islands.

From the outset, the heavy defensive armament of the Boeing B-17 Fortress heavy bomber enabled the USAAF to conduct daylight raids over enemy territory, while British and German bomber forces had been forced to concentrate on night raids to minimise their losses. Nevertheless, at first the USAAF was also to suffer heavy losses on its daylight raids while it awaited long-range fighters.

Chapter 3

War in Europe – Will it be Like the Last Time?

The outbreak of war on 3 September 1939 was not a surprise to many in the UK, and some actually recalled that the news was greeted with relief that the waiting was all over. As soon as the Prime Minister, Neville Chamberlain, finished his radio broadcast, the first air raid sirens began to wail, but no enemy aircraft appeared as this was just a case of accustoming the population to a sound that many would come to dread in the years ahead.

By contrast, many in Germany, including the armed forces, did not believe that war would come, and amongst those who did, many had been assured by the Führer, Adolf Hitler, that war with the United Kingdom would not break out until 1942 or even 1943.

The years of appeasement had lulled many Germans into a false sense of security. After all, the League of Nations had not intervened when Italy invaded Abyssinia, and, while the United Kingdom had prepared for action, the French had held back, and without the support of the strong French naval and air power deployed in the Mediterranean, the UK felt that it could not act alone. The Germans had been allowed to take the Sudetenland, and many in British political life had been sympathetic to German claims. No one had taken action when German forces occupied Austria, or when the rest of Czechoslovakia was occupied. Perhaps many in Germany felt that some at least amongst the British would also be sympathetic to Germany taking at least part of Poland – those areas that had been taken from Germany after the First World War.

They were proved wrong, and this time the UK and France were acting in concert, at least for the time being.

While the British made the most of the year's grace bought by the Munich Agreement, progress in France was hampered as the aircraft industry was being nationalised and reorganised, and, in the confusion, re-equipment did not receive the attention it needed. Italy, on the other hand, had another nine months in which to prepare for war as, to Hitler's surprise and disappointment, the country did not enter the war on 3 September 1939, but waited until June 1940, as France fell. Italy's timing led to the Germans describing their new ally as the 'harvest hands', sitting on the sidelines until the fruits of victory were ready.

POLAND

It had been Germany's invasion of Poland on 1 September 1939 that had provoked an ultimatum from the British and French governments that eventually resulted in the declaration of war on 3 September. Many German military planners were planning for war with the United Kingdom and her empire to start in 1945, suggesting that Hitler was counting on an Anglo-French acceptance of the situation as had happened the previous year when Germany had invaded Czechoslovakia. This time, Germany was not entirely alone as the Soviet Union invaded and occupied the eastern provinces of Poland on 17 September.

While the Poles fought valiantly, their armed forces were outnumbered and outclassed. Poland at the time was amongst the poorest nations in Europe, and the equipment of the armed forces reflected this situation. The Polish Air Force had achieved autonomy from army control the previous year, and had ambitious re-equipment plans, but for the most part the Poles had too few aircraft, and too many of these were obsolete. Even so, the *Luftwaffe* did not have everything its own way, and Second Lieutenant Wladyshaw Gnys of 122 Fighter Squadron, Polish Air Force, was the first man to shoot down a *Luftwaffe* aircraft.

German troops had moved swiftly across the border with Poland early in the morning of Friday, 1 September, with the first bombing raids following at daylight, designed to cripple Polish airfields and destroy the Polish Air Force, giving Germany early aerial superiority so that the *Luftwaffe* could then provide support for the German ground forces. A few days after the invasion started, a newspaper, the Nazi *Volkischer Beobachter*, carried this report from a German airman in a Do17 bomber squadron who was involved in the campaign against the Polish Air Force on that first day:

> ... the telephone rings shrilly. We all read the announcement from the adjutant's face: 'Be ready to take off tomorrow morning at 4.20am.' Rapidly the needed instructions are passed to the squadrons: 'Wake-up time 2.00am. Breakfast 2.30am, flight briefing at 3.15, crews man their planes at 4.00. Machines warmed up at 4.10. Now everyone go to sleep at once!'
>
> A cool morning greets us as we go to our flight briefing ... 'The group is going to make a ground attack on Krakow Airfield. Attack time 5:45am.'
>
> We are on course. At first it is hard to keep our bearings in the thick morning haze. We know that at this same moment our comrades on

the ground are tearing down the boundary posts and beginning the attack ... Slowly it gets light, visibility is good now. We are flying over enemy land ... Another squadron is flying to our left: we see that it is being fired on. Then a cloud of black smoke on the horizon shows us our target. We are alongside, we see fire, smoke, more fire and explosion after explosion. We nose our aircraft to 150 feet so that the bombs will bite on impact ... a short distance ahead at the edge of the airfield, we see a neatly-arranged string of Polish fighter planes. The bomb trail is launched ... Red explosions are bursting all over the ground, the threads of enemy anti-aircraft shells pull around us. Our machine-gun barrels are hot; probably the turrets have never rotated so fast. Then, pressed close to the ground, we race off on the course for home.[1]

The German desire to eliminate all aerial opposition was obviously the right one from both the strategic and the tactical aspect, while the Polish Air Force was caught unprepared so that many of its aircraft were destroyed on the ground. A lack of combat experience on the Polish side was also apparent, with aircraft parked in lines, so that a bomber or even a strafing fighter would have an easy target, having to make just one run over the airfield. Obviously, the newspaper account was tinged with propaganda, but there is no reason to doubt that, despite some losses, the *Luftwaffe* was continuing to have things very much its own way.

While Poland had been attempting to expand its armed forces in anticipation of war with Germany, the country was nevertheless caught before expansion was complete. Typical of those who missed their chance to fight was Tadeusz Andersz. Ironically, it was a gliding course that had filled him with the ambition to become a fighter pilot, just as the Germans had organised gliding schools to prepare for the creation of the *Luftwaffe*. Andersz and the rest of his intake were evacuated to Romania, where they were interned, but he escaped via Yugoslavia and Greece to France, where Polish forces were being reformed. Based on Lyon, he flew a few sorties on Dewoitine D501 fighters before the fall of France, and escaped by sea from Bordeaux aboard a British ship. He joined the RAF on arrival and eventually became a squadron leader.

THE PHONEY WAR

In 1938 and 1939, the general expectation was that any war in Europe would follow the pattern of the First World War, with rapid German advances followed by stalemate on a new front. The French put much faith into the Maginot Line, a series of strongly defended positions stretching from the border with Switzerland to the Belgian frontier. This was part of its inherent weakness, as Belgium was exposed and weakly armed, while there had been no effective co-ordination of training or exercising with British and French forces.

A German invasion of Belgium was widely expected, which makes the lack of any detailed planning and joint exercises so much more inexcusable, but what the British and French had not counted on was that German forces would invade Denmark, Norway and the Netherlands, as all three countries had managed to remain neutral during the First World War.

On the day after war was declared, the British Expeditionary Force (BEF) had started its move to France, with an initial 152,000 men supported by an air component of twelve RAF squadrons and 9,393 personnel. In addition, the BEF was supported by the AASF drawn from No. 1 Group, Bomber Command, with ten squadrons of Fairey Battles, to which were added two squadrons of Bristol Blenheims and, later, two squadrons of Gladiators. Eventually, the BEF's Air Component was to rise to four squadrons of Hurricanes, four squadrons of Blenheims and five Lysander army co-operation squadrons. Ten additional Hurricane squadrons were moved to France within hours when the German advance started on 10 May 1940.

The force deployed was hopeless, not only being numerically inferior to the forces at the disposal of the *Luftwaffe*, but the aircraft were all hopelessly outclassed. Although highly manoeuvrable and easy to repair, the Hurricane lacked the speed of the Messerschmitt Bf109, while the Gladiator was almost a museum piece. The Fairey Battle stemmed from a belief that a single-engined bomber could have the manoeuvrability of a fighter and much of its speed, but it didn't. Worse still, it had still to be appreciated that bombing raids were best conducted by a concentration of as many aircraft as possible to force the defences to divide their fire. Surprise was also often lacking. In any event, there was strong French resistance for bombing raids against German cities for fear that this would bring reprisal raids against French cities.

Meanwhile, despite the fact that hostilities had started and both the United Kingdom and France were at war with Germany, there seemed to be a lack of offensive spirit and desire to avoid civilian casualties if at all possible, at least between Britain and Germany. RAF Bomber Command's early operations consisted mainly of leaflet dropping, eventually known as the 'Nickel' operations and the laying of mines in the Schillig Roads, an important part of the war effort known as the 'gardening' sorties. Even Hitler insisted that only military and naval targets be attacked, and that no action should proceed if there was a danger of death or injury to British civilians. The use of precision dive-bombers was favoured over high-altitude bombing.

All of this contrasted sharply with the months of the Blitz that were to follow.

24

After the invasion of Poland, nothing seemed to happen, at least in the recollection of most of the populations of the supposedly warring nations. In fact, a great deal had been happening on certain fronts, especially at sea, and the Royal Air Force and the *Luftwaffe* had both expended energy and lives on attacking each others' fleets. To the British, this period from September 1939 to May 1940 was known popularly as the 'phoney war', while to the Germans it was known as the 'sitting war', which was probably more accurate with the opposing Anglo-French and German armies sitting on either side of the Franco-German border.

The need to avoid civilian casualties was also very much in mind when, on 16 October 1939, nine Junkers Ju88 bombers of *I Gruppe* of *Kampfgeschwader 30* were sent to attack the giant battle cruiser *Hood*, believed to be at anchor in the Firth of Forth on the east coast of Scotland. The information was not quite right, for they found her in Rosyth Dockyard, on the north shore of the Firth, where there was a risk of civilian casualties placing her effectively 'out of bounds' for the *Luftwaffe*. *Hauptmann* Helmut Pohl, leading the attack, ordered his crews to turn their attention to other warships anchored in the Firth of Forth, which included the two cruisers *Edinburgh* and *Southampton*. Pohl attacked *Southampton*, sending a 1,100lb armour-piercing bomb into the ship, through her port side and through three decks and out through the starboard side, before exploding below the waterline and causing further structural damage. *Edinburgh* also came under attack, suffering minor damage from bomb splinters, as did a destroyer. At this stage, Spitfires from No. 602 (City of Glasgow) and No. 603 (City of Edinburgh) Squadrons flying from RAF Turnhouse (now Edinburgh Airport) caught the bombers, forcing them to break off their attack, and then chasing them out to sea, shooting down two aircraft, including that of Pohl.

Leutnant Horst von Riesen, the pilot of one of the bombers, recalls being under attack by the Spitfires:

> Now I thought I was finished. Guns were firing at me from all sides and the Spitfires behind seemed to be taking turns at attacking. But I think my speed gave them all a bit of a surprise – I was doing more than 400 kilometres per hour [250mph], which must have been somewhat faster than any other bomber they had trained against at low level – and of course I jinked from side to side to make their aim as difficult as possible. At one stage in the pursuit I remember looking down and seeing what looked like rain drops hitting the water. It was all very strange. Then I realised what it was: those splashes marked the impact of bullets being aimed at me from above.[2]

Fortunately for von Riesen, the Spitfires, with their limited range, soon had to break off their attack, but not before one of them had managed to damage the Ju88's starboard engine cooling system, leaving the aircraft with just one engine labouring to keep it airborne. This gave von Riesen a problem, since during training he had been told that a Ju88 would not maintain height on one engine – and his damaged aircraft was now struggling. He rejected the idea of ditching as it was getting dark, and it was unlikely that they would be picked up, leaving them to drown or die of exposure.

A crew member suggested turning back to Scotland, and crash-landing there, but one of the others shouted over the intercom, 'No, no, never!'[3] adding forcibly that Spitfires would be waiting for them.

The crew struggled to keep their aircraft airborne, even hand-pumping fuel from the starboard wing tank to the port wing tank, to keep the good engine running, while the navigator wrapped his belt around the left rudder pedal and pulled hard, in an attempt to take the pressure off von Riesen. As fuel burnt off and the aircraft became lighter, it was possible to regain some altitude, but even so the aircraft was still only at 2,000 feet when, after three hours' flying, it managed to struggle home to its base on Westerland.

On 28 October, in a further attack, a Heinkel He111 was brought down near Gifford, in East Lothian. This was the first German aircraft to be brought down in Scotland and the second in Great Britain after Hurricanes of No. 43 Squadron had shot down a He111 near Whitby on 3 February 1940.

FRIENDLY FIRE

Throughout the Second World War, there were doubts about aircraft recognition, but naturally this was at its worst during the early days when few fighter pilots had seen an enemy plane. On 4 September 1939, several Hurricane and Spitfire squadrons were scrambled over the Essex coast, including No. 74 Squadron, flying Spitfires from RAF Hornchurch. Two of the squadron's pilots, Pilot Officers John Freeborn and Vincent Byrne, spotted two aircraft that they took to be Bf109s and were ordered to attack by their CO, Squadron Leader 'Sailor' Malan. Freeborn became the first Spitfire pilot to shoot down an aircraft, but unfortunately the two 'Bf109s' were in fact Hurricanes of No. 56 Squadron flying from North Weald that had been scrambled earlier. The pilot of the aircraft shot down by Byrne managed to bale out and survived, but Montague Hulton-Harrop, shot down by Freeborn, had the unwanted distinction of being the first British pilot to be killed during the war.

Both men were exonerated in the resulting court martial, although they felt let down by Malan, who gave evidence against them.

The causes of the incident were various. Fighter control and direction was not as polished as it became under the experience gained in the Battle of Britain, while the ugly cockpit canopy of the Hurricane bore a passing resemblance to that of the Bf109. In the end, of course, it was a case of two very inexperienced pilots who had never seen a Bf109 and possibly never having seen a Hurricane either, on their first sortie in which they were likely to meet an enemy aircraft, and no doubt excited and nervous, making a mistake while acting in haste, realising that in aerial combat it is a case of shoot down or be shot down.

With the usual gallows humour of the fighting man, this event was nicknamed the 'Battle of Barking Creek' by their fellow pilots.

DENMARK AND NORWAY

During the first winter of war, many believed that a negotiated settlement might be achieved and both sides sent aircraft on leaflet raids, but any hopes that the Germans might change their minds were dashed when Germany invaded Norway and Denmark on 9 April 1940. This was the end of the 'phoney war'. Denmark, with a land border with Germany, was overrun quickly, but in Norway, despite the Germans using air- and sea-landed troops, bad luck and the greater size of the country meant that the government was able to escape and mobilise the armed forces to resist the invaders.

The country was of immense strategic importance to both sides. Seizing both Norway and Denmark gave the Germans far easier movement between the Baltic and the Atlantic and meant that a repeat of the First World War British naval blockade and submarine operations in the Baltic became far more difficult. No less important, securing Norwegian ports meant that iron ore from Sweden could be moved all year round, which otherwise would have been difficult during the winter months when the Gulf of Bothnia froze. Norwegian airfields and naval bases meant that operations against British shipping in the North Atlantic became far easier, and, although this was not apparent at the time, it would make support of the Soviet Union by British and American forces far more difficult once Operation Barbarossa got under way.

Appreciating the importance of Narvik for the movement of Swedish iron ore, the British and French governments had been planning an invasion of the port during the Russo-Finnish War of 1939–1940 – the so-called Winter War. This was to be done under the guise of aiding Finland, but the plans had to be dropped after an armistice came into effect. Nevertheless, the Germans had obtained intelligence about the plans, which made them determined to seize Norway, especially after the *Altmark* incident, in which the *Graf Spee*'s supply ship was boarded in Norwegian waters and British prisoners released by the Royal Navy. Meanwhile, the Anglo-French Supreme War Council, under pressure to do something as the 'phoney war' dragged on, decided that if a pretext to establish a presence in Norway could not be found, then mines should be laid in Norwegian waters to force German merchant shipping out of territorial waters and onto the high seas, where they could be legally attacked by British and French forces. While the first mines were being laid on 8 April, it became clear to the Allies that Germans were themselves planning a major move against the two Scandinavian countries.

The invasion when it came the following day was a textbook example of how to mount an assault, especially on territory over which land communications could be difficult, even in high summer. Despite the loss of the cruiser *Blucher* to Norwegian shore batteries at Oslo, by noon, the Germans were in control of Bergen, Kristiansand, Narvik, Stavanger and Trondheim.

After the Norwegian government accepted British and French promises of support, an Anglo-French expeditionary force was immediately dispatched. Before the advance formations of British and Free Polish troops arrived at Narvik on 12 April, the Royal Navy had already enjoyed success in the First Battle of Narvik and had used shore-based aircraft to sink the light cruiser *Konigsberg*. Improvised airstrips and frozen lakes were all that the country could offer by way of airfields. With few airfields ashore and the country deep in snow, the campaign would have been well suited to the use of carrier-borne air power, had sufficient ships and high performance aircraft been available. As it was, aircraft had to be moved by sea aboard the aircraft carrier *Glorious,* which took the Hurricanes of the RAF's No. 46 Squadron to Norway. When the aircraft were flown off, two crashed on the soft landing ground, so the rest were moved north to Bardufoss, where they provided fighter cover for Narvik. Meanwhile, No. 263 Squadron arrived with its Gloster Gladiator biplanes, but all of these obsolete aircraft were either destroyed or badly damaged within three days. The squadron returned home to re-equip, but again still with Gladiators, so that when it returned, the outcome was much the same.

In Scotland, bombing sorties were mounted from Lossiemouth, with anti-shipping strikes from RAF Leuchars.

Nevertheless, these were small forces with which to contest the well-equipped Germans, and, clearly, British equipment was insufficient and dated. Apart from the Advanced Air Striking Force already deployed to France, many fighter units were being held back in the UK in expectation of German aerial attack. Despite British and French troops pushing the German forces back towards the Swedish border, it soon became clear that the air and ground forces deployed in Norway were more urgently needed in France as the German assault on the Low Countries and then France forged ahead. On 7 June, the members of Nos 46 and 263 Squadrons were ordered to destroy their remaining aircraft and join the aircraft carriers HMS *Glorious* and *Ark Royal* for the passage home. Believing that their Hurricanes were too valuable to destroy, the pilots of No. 46, without arrestor hooks or carrier deck landing training, succeeded in flying their aircraft aboard *Glorious* by the expedient fitting of sandbags to the tail wheels. The carrier had been chosen because her larger lifts meant that the

28

aircraft could be 'struck down' safely into her hangar deck. Not equipped with radar, it seems incredible that the ship did not send off reconnaissance flights or even have a look-out posted in the crow's nest. The ship's own aircraft were disarmed and torpedoes returned to the magazines. The next day, while the ship was steaming at a leisurely pace, to save fuel, towards Scapa Flow in Orkney, she was caught by the German battle cruisers *Scharnhorst* and *Gneisenau* – both of which were equipped with radar – shelled and sunk. Many members of the RAF were amongst more than 1,500 men who died, either during the action or in the cold seas afterwards.

It was not just the aircraft that had needed to be saved as in the months ahead it was to be the shortage of fighter pilots that was to be the biggest problem. Their loss at sea could not be afforded.

FALL GELB – THE GERMAN INVASION OF THE LOW COUNTRIES AND FRANCE

Having secured Denmark and Norway, Germany could now strike west towards the Channel coast. Belgium had just 180 aircraft, of which 81 were fighters, while the Netherlands had 132 aircraft, of which 35 were fighters and twenty-three fighter-destroyers. Inevitably, both Belgium and the Netherlands were quickly overrun with tightly co-ordinated air and ground attack aided by the use of glider-borne troops and paratroops, perhaps most spectacularly deployed in the case of Fort Eben-Emael, which enabled the Rhine bridges to be secured.

France was a larger, better defended and more difficult territory, but the seizure of Belgium meant that the Maginot Line could be bypassed while in terms of equipment, the odds were once again stacked against the defenders. The *Luftwaffe* had 3,834 aircraft, including 1,482 bombers and dive-bombers, 42 ground attack aircraft, 248 fighter destroyers or *Zerstorer* (fighter-bombers), and 1,016 fighters. By contrast, the RAF had 456 aircraft, of which 261 were fighters, 135 bombers and 60 reconnaissance aircraft. Somewhat larger, the French Armée de l' Air had 1,604 aircraft, many of them also obsolete or obsolescent, of which 260 were bombers, 764 fighters, 180 reconnaissance aircraft and another 400 or so aircraft in army support duties.

The Germans scored in both quality and quantity, and through having combat-hardened aircrew. The situation was not helped by the French insisting that neither of the two Allied air forces should press heavy bombing raids against German industry for fear of German reprisals against French targets.

At the time, it was an achievement for a nation to have a radar network on the scale of the Chain Home network. Mobile air defence radars were still some way off, and so the air force units accompanying the BEF were at a big disadvantage. Billy Drake was with the first squadrons to cross the Channel and be based in France.

At the beginning of the war we were one of four squadrons that were sent to France to look after the Expeditionary Force. We had no organisation looking after us as we did in England during the Battle of Britain, telling us what or what not to do. In France we had no radar and no Observer Corps. The French themselves had no concept of how to operate their air force and therefore our only contact with the Germans was to see contrails flying over us, at which we would take off, intercept them where possible, and do whatever we could.

There was an occasion where I caught up with a 109 but he saw me and just stuck his nose down and went back to his base as fast as possible. I followed him and we crossed the Rhine. He obviously knew the area well, and when I looked up from him I suddenly saw we were flying towards high tension cables. We dived underneath them and eventually he pulled up, which was his fatal mistake, because as he pulled up he lost speed and I was able to get close behind him, close enough to shoot him down in flames.[4]

It took just two days for the RAF's bomber strength in France to be cut from 135 aircraft to 72, and of these another 40 were shot down by the third day. Bomber squadrons based in southern England also attacked the advancing German forces, but to little effect and at great cost. Typical of the actions that took place was on 12 May, when six AASF Battles, with an escort of two Hurricane fighters, were sent against the Vroenhoven and Veldwezelt bridges, across which the German forces were streaming.

Four of the aircraft were shot down as they approached the targets, which were left undamaged. One of the Battles was burning 'like a torch' as it dropped its bombs, but its pilot, Flying Officer McIntosh, managed to land it safely behind enemy lines, and the crew spent the rest of the war as prisoners. One German officer pointed out to McIntosh that they had taken the bridges early on the Friday morning, but the Germans had been left with the whole of Friday and Saturday to build up AA defences before the RAF had arrived on the Sunday.

By 21 May, the air component of the BEF was down to its last few Lysanders, while the few surviving Battles were limited to night operations to keep losses to an acceptable level. As the Germans swept through Belgium and the Netherlands, forcing British forces that had ventured into Belgium back into France, the British soon started to husband scarce resources and trained aircrew for the defence of the British Isles. Two more Hurricane squadrons had been despatched to France in response to desperate pleas from the Army, but Air Chief Marshal Sir Hugh Dowding, AOC-in-C, Fighter Command, successfully opposed sending more, arguing that to do so would 'bleed white' the air defences of the United

Kingdom. During the withdrawal and then the evacuation from Dunkirk, the RAF used units based in the south of England to provide air cover. Hitler had been persuaded to let the *Luftwaffe* finish off the British troops with their backs to the sea at Dunkirk, but at huge cost Fighter Command expended valuable resources in an attempt to ward off the *Luftwaffe*, even obtaining local air superiority at times. This was despite the difficulty of providing constant fighter cover over the beaches at Dunkirk given the short range of fighter aircraft at this stage of the war. While Fighter Command could not always stop ships being bombed as they loaded troops, Coastal Command and the Fleet Air Arm helped by ensuring that enemy U-boats (submarines) and E-boats (fast motor gunboats and torpedo-boats) were prevented from attacking the evacuation fleet.

The aircraft of the AASF remained in France after the evacuation of Dunkirk ended, with its Blenheims and Battles continuing to make offensive sorties as the remnants of the BEF and French forces were squeezed into the Cherbourg peninsula. Only as these too were evacuated did the aircraft return to the UK, with the fighter squadrons acting as a rear guard and being last to return.

In all, during the Battle of France, RAF losses totalled 931 aircraft with 1,526 casualties. Of these aircraft, 229 were from the AASF and a further 279 were from the BEF's air component, with around 200 from Fighter Command and more than 150 from Bomber Command, while around 60 were from Coastal Command.

One thing was clear from the outcome, which was that the Second World War was not going to follow the pattern of the First World War. From the North Cape to just a few miles north of Bordeaux, continental Europe was in German hands.

Notes

1. Janusz Piekalkiewicz, *The Air War: 1939–45*, Blandford, London, 1985.
2. Alfred Price, *Blitz On Britain 1939–45*, Ian Allan, London, 1977.
3. Alfred Price, *Blitz On Britain 1939–45*, Ian Allan, London, 1977.
4. Imperial War Museum Sound Archive.

Chapter 4

Battle of Britain

The first battle that was almost entirely between opposing air forces, the term 'Battle of Britain' was coined by Britain's wartime leader, Winston Churchill, in a speech to the House of Commons on 18 June 1940. He told the Members of Parliament that the Battle of France had ended and the Battle of Britain was about to begin. He saw clearly that the German navy, the Kriegsmarine, lacked the power to put an adequate number of troops ashore or to confront the Royal Navy, especially after it had lost so many ships during the Norwegian campaign. He realised that the first priority for the *Luftwaffe* would have to be the destruction of the Royal Air Force, possibly combined with airborne landings.

Nevertheless, the Germans also had a name for the operation: *Luftschlacht um England* or *Luftschlacht um Grossbritannien*, meaning either 'air battle against England' or 'air battle against Great Britain'. For once, both sides had much the same name for the conflict.

It is a myth of British folklore that the Battle of Britain was won by the Supermarine Spitfire; the Spitfire was very much in the minority of fighter aircraft at the time, having only started to enter service early in 1939. The mainstay of RAF Fighter Command was the Hawker Hurricane, a slower aircraft, albeit easier to repair and with a tighter turning circle. Both aircraft used the Rolls-Royce Merlin engine. Even the Hurricane excelled when compared not just with the Gloster Gladiator that had suffered so badly in Norway and in France, but with the Boulton Paul Defiant, which was hampered by its rear turret. Winston Churchill, who became Britain's wartime premier on 10 May 1940, believed that all fighters should have a rear gunner, as many had during the First World War. The problem was that the extra weight seriously diminished aircraft performance, while enemy fighter pilots soon realised that there was a rear gunner and adjusted their tactics accordingly. Meanwhile, the Minister for Aircraft Production, Lord Beaverbrook, believed that all fighters should have twin engines, as with the Bristol Beaufighter, ignoring the fact that a single-engined fighter in piston days was far more manoeuvrable than the twin-engined equivalent.

During the Second World War, Britain's top-scoring surviving fighter ace was Group Captain J.E. Johnson, more commonly known as 'Johnnie' Johnson. In his memoirs, *Wing Leader*, he recalled the state of the Royal Air Force's fighter defences during the Battle of Britain. Despite many having recognised that war with Germany was inevitable, and the time bought by the Munich Agreement and more than seven months of the 'phoney war', all was not well with the pilots or with the aircraft.

The German Messerschmitt Bf109 had the novel feature of a cannon firing through the propeller boss, and cannon fire was far more effective than machine-gun fire, although the aircraft also had eight wing-mounted machine guns. Only the unsuccessful Bell Airacobra also had a gun in the propeller hub. The Spitfire originally had eight machine guns, four in each wing, but although Spitfires fitted with a cannon in each wing appeared in 1940, this improvement failed to meet expectations simply because the cannon jammed, and pilots soon demanded their eight machine guns back!

British pilots also lacked the hard core of experience in the Spanish Civil War and over Poland that the *Luftwaffe* enjoyed. Neither side had conversion trainers, although much later twin-seat Spitfires and Hurricanes appeared for Ireland and Iran respectively. This was typical of the time. More serious was that in training fighter pilots, there were no lectures on tactics at this early stage of the war. Newly-fledged pilots, some with less than twenty hours on Spitfires, were sent to fighter squadrons wondering whether their aircraft could out-turn a Bf109, knowing full well if they were Hurricane pilots that they couldn't outrun one, as indeed the Bf109 was even faster than a Spitfire. The fact that the British aircraft were better armoured, and protected the pilot, wasn't known at first, nor was the fact that the Bf109's Achilles heel was its weak tailplane.

'What went on when flights of Spitfires and Messerschmitts met?' Johnnie Johnson asked himself. 'When squadron met squadron and wing encountered wing? Could the 109s turn inside us? ... What was the most important asset of a fighter pilot – to shoot straight, to keep a good lookout or to be able to stay with his leader at all times?'[1]

The other enduring myth of this stage of the war was that the battle was won by 'The Few', but this term is relative. There were less than 3,000, which by today's much diminished standards would be a very large number indeed, but what is true is that they were initially outnumbered by their *Luftwaffe* opponents. Had not Dowding safeguarded sufficient airmen and aircraft rather than hazard everything in the Battle of France, there would indeed have been very many fewer and probably insufficient numbers to win the battle. Augmenting the RAF airmen were a number of Fleet Air Arm pilots as the Royal Navy had more trained pilots than aircraft, and no high performance aircraft at all. There were also the first of those airmen from the nations overrun by the German advance who had gone to great lengths to continue the fight – some of whom had experience of aerial combat over Poland and then France before crossing the Channel.

The 'battle' was not simply one for RAF Fighter Command. While control of the air was essential, at no stage did the Royal Navy lose control of the seas, while Coastal Command and Bomber Command, with help from shore-based Fleet Air Arm Swordfish, did their best to attack the growing fleet of invasion barges being built up in the French and Belgian Channel ports, and laid mines to further hamper enemy shipping of all kinds.

THE BATTLE BEGINS

Unlike most conflicts the dates for the Battle of Britain are not fixed. There was a lull after the fall of France on 22 June 1940, although there were numerous isolated sorties against Britain. Some German sources suggest that the battle started on 4 July, although others put the start date as late as 13 August. In Great Britain, the official starting date is taken as 10 July. The difference could be because the British view is that the first phase of the battle ran until 12 August, and the second phase ran from 13 August. In the first phase, the primary targets were British shipping and ports. This was known to the *Luftwaffe* as the *Kanalkampf*, or 'Channel Struggle'.

The day started quietly enough. During the morning a solitary Dornier Do17Z bomber escorted by ten Messerschmitt Bf109s had attacked a coastal convoy off the North Foreland in Kent. This opportunist hit-and-run raid was not uncommon and damage was limited.

By this time, RAF Fighter Command had already lost its first pilot of the period of the Battle of Britain. Sergeant Pilot Ian Clenshaw of No. 253 Squadron from Kirton-in-Lindsey had been on an early patrol over the Humber Estuary in poor visibility when he lost control of his aircraft and it crashed. He was just twenty-two years old, a bank clerk who had joined the RAFVR in spring 1939.

Early in the afternoon, around 13.25, the Chain Home RDF stations near Dover noted that large numbers of aircraft were massing beyond the Pas de Calais, and as these were reported to the operations room for 11 Group at RAF Uxbridge, it soon became clear that something was afoot. Six Hurricanes of No. 32 Squadron from RAF Biggin Hill were on patrol and immediately vectored to the area, while another six Hurricanes of No. 56 Squadron on standby at Manston were scrambled. They arrived over the Channel to find a convoy already under attack by *Luftflotte* 2, with the German aircraft arranged on three levels, with the ships being attacked by some twenty Dornier Do17Z bombers that formed the lowest level, with thirty Messerschmitt Me110s providing close support in the middle level and twenty Messerschmitt Bf109s providing top cover.

With the experience of Spain, Poland, the Low Countries and France behind them, this formation had evolved as the *Luftwaffe* standard at this stage of the air war. The Me110s were to form a defensive circle around the bombers while the Bf109s would swoop down for the kill. Outnumbered and outclassed, the Hurricane pilots divided their forces with some aircraft attacking the bombers while the remainder tackled the Me110s. Climbing to counter the Bf109s would have taken too long, and in any case wasn't necessary as the Bf109s swooped down on the slower British fighters, doubtless anticipating an easy victory.

The Hurricanes all survived this first battle, however, and returned to their bases, but one of those from No. 56 Squadron crash-landed at Manston and two of those from No. 32 also crash-landed, one at Hawkinge and the other at Lympne. Meanwhile, other fighters had reached the battle area and eventually the attack was repelled, but at the cost of one ship sunk.

The rest of the long summer afternoon and evening saw further raids and further air battles from as far south as Beachy Head on the Sussex coast to as far north as the Firth of Tay, north of St Andrews, in Scotland. By nightfall, the RAF had flown 641 sorties and lost 6 aircraft, while the *Luftwaffe* had lost 12 aircraft, 8 of them fighters and the other 4 bombers.

With attacks likely to come from a wide area stretching from France to Norway, at least in theory, co-ordination was essential. At RAF Bentley Priory, a complete picture of what became known as the Air Defence of Great Britain was possible and it was important that the groups reinforced one another. This was not a major problem at the outset, but later in the Battle of Britain, aircraft were often vectored in the airspace of another group, usually with either 10 or 12 Groups being called on to assist 11 Group as it came under heavy pressure. Each group would have its own controller and plotting room with the controllers assisted by members of the Women's Auxiliary Air Force, each with teams working four shifts, twenty-four hours on and twenty-four hours off.

The system of having groups overlap when the next needed assistance seemed to work very well, at least between 10 and 11 Groups. Keith Lawrence was a young pilot officer from New Zealand flying Spitfires with No. 234 Squadron, moved to Middle Wallop during the battle.

The majority of fighting was, of course, over Kent and the south-east. No. 11 Group was well supported by Air Vice-Marshal Brand at 10 Group. He co-operated well with AVM Park, and whenever Park needed reinforcements from 10 Group he would call on some of the squadrons at Middle Wallop, Warmwell or other airfields that were close to 11 Group. A good two-thirds of our flying was in support of 11 Group as there were fewer enemy raids along the south coast, partly because such raids were at the extreme range of fighter escort.

When we were scrambled to reinforce 11 Group, with the order 'Scramble 234 Squadron' we were off the ground within 5–6 minutes.

Once airborne, the CO would report 'Crecy Squadron airborne' and then we would get our orders from the Middle Wallop sector controller: 'Crecy Squadron patrol Guildford [or patrol Brooklands] angels 20' [their altitude]. That was an easy 15 minutes' climb up to Guildford or Brooklands. Brooklands was quite a landmark and when we got there the CO would report 'Crecy Squadron Brooklands angels 20'.

The controller at Wallop could see on his table the whole of the raid, the numbers of German bombers and where they were coming in. We continued to be controlled from our sector station even when over Kent. The Wallop controller was co-operating with the controller at 11 Group, who would know from his ops room table what 11 Group squadrons had been scrambled and which formations they were intercepting. Likewise, the 10 Group controller would have been told which formations he was to tackle and so on.

With our wonderful system of radar, the controller could track the incoming bombers once they had reached more than 15,000 feet. The difficulty was that, by the time they got to 18,000 feet and set course for England, it was only a matter of 10 to 15 minutes before they crossed the coast. The controllers were pilots who had either been on ops themselves, or had been experienced fighter pilots. For the most part the VHF radio was good and we could hear them quite well. The ... controller could position us at a reasonable height to intercept and make an attack.

At the time we didn't know much about what was going on in 12 Group. We didn't know anything about the co-operation (or lack of it) between 11 and 12 Groups, and only learnt about that afterwards. All we had to do was to go on readiness every morning at first light and remain on readiness until 'scrambled' or relieved by the pilots on the duty roster.[2]

The outstanding success of the Battle of Britain was the Chain Home radar network. This minimised the relative disadvantage in numbers of the RAF compared to the *Luftwaffe* by ensuring that aircraft were only in the air when they needed to be, saving the waste of fuel and manpower in standing patrols, and also ensured that aircraft were directed to where they were needed as and when they were needed. There was also the problem that even when standing patrols could be mounted, the aircraft on patrol could be running low on fuel just at the moment they were needed.

It was also important that RAF aircraft were not mistaken for those of the *Luftwaffe* by the radar stations, and at first this was a problem, but before long an early form of identification friend or foe (IFF) equipment was deployed aboard the RAF's fighters.

The brunt of the Battle of Britain was borne by the less glamorous Hawker Hurricane, first flown by No. 111 Squadron. Closest to the 'front line' of this air war were those squadrons along the south coast of England, with one of the busiest bases, and most vulnerable, being RAF Tangmere in West Sussex. One of the Tangmere Hurricane squadrons was No. 501, with which Pilot Officer Peter Hairs served. He was very appreciative of the value of radar and also explained how the IFF worked.

The very effective system of radar, which, although in its infancy, was remarkably accurate, and enabled the ground control to use the limited aircraft at their disposal to the fullest extent and minimised standing patrols, which are not only wasteful but tiring for those slogging around. Radar was able to pick up the enemy aircraft before they left the French coast while still forming up, and so ample warning was received and the defending squadrons could be deployed and sent off in time to meet the attack at the most convenient point.

Often we would get a phone call through from control to say that things were building up over the Channel some time before the order to scramble came through. To ensure that our own fighters were not plotted as enemy aircraft, our aircraft were equipped with an instrument which gave out a regular signal for 15 seconds each minute – this was synchronised with the controller by a small instrument like a clock in the cockpit. On one occasion we were scrambled from Hawkinge as evening was drawing and climbed through a thin layer of cloud near Dungeness and control came through to say some enemy aircraft were in the vicinity.

Nothing could be seen so a section of us broke away and came down below the cloud once again. We broke cloud only to find ourselves in the middle of some twelve Bf109s which were on their way home. I don't know who were the more surprised! What I recall mostly about the mix-up was the patterns weaved by the tracer bullets, which showed up so brightly in the gathering dusk and I was intrigued by the way the tracers seemed to travel through the air so lazily. I was, however, brought back to earth (not literally) by a thump behind and looking in my rear-view mirror saw my tailplane in tatters.[3]

The keen interest shown by Hairs in tracer was something shared by many pilots, especially those in bombers, over the war years.

While the first phase of the battle was inconclusive, the losses to British shipping and the strain on the Royal Navy, which also had convoys across the Atlantic and the Bay of Biscay to protect, was such that the Admiralty soon decided not to run convoys through the English Channel. In this sense, the *Kanalkampf* was a success for the Germans. This was not surprising as attacks on shipping off the coast always meant that RAF Fighter Command had further to go to defend the convoys and the *Luftwaffe* fighter pilots were still well within their range of action. Ships were also more vulnerable, especially at the time when the average size of a coasting merchant ship was small, often less than a thousand tons.

THE MAIN ATTACK

Much had been learnt about tactics by both sides during the opening phase of the Battle of Britain. While the RAF had soon realised that the Boulton Paul Defiant with its heavy aft-facing gun turret was no match for an agile German fighter, the *Luftwaffe* in turn soon realised that a twin-engined fighter such as the Messerschmitt Me110 was at a disadvantage in a dogfight.

No less important, the Germans had come to realise that the big advantage possessed by the British was radar, and the Chain Home network in particular. This was the 'brain' behind the British defences, always ensuring that timely warning was given and that the nation's fighter defences were well directed and well co-ordinated. It was clear that if the planned invasion was to go ahead, the Royal Air Force would have to be destroyed. An operation was planned for this *Adlerangriff* (Eagle Attack), and the start date was known to the Germans as *Adlertag* (Eagle Day), but as so often happens, the start was delayed by the weather until 13 August 1940. This time the targets were not shipping or ports, but RAF stations and the Chain Home radar network.

The *Luftwaffe*'s planning was impeccable, as the operation was preceded by a determined assault on four of the Chain Home stations on 12 August, the day before the start date, by the specialised fighter-bomber unit *Erprobungsgruppe* 210, which attacked four of the stations, but only three of them became non-operational, and all were back in service within six hours. It was clear that the radar stations presented difficult targets. Not only were the masts difficult to hit, but their lattice structure meant that only a direct hit or very near miss was likely to cause significant damage.

On 13 August, *Adlertag*, *Erprobungsgruppe* 210 (or *Epro* 210) opened the attacks on RAF airfields and forward landing grounds, initially striking at those closest to the Channel coast, including RAF Manston and Hawkinge. There were further attacks on the Chain Home network as the week progressed and attention also turned to fighter bases further inland such as Biggin Hill and Croydon. The operation quickly built up to a climax on 15 August[4] when the *Luftwaffe* effort peaked with the largest number of sorties during the entire Battle of Britain. In the mistaken belief that RAF Fighter Command had concentrated all of its strength in the south, *Luftflotte* 5 attacked the north of England with aircraft flying from bases in Denmark and Norway. The target area was beyond the range of the Bf109 and instead the attackers had to rely on Me110s, and suffered heavy casualties as a result. The lesson was learnt, and *Luftflotte* 5 did not return in strength during the battle.

It was another three days before casualties peaked, however, as this was on 18 August, sometimes described as 'The Hardest Day'. Both sides suffered their heaviest losses on this day, but the big lesson for the *Luftwaffe* was that the Junkers Ju87 Stuka dive-bomber, which had served it so well in Spain, Poland, Norway, the Low Countries and France, was easy prey for British fighters. Yet, this was the aircraft on which the *Luftwaffe* relied for precision bombing, and it left the Germans at a disadvantage, forced to depend on *Erprobungsgruppe* 210, already heavily committed.

It was a blessing for both sides that the weather intervened once again and for almost a week operations were limited to reconnaissance flights. Nevertheless, the opportunity was taken to move other squadrons forward.

One squadron that was moved forward to Middle Wallop, in Hampshire, on 14 August, the day after the main part of the campaign had begun, was No. 234, with Pilot Officer Keith Lawrence. He recalls the way in which operations were conducted:

When we got to Middle Wallop it was straight into action. On the very first day, one of the chaps I came over on the boat with from New Zealand was killed, Cecil Hight. At the end of the first week of September the squadron returned to St Eval [in Cornwall] to 'rest' and train new pilots. During four weeks' fighting, we lost eighteen Spitfires in action.

At that time, the end of August, whenever we lost an aircraft, a replacement was soon flown in as there was, by now, a steady flow of new Spitfires from the factories at Castle Bromwich.[5] The ATA[6] pilots would usually fly them in, but also pilots from Ferry Command. I can remember them being flown in and going to the hangar for inspection. They were supposed to be ready for immediate action, but not before our ground crews were satisfied. Twenty-four pilots and twenty aircraft was roughly the disposition of the squadron which was aimed for. We flew as a squadron in twelves and rotated the on and off-duty times so that the twenty-four pilots shared the flying.

We had quite a few actions over the south coast. On one particular scramble (which I missed) there was a big raid over Sussex during which No. 234 Squadron probably destroyed or damaged ten Me110s.[7]

The inspection of newly arrived aircraft by the squadron's own mechanics was probably very reassuring to the pilots as aircraft produced by hastily trained factory workers during wartime were known to have left the factory and the pre-delivery test flight with some faults. One of the worst on record was an Avro Lancaster bomber delivered to No. 617 Squadron, the famous 'Dam Busters' later in the war with the control wires fitted so that every control movement resulted in the aircraft doing the opposite to that intended.

At the time, RAF fighter squadrons would fly in close formation with only the formation leader (the CO) searching the sky for other aircraft. The twelve aircraft would fly in four tight vics of three, although some squadrons would have an 'arse-end Charlie', or 'tail-arse Charlie', to weave on the watch for enemy fighters attempting to attack from behind. The squadron did not break formation until the CO had spotted an incoming German formation, called out its position on the radio, and then shouted 'tally ho'. As they headed for the bombers, they often found themselves engaged in a dogfight with the escorting Bf109s.

While there was an attempt to ensure that the initial attack was guided and co-ordinated, in the melee that followed it was every man for himself, so the squadron formation was lost and the aircraft were widely scattered. Aircraft were either attacking German aircraft or being attacked, but in just two or three minutes it would be over and the sky deserted. The pilots, many of them still very young and inexperienced, would then have to make their way back to base. It was usual for a newcomer to a squadron to be taken up with his aircraft accompanied by that of a more experienced pilot so that he could see the local landmarks and, if visibility was good, be able to find his own way home after action.

If there was cloud obscuring the view of the ground, the fighter pilots would call their base for a homing beacon, transmitting for four seconds or so. Most air stations had three homing stations, and by triangulation could identify the location of the fighter, and provide a course for the homeward flight. It was not usual to re-formate. Indeed, if aircraft returned in formation, those on the ground could safely assume that they had not found the enemy. After an encounter, the aircraft returned to base in ones and twos, usually over a period of around twenty minutes. After this time, any that had not arrived were feared to have either force-landed or baled out, or worse. Usually news of those who had survived a mishap came fairly quickly, but after thirty or forty minutes, often the worst was assumed. This was not unreasonable as downed pilots could be back with their units within hours.

By contrast, with the experience of the Spanish Civil War behind them, the *Luftwaffe* fighter pilots had evolved different tactics from the RAF. Instead of tight formations, fighters were sent in loose sections of two aircraft, known as a *Rotte*, with the leader followed by a wingman about 600 feet behind him, flying slightly higher. The leader searched for enemy aircraft and both covered the other's blind spots. Anyone attacking the leader could find himself sandwiched between the two aircraft.

Some credit this formation to that evolved by Oswald Boelcke in 1916, or to the Finnish Air Force, which decided on a similar tactic in 1934. Nevertheless, it was the *Luftwaffe* that used this tactic with modern aircraft and the RAF that did not use it at first.

The two-fighter patrol evolved into a four-fighter *Schwarm* with each pilot flying at a different height and all four keeping a lookout. It also had the advantage of making the formation more difficult to spot at a distance, while a tight crossover turn enabled the *Schwarm* to change direction quickly. This was far better than the RAF's dependence on the formation leader, and possibly also the 'tail-arse Charlie' to spot enemy aircraft.

Naturally, the more experienced RAF fighter pilots soon realised that their formations were far from ideal. Some units introduced more weavers flying slightly above the main formation to keep an additional lookout, but these tended to be the less experienced pilots and were often the first to be shot down, sometimes without the other pilots realising what had happened. As the battle continued, Squadron Leader Adolph 'Sailor' Malan, in command of No. 74 Squadron, decided on a variant of the *Luftwaffe* tactics that became known as the 'fours in line astern', which soon proved to be more effective and was later adopted throughout Fighter Command.

The air stations that had been completed before the war usually had decent accommodation for personnel and aircraft, although few fighter stations of the day had hard runways. The newer airfields, prepared rather than constructed in haste, often had bell tents for accommodation, with a marquee for the messes. Many of these airfields would have two or three squadrons, with the only communication being a shared field telephone that would ring once for one squadron, twice for another and three times for the third. This left everyone on edge until the ringing stopped!

Soon the airfields closest to the battles became untenable, including Manston, Ford and Tangmere, and the Fleet Air Arm's main station at RNAS Lee-on-the-Solent, more usually known simply as 'Lee'. Not all airfields were convenient for the Battle of Britain, and often squadrons could be accommodated at an airfield other than that from which they flew their missions.

Even airfields such as North Weald, less exposed, were often bombed. Aircrew could return to find that their accommodation had been destroyed, along with their possessions. Many had just the clothes they stood up in, and one pilot recalls having to go to a pub in order to have a bath! With his comrades, at one time he had to sleep on mattresses laid in rows in a shed.

Life for the pilots was demanding – either waiting for action or actually engaged in action, none of them knowing at breakfast whether they would survive the day, or even the morning. Pilot Officer Irving 'Black' Smith served with No. 151 Squadron, a Hurricane unit at North Weald. He recalls daily life.

> Throughout August 1940 ... the squadron would be released at nautical twilight (22.00 to 22.30 hours), go to bed, and be up again at 02.30 to 03.00 hours, having a cup of tea and probably an egg for breakfast, to be airborne from North Weald at nautical twilight at around 04.00 hours, in a formation of twelve aircraft, no lights, dimly in sight of each other and flying at low level about 50 feet above the ground, to land at first light at Rochford to be on readiness at dawn.
>
> If nothing was happening, No. 151 would be relieved by No. 56 Squadron at midday, but if things were happening, there was no relief. If No. 151 was on afternoon readiness at Rochford, they would fly back to North Weald at dusk, the aircraft being serviced overnight. This was an efficient but tiring routine, and getting enough sleep was a problem.
>
> Food was also a problem. All food at Rochford had to be sent in boxes to the tents. One often missed it and on occasions we did not get anything to eat until we were back at North Weald. But North Weald was not organised to serve the needs of pilots, and I remember often pleading with the mess staff to boil an egg or two out of hours. This is not a criticism, as the RAF was just starting to learn what it was all about, and it takes quite a long time to change entrenched attitudes and procedures during wartime, especially administrative ones.[8]

This clearly shows that the RAF, supposedly *the* service for airmen, had no idea and had given no thought to what life would be like under actual combat conditions. There was worse, as one pilot had no change of clothes at all and the uniform he was wearing was frayed and a 'greenish-colour', in his own words. His superiors at RAF Digby were unimpressed as they had not seen action and had no idea of how bad the situation was in the forward stations. He was lucky to escape punishment.

THE THIRD AND FOURTH PHASES

The *Luftwaffe* soon extended its campaign into a third phase, attacking RAF airfields and aircraft factories, as well as other industries such as tyre and engine factories that supplied the aircraft industry. The aircraft factories were attacked from 19 August and on 23 August the campaign extended to the RAF's airfields, although some had been attacked earlier. On the night of 24/25 August, several parts of the East End of London were attacked, setting a large area ablaze. This, the first big raid, is believed by some to have been a mistake as a formation of He111 bombers failed to find their target and ditched their bombs, but others feel that the attack was deliberate in an attempt to undermine the will of the civilian population. It is almost inevitable that any attack on industrial targets can lead to bombs drifting off-target and onto surrounding housing or other civilian areas such as shopping areas, hospitals or schools. The following night saw a further escalation in the air war as the RAF mounted a retaliatory raid on Berlin, much to the chagrin of Goering, who had boasted that Berlin would never be bombed. In his fury, Hitler demanded attacks on London.

Starting on 24 August, the crux of the battle became a contest between AVM Keith Park's 11 Group and Kesselring's *Luftflotte* 2. In the fortnight that followed, there were no less than thirty-three heavy attacks, of which no less than twenty-four were against airfields. RAF Eastchurch, a Coastal Command station, was attacked no less than seven times because it was thought to be a Fighter Command station, while Biggin Hill and Horn-church were struck four times each; Debden and North Weald twice; while Croydon, Gravesend, Hawkinge, Manston and Rochford were attacked once.

Spitfires continued to arrive at RAF stations to replace losses, but it took longer to train new pilots than build new aircraft, and new pilots were also those most likely to be lost once they joined an operational squadron. The typical replacement had had nine hours' flying time in an operational training unit (OTU), but no weapons or air-to-air combat training. Some sixty Fairey Battle bomber pilots were transferred to Fighter Command, where at least they could fly a useful aircraft! Around fifty-eight Fleet Air Arm fighter pilots also volunteered for secondment to the RAF, which at least had high performance fighters. By this time, the RAF had many air-crew from the British Empire, and especially the dominions of Australia, Canada, New Zealand and South Africa, while French and Belgian pilots had escaped to continue the war, although the Free French forces were still to be organised. They were soon joined by Czechoslovak and Polish pilots, usually flying in their own squadrons such as No. 303 (Polish) Squadron, but who had been held by Dowding until this late in the Battle of Britain as he was concerned about their lack of English. In fact, his fears were unjustified as one Czech, Josef Frantisek, who had the distinction of having flown first in his own country, then with the Polish Air Force and then the French *Armée de l'Air*, before finally joining the RAF, became the battle's top-scoring ace. Doubtless he was highly motivated!

What today might be described as 'mission creep' meant that the third phase led inexorably to the fourth phase, which was really the start of the blitz against British cities.

THE BIG WING
There was much for both sides to learn. The Battle of Britain was the first time that the *Luftwaffe* had met determined and successful resistance, but at least the *Luftwaffe* pilots and their leaders had several years of experience behind them while the RAF was learning as the war progressed.

At Duxford, Wing Commander Douglas Bader's 12 Group had been organised to operate as a 'Big Wing' of Nos 242, 302 and 310 Hurricane Squadrons and Nos 19 and 611 Spitfire Squadrons. The thinking behind this idea of Trafford Leigh Mallory was to meet the enemy formations with as large a concentration of defensive fighter power as possible, with the Hurricanes tackling the bombers while the faster Spitfires dealt with the fighter escorts. Ideally, this would break up the enemy formation and individual squadrons of 11 Group would deal with these.

This was the theory. Bader knew that for this system to work, his wing would have to be scrambled early. In practice, the wing was only called into action by the controllers of 11 Group if their aircraft were having difficulty containing the enemy attack, which meant that almost always the Duxford wing was scrambled late. With such a large formation of aircraft, it took time to form up into the Big Wing, which delayed their arrival further. AVM Keith Park criticised the Big Wing for arriving too late, while his frustration was shared by the pilots of the wing. Often, the wing would consist only of three squadrons instead of all five.

It was decided to simplify the start of the formation by the Hurricanes of Nos 242 and 310 taking off from Duxford and the Spitfires of No. 19 taking off from Fowlmere, and instead of forming up, all the aircraft would head for the rendezvous climbing as quickly as possible. The Spitfires were intended to arrive at the rendezvous slightly to one side of the Hurricanes and between 3,000 and 4,000 feet above them, so that the Hurricanes were on the bomber level and the Spitfires at the Bf109 fighter level.

Part of the problem was, of course, that Duxford reinforced 11 Group and possibly the Big Wing would have worked better had it consisted of 11 Group rather than 12 Group. The late arrival did have one advantage, however, as often the Duxford squadrons would be asked to patrol over 11 Group's airfields so that their aircraft could land safely because any aircraft is at its most vulnerable to enemy attack while landing.

OUTCOME

So, could the *Luftwaffe* have destroyed the RAF? Goering was prone to bombast. He had promised to finish off the British and French armies at Dunkirk, but had failed; he had promised that Berlin would not suffer an air raid, but in this too he was wrong. He had also promised to finish the RAF, but, as history shows, once again he had failed. More sober and contemplative minds, such as the head of the German Navy, or *Kriegsmarine*, Admiral Raeder, knew that they could not rule the waves and that Germany could not have absolute air superiority over British coastal waters let alone the mainland, and that an invasion of the United Kingdom was impossible.

Dowding, in a report to the Chief of the Air Staff, Sir Hugh Trenchard, maintained that the *Luftwaffe* had achieved 'very little' at the end of August and beginning of September. Only Biggin Hill was shut down amongst the sector stations, and that for just two hours.

Others, with access to records, contend that not only was aircraft production keeping pace with losses, aided by the Civilian Repair Organisation (CRO) and Air Servicing Unit (ASU) airfields, which between them repaired just under 5,000 aircraft, but the supply of new pilots also held up better than many believed at the time. The statistics indicate that on 1 July, RAF Fighter Command had 1,200 pilots, and a month later there were 1,400, a figure that rose to 1,600 by October and 1,800 in November. In addition to the repaired aircraft, 496 new aircraft were produced in July, although this fell to 467 in August and the same again in September. On 3 August, RAF Fighter Command had 1,061 fighters on its strength and of these, 708 were serviceable, while on 7 September, there were 1,161 on strength, and of these, 746 were serviceable. During the battle, there were 1,400 pilots and in the second half of September this rose to 1,500. By contrast, the *Luftwaffe* never had more than 1,200 pilots.

So much for the myth of 'The Few'. The Germans were even fewer.

This apart, without control of the sea, the invasion, Operation Sea Lion, could never have taken place. This was to be proved later in the war during the invasion of Crete, when the British and Greek forces lost control of the skies and the Germans were able to drop paratroops and land glider-borne troops, with heavy losses, but the Mediterranean Fleet wiped out the invasion barges.

Notes

1. Johnson, Group Captain 'Johnnie', *Wing Leader*, Chatto & Windus, London, 1956.
2. Imperial War Museum Sound Archive.
3. Imperial War Museum Sound Archive.
4. Now celebrated in the UK as Battle of Britain Day.
5. A shadow factory as Supermarine was based at Hamble, near Southampton.
6. Air Transport Auxiliary.
7. Imperial War Museum Sound Archive.
8. Imperial War Museum Sound Archive.

Chapter 5

Blitzkrieg and Fighter Sweeps

As shown in the previous chapter, the start of the bomber campaign against British cities, and especially London, overlapped with the Battle of Britain. Known popularly as the 'Blitz', short for the German *Blitzkrieg* or 'Lightning War', it started with day raids but soon evolved into night raids as the *Luftwaffe*, like the RAF, soon discovered that day raids were too costly in aircraft and men. The ability to attack at night was aided by Germany's advanced aircraft direction systems that made accurate attack possible until the RAF started to deflect the guiding beams. It was also aided by the initial lack of night fighters with airborne radar in the RAF as this development was still in its infancy.

The Blitz ran from August 1940 to May 1941, although some doubt whether the first raid in August was deliberate. The change from attacking the RAF to attacking British cities was intended to undermine the overall war effort, but not only had the *Luftwaffe* manifestly failed to destroy the RAF, as we have seen in the previous chapter, the RAF had grown stronger, not least in Fighter Command.

LUFTWAFFE TACTICS

In mounting a major strategic bombing campaign, the *Luftwaffe* was faced, as was the RAF, with the need to ensure both accurate navigation and then bombing accuracy over the target, not easy at night or in dense cloud. Night operations were preferred for high-level bombing, since the risk of fighter interception during the early months of the war was minimal. The *Luftwaffe* was well prepared for a major strategic bombing campaign in the sense that it had the technology in place to ensure accuracy, but was ill-prepared in that it lacked aircraft with sufficient range or war-load to sustain strategic bombing. This was the result of a decision taken in the late 1930s to concentrate on dive-bombers and what were at best medium bombers, partly because this ensured that great numbers of aircraft could be produced for the same money and raw materials, and partly because the *Luftwaffe* had not developed as a strategic air force. Despite the *Luftwaffe* controlling all German service aviation, or perhaps because of it, the service had developed as a tactical air force designed to operate in close support of fast-moving ground formations led by the Panzer tanks. In fact, the term *blitzkrieg* actually referred to this form of land and air close co-ordination rather than a bombing campaign as the British would have it.

The first of the techniques used by the *Luftwaffe* to ensure accuracy was called *Knickebein*, essentially radio beams transmitted by ground-based stations in occupied Europe, from northern France to the south of Norway, capable of covering the whole of the British Isles. By the end of August 1940, there were twelve of these stations, but by this time, too, No. 80 Wing of the RAF had started jamming the *Knickebein* beams. *Luftwaffe* pilot Otto von Ballasko recalls:

> At first we were very excited about *Knickebein*. But after we had used it on operations once or twice, we realised that the British were inter-fering with it ... the fact that our enemy obviously knew that the beams existed and that they were pointing towards the target for the night, was very disconcerting. For all we knew, the night fighters might be concentrating all the way along the beam to the target; more and more crews began to use the *Knickebein* beams only for range and kept out of them on the run up to the target.[1]

Eventually the RAF's countermeasures became more sophisticated and effective, with ground-based 'Meacons' bending the beams. The *Luftwaffe* then introduced more sophisticated radio beams, *X-Geraet* and *Y-Geraet*. The first of these used four beams, with the first pointed at the target for navigation, while the other three crossed the main beam at pre-set points in advance of the bomb release point, assisting accurate bomb-aiming. The first beam was 50 kilometres (31 miles) from the bomb release point; the second was at 20 kilometres (12.5 miles) from the bomb release point, at which the observer started a special clock which effectively acted as a stop-watch, and then the third beam was at 5 kilometres (3 miles) from the bomb release point. At the third beam, the observer pressed the button on the clock which stopped the first hand, and when the second hand caught up with it, electrical contacts were closed and the bombs were released automatically. The clock was essential to accurate bombing, complement-ing the beams by providing accurate information about the aircraft's ground speed, which of course could otherwise put accuracy at the mercy of the prevailing winds.

A refinement, *Y-Geraet* used a single ground station that produced a complicated beam that comprised 180 directional signals per minute, which had to be interpreted by a special device aboard the aircraft, whose functions included re-radiating the signal back to the ground station, ensuring that the operators on the ground knew the aircraft's position exactly. This meant that they could then signal the aircraft at the bomb-release point. The sophistication of the equipment, with both *Geraet* systems using higher frequency and more accurate radio signals than the original *Knickebein*, meant that specially trained crews had to be used, effectively the German equivalent of the RAF's Pathfinders, and working within a special unit, *Kampfgruppe* 100, flying Heinkel He111s.

This unit was moved forward from Germany to a base at Vannes, in Brittany, on 11 August 1940. The unit's first operation was two days later, on the night of 13/14 August, against Castle Bromwich, in the English Midlands, where a 'shadow' factory was preparing to start production of Spitfires. There were another eight operations before the end of the month.

Not all of the measures were necessarily sophisticated. A defensive measure used by both sides during the war was to operate aircraft with their engines desynchronised – one running faster than the other – so that the resultant throbbing note made the use of sound locators to detect the position of aircraft about to fly overhead extremely difficult.

THE START OF THE BLITZ

The impact of the bombing on those on the ground was considerable. The first heavy daylight attack on London was on 7 September. It was followed after dark on the night of 7/8 September 1940, by the first heavy German night raid on London, with 318 German bombers sent against the city, with no risk of interception by night fighters. In contrast to raids later in the war, no effort was made to concentrate the attack, which lasted from 20.10 on 7 September until 04.30 the following morning.

Amongst the squadrons scrambled to intercept the approaching German bombers was No. 72 with Spitfires from RAF Croydon, the site of London's pre-war civil airport. They were directed to meet more than fifty Dornier Do17 bombers with their fighter escorts. One of those involved was Sergeant Pilot William Rolls, who was flying in a section led by Flying Officer Elsdon.

As we approached the enemy aircraft, Elsdon ordered echelon to port and I went underneath to come up on John White's port-side. This way we went in to the bombers. As we were almost head-on, there was little chance to get a single target in your sight, so it left you open to fire at everything in front of you as you flew through the formation of enemy bombers. At the same time the gunners in the front and rear turrets of the bombers were firing at us.

I saw a hell of a lot of crosses, but did not see any going down, and by the time I had got through the formation I was on my own without ammunition, and was diving as fast as I could away from a Bf109 that I saw in my mirror. There were dozens of Spitfires from other squadrons attacking the bombers and I could see the fires down by the docks.

I was now over the reservoirs at Chingford and not far from my parents' home at Edmonton. I flew low over the house and waggled my wings; I knew that if my parents did not see me, one of the neighbours would and they would tell my mother.[2]

William Rolls was the lucky one of his formation, a vic of just three aircraft. He reached Croydon safely to find that the other two had not returned. He soon learned that Elsdon had baled out and White had crash-landed near the docks. Nevertheless, all ended well as they were soon told that both were safe. White telephoned to say that he was in a pub in Rotherhithe, and Rolls accompanied the station motor transport section driver to pick him up, finding him surrounded by the local ladies and being treated to free drinks, including a few Scotches. Rolls was given the same generous treatment.

For the *Luftwaffe* that night, finding the target was not a problem, since the fires from the daylight attack were still burning. Of nine major fires, defined by the London Fire Brigade as a 'conflagration' – one that is spreading and requires more than one hundred pumps – that in the Surrey Docks, at the Quebec Yard, was the fiercest recorded in Britain. Elsewhere, there were other hazards, as the London Fire Brigade's official history of the Second World War recalls.

At Woolwich Arsenal men fought the flames amongst boxes of live ammunition and crates of nitro-glycerine under a hail of bombs directed at London's No. 1 military target. But in the docks themselves strange things were going on. There were pepper fires, loading the surrounding air heavily with stinging particles, so that when the firemen took a deep breath it felt like burning fire itself. There were rum fires, with torrents of blazing liquid pouring from the warehouse doors and barrels exploding like bombs themselves. There was a paint fire, another cascade of white hot flame, coating the pumps with varnish that could not be cleaned for weeks. A rubber fire gave forth black clouds of smoke so asphyxiating that it could only be fought from a distance, and was always threatening to choke the attackers. Sugar, it seems, burns well in liquid form as it floats on the water in dockyard basins. Tea makes a blaze that is 'sweet, sickly and very intense'. One man found it odd to be pouring cold water on hot tea leaves. A grain warehouse when burning produced great clouds of black flies that settled in banks upon the walls, whence the firemen washed them off with their jets. There were rats in their hundreds. And the residue of burned wheat was 'a sticky mess that pulls your boots off'.[3]

There were also nineteen major fires, that is fires requiring thirty or more pumps, forty serious fires and a thousand smaller fires. Set against this, it seems almost miraculous that the death toll was no higher than 430 killed and 1,600 injured.

The volume of anti-aircraft fire aimed at the attackers was largely wild and uncontrolled shooting as the control systems broke down. Londoners would afterwards claim that they could tell German bombers from British because of the distinctive engine note, but as mentioned earlier, the German pilots put their engines on different power settings whilst over the target area to confuse sound direction-seeking equipment.

The *Luftwaffe* sent another 207 aircraft over the following night, aiming for the fires that had defeated the fire brigade's efforts, so that by the morning of 9 September, there were no less than 12 major conflagrations. Another 412 people had been killed and 747 seriously injured. The four main railway termini serving the south of England were so badly damaged that railway services could not be operated for a short period. Interestingly, many of these lines had been electrified by the Southern Railway between the wars, and electric trains proved as reliable amongst wartime damage as the hardier steam locomotives.

This was the result of two nights' bombing by medium bombers. The *Luftwaffe* was back for sixty-four of the following sixty-five nights – the exception being due to bad weather.

The *Luftwaffe* had a massive, indeed overwhelming, strength, but this did not mean that the bomber crews had an easy time with ample rest between sorties. *Unteroffizier* Horst Goetz flew with *Kampfgruppe* 100 during the blitz on London, and in one three-week period he flew against London: on 23 September, twice on 24 September (once in the morning and again in the evening), and then again on the evenings of 27, 28, 29, 30 September, and 2 and 4 October, before flying against Manchester on 7 and 9 October, and then against Coventry on 12 October. Coventry, in the Midlands, and Manchester, even further north in the north-west, were more distant targets than London, hence the less intensive nature of these operations.

An experienced pilot, Goetz had flown 1,800 hours before he even started operations against Britain. He recalls:

> I have no particular memories of individual operations. They were all quite routine, like running a bus service. The London flak defences put on a great show – at night the exploding shells gave the place the appearance of bubbling pea soup; but very few of our aircraft were hit – I myself never collected so much as a shell fragment.[4]

Goetz maintains that it was a rare occasion for one of his crew to catch sight of a British night fighter, and they never attacked. On the return flights the radio operator would often tune in his receiver to a music programme to provide some relief from the monotony.

One of the heaviest attacks during the London Blitz was that of the night of 15/16 October, starting at 20.40 on 15 October and continuing at 04.40 the following morning. A force of 400 bombers was sent against the city, approaching it at between 16,000 and 20,000 feet. The aircraft came from bases in the Netherlands, Belgium and northern France, crossing the coast at many points between West Sussex and Essex. One pilot, *Feldwebel* Guenther Unger, flew two sorties, one in the evening and another early the following morning, with a two-hour break on the ground between them. In an interesting contrast to bomber operations later in the war, he had to remain over the London Docks, circling for as long as possible to cause the maximum confusion for the defences, and dropping a bomb every five minutes or so, so that on each sortie he spent some twenty-five minutes over the target area. The anti-aircraft fire ranged from between 13,000 and 20,000 feet. Forty-one night fighters, including some Bristol Blenheims equipped with radar, were sent to intercept the bombers, but in desperation, the obsolete Boulton Paul Defiants were put into the air as night fighters, although lacking radar, and on the night of 15/16 October, one of these from 264 Squadron managed to shoot down a German bomber, believed to have been the only RAF success that night!

London's blitz lasted a total of sixty-seven nights from 7 September until the morning of 14 November, with just one night without attack from the air.

15 SEPTEMBER

One of the most decisive days in the Battle of Britain was Sunday, 15 September, when the *Luftwaffe* made two very heavy raids on London with the intention of drawing as many RAF fighters as possible into the action. They did, but had clearly underestimated just how many aircraft RAF Fighter Command could put into the air by this time, with more than 300 Hurricanes and Spitfires ready for the Germans.

By coincidence, Winston Churchill was visiting RAF Uxbridge that day, before anyone knew what was likely to happen. As he watched events unfold on the plotting table, he turned to AVM Keith Park and asked him what reserves he had left. 'None,' came the reply.

The driving force behind the all-out effort by the *Luftwaffe* on this day was simply that Kesselring knew that if he did not inflict serious damage on the RAF by mid-September, the chance of Germany mounting an invasion before the winter weather set in was gone. He was already short of aircraft and airmen. Hitler was determined to invade Great Britain, and Goering was not the man to face his leader with a sharp dose of reality, unlike the naval commanders who knew that their position was weak. After more than a month of intensive bombing of London and the south coast ports and airfields, Kesselring's bomber force had been reduced by around fifty per cent.

Despite this, there was almost a leisurely pace to the start of the first raid. The Chain Home network noted the first aircraft as they assembled over the French coast at 10.30, and then waited for the rest of the attacking force to form up so that more than 100 bombers and 400 fighters did not reach the English coast until 11.30. By this time, Park had scrambled eleven out of his twenty-one Spitfire and Hurricane squadrons. His 11 Group was not alone, as Brand sent a Spitfire squadron from Middle Wallop and Leigh-Mallory put the Duxford Wing into the air, led by Douglas Bader, with all five of its squadrons.

This was a formidable defence, and, as the Germans crossed the coast of Kent near Dover, it provided a gauntlet of fire all the way to London, dispersing the *Luftwaffe* formations. Even so, many aircraft still reached London and dropped their bombs. Then, they found themselves facing the Duxford Wing. There was criticism at the time of the Duxford Wing arriving late, and after the *Luftwaffe* had dropped their bombs and expended their ammunition.

Sergeant Pilot Michael Croskell was flying with No. 213 Squadron, in one of twenty-seven aircraft lost by Fighter Command that day. He took off from Tangmere.

> The first thing was we were called to get cracking when we were all drinking a cup of tea outside the tea van. I remember saying to the girl: 'Keep that warm, I'll be back in half an hour,' but of course I wasn't. We went charging off and flew straight through a large flock of Heinkel He111s.
>
> We had this old-fashioned idea of flying in vic formation. The Germans were much better, they flew in what were called finger fours. They used to fly four aircraft, so you could look out a lot more. In vic formation you're looking at the flipping leader and you aren't looking out for the opposition. Well, we turned very quickly after this bunch of He111s, so quickly that I was on the inside of the turn. I couldn't get the throttle back quickly enough and the bloke on the outside of the turn was left miles behind. We both got shot down.
>
> What happened was, I saw a Dornier Do17 below me and I thought that's for me and I went charging down. The next thing I knew I got four cannon shells into me because I didn't look in the rear-view mirror. There were two Bf109s behind me. I saw them too late of course. The Germans had much more advanced armament than we did, 20mm explosive shells, they did a hell of a lot of damage. Most of my tail end was shot away. So there we are, I got out at 200 feet, which was a bit low. I remember I got desperate. You had to pull a handle sideways in the cockpit to release the hood and slide it back, but that was all jammed by these cannon shells. I actually undid my belt and stood crouched on the seat and tried to use two hands to open the hood.
>
> Eventually it came open and I shot out just in time. The parachute opened almost as I hit the ground and the aeroplane exploded before

the parachute opened. I remember thinking, 'Christ, the parachute's on fire,' but it wasn't. I fortunately landed in a wood of young trees. I didn't know where I was of course. I was eventually found by some ack-ack people and I had a fair bit of blood coming out of me as I'd been hit by four cannon shells. There was a lot of blood coming out of my left shoe and they were determined to cut it off, but being a mean Yorkshireman I objected strongly, and whilst I was objecting they cut the other one off.

Anyway, I spent a bit of time in Maidstone hospital, then moved to Hatton and whilst my mates were finishing off the battle I chatted up the nursing sister and married the girl.[5]

The first raid was over by noon.

At around 14.00, enemy aircraft were seen starting to form up again, and this time they were much less leisurely than they had been in the morning. As in the morning, 10 and 12 Groups sent squadrons to support the hard-pressed 11 Group, but this time twelve squadrons were airborne even before the *Luftwaffe* aircraft crossed the coast. Kesselring had intended to mount an even heavier attack with *Luftflotte* 2, but his fighters had been badly depleted during the morning. He still sent a larger force of bombers, but, in a change of tactics, instead of having all of his fighters provide close support for the bombers, he sent a large number of them ahead of the bombers with the intention of engaging the RAF's fighters and so allowing his bombers to fly unchallenged to London.

The bomber force crossed the coast with one part engaged by RAF fighters near Edenbridge and the other near Canterbury. A running battle developed and the Germans were tackled by fresh fighters on their way to London, where the advance German fighters suddenly found themselves confronted by fifteen Hurricane and Spitfire squadrons. While an aerial battle of epic proportions continued, the main bomber force arrived and started to drop their bombs on London. So far it looked as if Kesselring's plan was working, but as the bombers dropped their loads, with the crews confident that they were safe from challenge by RAF fighters, the Duxford Wing appeared, led by Douglas Bader, and fell upon the attackers.

It was clear that the RAF had not been destroyed and that it was, if anything, more capable than ever of being able to send a substantial force into the sky whenever the *Luftwaffe* arrived.

While 10 Group had reinforced 11 Group that day, it was not without challenges in its own area. Sperrle's *Luftflotte* 3 had mounted daylight raids against the naval base at Portland and the Supermarine Spitfire factory some miles to the east at Eastleigh, near Southampton. This was done without a fighter escort, which perhaps is why they missed the factory even flying as low as 2,000 feet, as they were doubtless anxious to fly in, drop their bombs and get away again.

After such a strenuous day, it must have been a relief that Monday, 16 September was wet and operations were suspended.

While the crews rested and aircraft were repaired, Kesselring and Sperrle met Goering, only to find that he still maintained that four or five days of fine weather would see the RAF finished. The *Luftwaffe* officers knew that this would be impossible and that all that would result would be a further reduction in their numbers. Hitler must have had his own doubts as well by this time, as on 17 September he decided not to issue the preliminary order for the invasion, a decision doubtless also prompted by warnings of high winds and stormy seas by the *Kriegsmarine*. Operation Sealion was postponed.

COVENTRY

After the unsustainable losses suffered by the *Luftwaffe* during daylight raids, the strategy turned to night raids, mainly against London but many important provincial centres were also attacked, and, of these, the most notorious was that against Coventry, in the West Midlands.

The major raid on Coventry took place on the night of 14 November. No less than 449 bombers approached the target, which was marked by thirteen He111s of *Kampfgruppe* 100 using incendiary bombs. The bomber streams converged on the target, with one approaching over the Wash on Britain's east coast, another over Brighton and a third over the Isle of Wight, both on the south coast. *Feldwebel* Guenther Unger flew on the Coventry raid.

> While we were still over the Channel on the way in we caught sight of a small pinprick of white light in front of us, looking rather like a hand torch seen from 200 yards. My crew and I speculated as to what it might be – some form of beacon to guide British night fighters, perhaps? As we drew closer to our target the light gradually became larger until it suddenly dawned on us: we were looking at the burning city of Coventry.

The city of Coventry, in the English Midlands, was, as it still is, a major centre for manufacturing industry, including the motor industry, which had stopped producing cars and was producing military vehicles and aircraft under the 'shadow factory' programme, which had converted civilian manufacturing to the British war effort. The *Luftwaffe* had decided to attack British industrial centres in addition to London, which had relatively little heavy industry, although it was important from the point of view of communications and especially its massive dock system.

The night of 14/15 November 1940 saw 499 *Luftwaffe* bombers raid Coventry, devastating the city centre and causing civilian casualties. A much smaller city than London, Coventry was so seriously hit that production in its factories ground to a halt. Much of the city was flattened. A total of 506 people were killed, and another 432 seriously injured. Out of 119 night fighter sorties, just 7 sighted bombers, and none was shot down. Two bombers were shot down by anti-aircraft fire.

The Blitz continued throughout the winter and into the spring. On the night of 12/13 March 1941, the major port of Liverpool was the target. By this time, the British night fighter operations were becoming much more effective, with 178 aircraft put into the air to counter 339 *Luftwaffe* bombers converging on the target from their bases in France and the Low Countries, and, in this case, from Norway as well. Once again, fifteen He111s from *KG* 100 operated as pathfinders, dropping their incendiaries visually from around 12,000 feet, assisted by fourteen He111s from III/*KG* 26, who used *X-Geraet* and dropped their incendiaries from upwards of 16,000 feet. The bombers attacked from between 7,000 and 12,000 feet on a clear moonlit night.

As a defensive measure, Fighter Command despatched the Bristol Blenheims of No. 23 Squadron to patrol over airfields in northern France, and it is believed that one He111 from the pathfinder unit III/*KG* 26 was shot down, despite the absence of any claims by the RAF. Closer to the target, No. 93 Squadron had an elderly Harrow bomber on patrol off the south coast of England ready to drop aerial mines in front of the bombers, but the slow aircraft faced with relatively fast-moving bombers coming from a number of different bases was unable to get into position to drop its mines, despite remaining on station for three hours. The next line of defence were the night fighters, including the GCI (ground controlled interception) Bristol Beaufighters of No. 604 Squadron, whose seven aircraft that night reported one bomber shot down, another probable and two damaged. At least two more were then shot down by Defiants over southern England, and another was shot down by a Hurricane as it approached Liverpool. The bombers flew too low to be caught by Defiants and Hurricanes on patrol high over the target, although barrage balloons ensured that the bombers had to keep above 5,000 feet, but the improved accuracy of British anti-aircraft fire by this time accounted for a number of aircraft, including a new Junkers Ju88 being flown by *Feldwebel* Guenther Unger, who was just releasing his bomb load of four 550lb and ten 110lb bombs.

> I looked round and saw a small but very bright glow on the cowling immediately behind the starboard engine. The metal was actually burning, which meant that there must have been intense heat, probably from a fire inside the nacelle. At first the visible spot of fire was very small; but it grew rapidly and flames began to trail behind the aircraft. I could see there was no hope of our getting home so I ordered the crew to bail out.[6]

His flight engineer opened the escape hatch at the rear of the cabin and jumped, followed by the radio operator. After they had gone, Unger turned the bomber until it was pointing out to sea, so that when it crashed there would be nothing for the British to find. He left his seat as the observer dropped out of the hatch. The Junkers was flying properly trimmed, flying straight and level perfectly well on both engines. Unger recalls that, for a moment he considered trying to get home alone, but a further glance at the blaze made it clear that this would have been impossible. He moved to the rear of the aircraft and followed his crew out of the hatch.

Unger was flying with the II Gruppe on this occasion, rather than his own III/KG76, having volunteered while the rest of his unit was converting to the new type. He had attacked from 10,000 feet, aiming at shipping. On a typical bombing run such as this, his observer, *Feldwebel* 'Ast' Meier, sat next to the pilot, crouching over his *Lotfe* bombsight, with his left hand resting on Unger's right foot on the rudder pedal, finely adjusting the course of the bomber during the crucial seconds before bomb release.

Unger and his crew all landed safely, with Unger himself having the most difficult escape, landing in shallow water and then spending an hour wading ashore as he tried to avoid the deeper water channels cutting across the coastal mud banks. He gave himself up to a Home Guard member on reaching Wallasey.

While the loss of some seven bombers, four to fighters and three to gunners, was the heaviest *Luftwaffe* loss rate at that time of the war, such losses were affordable and far less in percentage terms than on many of the early RAF raids. Another two aircraft crashed on occupied territory, probably as a result of damage inflicted, although the less experienced pilots found landing very difficult on the many makeshift airfields in occupied France and Belgium. The bombs fell on Birkenhead and Wallasey, Liverpool and Bootle, starting more than 500 fires. The *Luftwaffe* force had carried 270 tons of high explosives and dropped almost 2,000 incendiaries.

A second attack on Liverpool took place the following night, although with just 65 aircraft, while another force attacked Hull, and the main force of 236 aircraft attacked Glasgow. It was on this evening that a Harrow of No. 93 Squadron, flown by Flight-Lieutenant Hayley-Bell, managed to strike a German bomber with one of its aerial mines. Having taken half an hour to climb to 17,000 feet, flying off Swanage, he was directed by ground radar to intercept a stream of bombers, being positioned 4 miles ahead of them and 3,000 feet above. The mines were dropped at 200-foot intervals in front of the bombers, and soon afterwards, Hayley-Bell heard an explosion, and then heard and felt a second one. One of his mines had hit an aircraft, which had then blown up. The irony was that his minefield had missed the bomber formation for which it had been intended by ground control, and struck an aircraft in another formation of four aircraft! Dropping aerial mines was a hopeless task and any success was due to good luck, at least for the mine droppers!

While the distance to Scotland from northern Germany and Scandinavia was enough to discourage *Luftwaffe* bombing on the scale that had affected London, Glasgow and nearby Clydebank suffered heavy attacks on the nights of 6/7 and 7/8 May 1941. One of the fighter pilots defending the city was Tom Dalton-Morgan, later a group captain, who was one of the few to succeed on night operations flying the Hurricane. He accounted for at least six enemy aircraft at night. On one occasion he shot down a Ju88 having first noticed its shadow on the moonlit sea.

On 24 July 1941, he was carrying out a practice interception with another pilot when he noticed another Ju88. He gave chase and was ready to attack when his engine began to give trouble and fumes filled the cockpit. He attacked the bomber three times, seeing it hit the sea, when his engine stopped. He was too low to bale out, so ditched, losing two front teeth when his face hit the gun sight. He was rescued by the Royal Navy.

'I consider this to be a classic example of how a first-class fighter pilot can attack an enemy while his engine is failing,' commented his station commander. 'Shoot it down, force land on the sea, and get away with it.'

Dalton-Morgan was awarded a bar to his DFC.

THE FIGHTER-BOMBER

The switch to night raids, which could not be escorted by the *Luftwaffe*'s fighters, all of which were day fighters, left the fighter units without a role. Goering ordered his Bf109s and Me110s to be converted into fighter-bombers. The single-engined Bf109 could carry a single 500lb bomb, while the twin-engined Me110 would carry two 500lb bombs and four 100lb bombs. Initially they were sent over in formations that varied between 50 and 100 aircraft, flying at between 20,000 feet and 30,000 feet, at which height they inflicted damage and bloodshed, despite being too high for accurate bomb-aiming. London, Portsmouth and Southampton first felt the effect of these raids on 1 October.

The following day, much smaller numbers of aircraft were sent against London and Biggin Hill, keeping up what was almost a nonstop series of raids between 09.30 and 13.30. That night there were bomber raids on a number of cities in addition to London, ranging from Manchester to Aberdeen. On 3 October, fighter-bombers attacked RAF Cardington, Cosford and Tangmere, as well as a number of smaller cities including Cambridge and Worcester, and the de Havilland aircraft factory at Hatfield.

Sergeant Pilot William Rolls was with No. 72 Squadron at RAF Biggin Hill.

Johnny White and I were on duty and at readiness when we got a call to scramble. We saw some Bf109s, but they were too high and too far away from us, so after a short patrol we landed. They had been intercepted by other squadrons. In the afternoon we were again scrambled and this time to 25,000 feet. We were to patrol a line between two points to stop any Bf109 bombers which had been coming over in place of the Ju88s and Do17s, etc. These fighter-bombers carried a bomb under each wing, and were used for scatter bombing by dropping their bombs directly they saw the Hurricanes or Spitfires approaching them. In many cases they would then turn tail back to France. It was not very encouraging to have to climb to these heights through cloud and weather, just to see them turn tail.[7]

The fighter-bomber raids continued into October, including attacks on London. By this time, there were also night bomber raids against airfields, where poor accuracy meant that little serious damage was done for the most part, and against London, where considerable damage was done. The 'tip-and-run' nature of the fighter-bomber attacks caused most havoc on the coast and at towns such as Bexhill-on-Sea. The low level and fast nature of the attacks often meant that air raid sirens were not sounded before the aircraft reached the towns and dropped their bombs and as quickly flew away again. This continued until the short, dull and cloudy grey days of December effectively put an end to such operations.

The *Luftwaffe* campaign against British cities caused considerable disruption and loss of life on the ground, for relatively light German losses at this stage in the war. As war progressed and improved equipment became available, the RAF's night fighters became a more formidable threat. Nevertheless, once again the Germans were paying the price of not having a heavy bomber fleet and lacking the bomb loads, bomb sizes and range to make effective strikes against British cities, despite having the benefit of advance bases in France and Belgium. The constant raids on London showed that even a persistent campaign could not break such a large target without large enough aircraft. It also overlooked the fact that much of Britain's industry had been widely dispersed, with relatively little heavy industry actually based in the capital itself.

The Germans did not maintain their blitz on Coventry, or any other British city other than London, in the way that the RAF and USAAF were to persist with their German targets later in the war. Some believe that had the Germans persisted in their raids on Coventry, or had not relieved the pressure on London by switching to provincial centres, civilian casualties and morale would have been so shaken that peace terms would have had to have been sought. Whether or not this would have been the case can only be guessed at. After the mauling received from the RAF during the Battle of Britain, German casualties during the onset of the night bombing campaign were relatively light, and the reason for such lack of persistence in the blitz on London and then in the campaign against Britain's industry, seems due simply to poor strategic planning and direction. On the other hand, would the *Luftwaffe*, lacking a true heavy bomber force, have been capable of causing the damage that the heavy bombers, sometimes attacking in twice the strength of the Coventry raid, inflicted upon German cities? Did the Germans seek surrender after these heavy and often repeated raids? They did not. It can be argued that even the RAF and USAAF probably moved on to their next target prematurely, since many, including Goebbels, Hitler's propaganda chief, doubted their country's ability to take much more punishment at times. In defence of the commanders of the bomber forces, they were always under massive military and, most of all, political pressure to attack many more targets than resources permitted, allowing targets time for reconstruction.

FIGHTER SWEEPS

Early in 1941, with fewer German day raids, even using fighter-bombers, RAF Fighter Command's pilots were beginning to feel under-employed. There had been attempts during the winter to use Spitfires to augment the still limited number of radar-equipped Bristol Beaufighters as night fighters, but this had resulted in little success and at least one occasion when a twin-engined Beaufighter was mistaken for a Junkers Ju88, probably the best medium bomber that the *Luftwaffe* employed. The risk of being shot down by British anti-aircraft fire was another problem, while heavy smoke from the industrial installations of the day made flying at night even more dangerous for day fighters without radar.

There were other problems. The Spitfire was the livelier and more modern aircraft, overall with a better performance, but if one had to use a day fighter on a night patrol the Hurricane had a better view than the early Spitfires and a roomier cockpit, and a wider undercarriage as the narrow undercarriage of the Spitfire made it more difficult to land at night.

While improved marks of Spitfire were entering service and the squadrons south of the river Thames had priority for these, the Messerschmitt Bf109 was also improving with the arrival of the Bf109F, the first to have the cannon fitted into the propeller boss that gave improved accuracy as well as the benefit of the more lethal cannon shell.

At the time, Johnnie Johnson, later a group captain and one of Britain's top-scoring fighter aces, was a young pilot officer with No. 616 Squadron, which had just been moved south to RAF Tangmere in West Sussex, where his wing was commanded by the legendary Douglas Bader. It was Bader who declared one day that '... if the Huns won't come up, we'll put on a show over St Omer!' St Omer was one of the main *Luftwaffe* fighter bases in occupied France. He recalls one of the first.

Soon after Bader's arrival we flew on a two-squadron sweep. We were to climb across the Channel, poke our noses over Boulogne, skirt down the Somme estuary and withdraw. Although the *Luftwaffe* had withdrawn some of its fighter units from northern France to Rumania, to support the campaign in the Balkans, a considerable number of fighters and bombers remained to oppose us. During these early spring days of 1941 both sides regarded the Channel as neutral territory and Spitfires and Messerschmitts often clashed in bitter air battles.

There had been no time for Bader to teach us his own theories of combat formations and tactics. For this show we could fly in the old, tight, line-astern style and he would lead our squadron.

Climbing and still holding a close formation, we curved across the Channel. I was in the number three position in Bader's section and ahead of me were Cocky and the wing commander. Behind me, in the unenviable tail-end Charlie position, was an apprehensive Nip. Suddenly I spotted three lean 109s only a few hundred feet higher than our formation and travelling in the same direction. Obviously they hadn't seen us and would make an ideal target for a section of 145 Squadron who were still higher than the 109s. I should have calmly reported the number, type and position of the 109s to our leader, but I was excited and shouted, 'Look out, Dogsbody.' ['Dogsbody' – the call sign for the formation leader, derived from his initials.]

But the other pilots of the wing weren't waiting for further advice from me. To them 'look out' was a warning of the utmost danger – of the dreaded bounce by a strong force of 109s. Now they took swift evasive action and half-rolled, dived, aileron-turned and swung out in all directions, like a wedge of fast-moving teal avoiding a wildfowler on the coast. In far less time than it takes to tell, a highly organised wing was reduced to a shambles and the scattered sections could never be reformed in time to continue the planned flight ...[8]

As Johnson suspected, on landing Bader was anxious to find the 'clot' who shouted 'look out'. He was very unimpressed with Johnson's explanation that there were three Bf109s above his formation, telling him that the two squadrons could have clobbered the lot. Bader then delivered a short, but clearly timely, lecture. In future, *in extremis* the pilot who identified a threat was to call out 'break port' or 'break starboard' using either the section's name, such as blue section, or using the Christian name of the section leader, which Bader much preferred. The expression 'look out' was not to be used, to avoid mass panic. Otherwise, enemy aircraft were to be reported using the clock code, so it would be: 'Dogsbody from red two. Three 109s at two o'clock high', with the distance in yards.

Bader was not a man to hold a grudge or be angry for long. A few days later Johnson was sent to check the squadron's Spitfires while most of the rest of the pilots were snatching a few hours in bed having been on night patrols. He was to check with the flight sergeant in charge of maintenance to see if any aircraft needed air tests. Bader appeared, and on hearing that a couple of aircraft required air tests, decided that he would take Johnson on a trip across the Channel to 'see if we can bag a couple of Huns before lunch'.

They took off and climbed through the clouds and out into bright sunshine. Bader waved his hand across his face, signalling to Johnson that he was to take up a wide abreast position. The hand signal was meant to ensure that radio silence was maintained, but the radio crackled into life, challenging them as to their intentions. At first Bader ignored the request, but when told that the station commander wanted to know, Bader had to reply, telling the controller that two aircraft were on a 'little snoop across the Channel'. Within a few moments the radio crackled into life again, ordering Bader and Johnson back to base. Nevertheless, never one to let an opportunity be lost, on the return flight along the Sussex coast Bader showed the younger pilot how to get onto the tail of a Bf109, with a steep climb and a tight turn.

'RHUBARB'

After such a discouraging start, low-level fighter sweeps over France, code-named 'Rhubarb', became very much the standard pattern of operations for the day fighters based at Tangmere. Days of low cloud or poor visibility were to provide the chance to drop below cloud level and look for 'targets of opportunity', such as aircraft on the ground, troops and staff cars, as well as transport targets such as railway rolling stock and locomotives. These aircraft were usually conducted by a section or pair of Spitfires hunting together.

Views on the usefulness of such operations varied. So pilots preferred the excitement and teamwork of dogfights, and some also believed that the gains from fighter sweeps did not justify the risk to aircraft or pilots. On the other hand, a fast-moving fighter, especially if fitted with the more lethal cannon, was more likely to succeed in an attack against aircraft on the ground or railway rolling stock than a bomber. A few cannon shells through the boiler of a steam locomotive was a very effective way of putting it out of action for some weeks, if not longer. Sadly, at the time the squadron's Spitfires had machine guns and so their efforts were puny by comparison.

These operations were not a soft option and certainly not easy or without risk. While the poor weather helped to conceal the impending attack, often the cloud base was below 1,000 feet and, while most of the target area was low and level, there were small hills that could provide an unwelcome and sudden landing should they be waiting as the Spitfires dropped down through the cloud. The one safety precaution was that if the aircraft weren't below cloud level at 500 feet, the operation was called off. This in itself was hardly a comforting precaution as the pressure altimeters in use needed local calibration for accuracy and this was hardly likely to be provided by the local *Luftwaffe* controllers!

Another pilot engaged in fighter sweeps was Captain Hamish Pelham-Burn, a Seaforth Highlander who had volunteered for a temporary transfer to the RAF after being evacuated from Cherbourg. He actually enjoyed the fighter sweeps, flying his Hurricane at close to treetop level to attack armed trains.

'Try to take out the gunner on the first pass,' as he described his technique later. 'Then pull up and have a go at the locomotive on the second time round. Ammunition finished, then streak for home.'

His brief career with the RAF was ended with a bout of sinusitis, after which he was transferred to special operations.

Flying in close formation so as not to lose one another in the cloud, the promises that most of the heavy AA fire would be concentrated on the coast soon proved to be false as *Luftwaffe* bases were, inevitably, always heavily defended and the gunners could hear the aircraft coming. Often decoy targets were placed, such as railway locomotives, drawing the attackers towards them and into a trap with surrounding heavy AA fire. The only way of having a chance of survival was to make one fast low-level attack and then climb away. Making a second run at a heavily defended target was suicidal.

While the Spitfire provided reasonably good armour protection for the pilot, its Achilles' heel was the coolant, glycol, contained in a small tank just below the propeller spinner. If fractured by a lucky machine-gun bullet, this leaked and the aircraft engine seized up or caught fire within minutes.

Johnson was one of those who believed that the 'Rhubarb' operations were a dangerous and costly waste of time, but they continued until late 1943, during which time he believed that hundreds of pilots had been lost, when he had an appointment at 11 Group and was in a position to make his views known.

The problem was partly one of poor armament; the early attempts at fitting cannon to the Spitfire had, as mentioned earlier, been unsuccessful. There were steady improvements to the Spitfire, especially to the Merlin engines, and with later versions having the Griffin engine, the Spitfire, and its naval cousin, the Seafire, was produced in more marks than any other British aircraft. At the time of the fighter sweeps, Johnnie Johnson was flying Spitfire 2s, while other squadrons in 11 Group were flying Spitfire 5s, with a slightly more powerful engine. The 5A had eight machine guns, but the 5B had two cannon and four machine-guns. The cannon was seen as being able to smash through the armour of enemy bombers, but would also have been even more effective at targets such as railway locomotives.

A big difference between the Spitfire 2 and the 5 was that the latter had metal ailerons rather than the fabric ailerons of the former, which made the aircraft much more manoeuvrable, requiring less stick pressure while the rate of roll at high speeds more than doubled. No. 616 Squadron approached the factory and had their fabric ailerons replaced with metal ones. All went well until a year later, when the authorities wanted to know who had authorised such a change. Nothing could be done, however, as by this time Bader was a prisoner of war and the squadron commander at the time of the change was on operations over the Western Desert.

BOMBER ESCORT

The *Luftwaffe* soon began to ignore high-level fighter sweeps over France, intended to draw the enemy into battle, as they realised that fighters flying at high altitude could do little damage whilst flying over the Pas de Calais. The RAF changed its tactics to 'Circus' operations, in which a dozen or so Bristol Blenheim bombers would be escorted by fighters to short-range targets in France.

Despite its modern appearance, the Bristol Blenheim did not distinguish itself during the early years of the war. Its operations prior to the fall of France had resulted in heavy losses. Much of this was doubtless due to the relatively small numbers employed on any one operation during the early years, whereas larger numbers would have forced the enemy to divide their fire. Another problem was the relatively poor defensive armament of the Blenheim. Yet, despite this, there were even ambitious attempts to use the Blenheim as a night fighter before the Beaufighter came into service in greater numbers. In short, despite its modern appearance, this aircraft was inferior to the Handley Page Hampden and simply did not compare with the larger Vickers Wellington, which was initially described as a 'heavy' bomber until the arrival of the four-engined Short Stirling, Avro Lancaster and Handley Page saw it downgraded to 'medium'.

The idea was that, faced with an attack on targets in the Pas de Calais, the *Luftwaffe* would not fail to respond. The force of twelve Blenheims was often accompanied by as many as twelve fighter squadrons, placed as close-escort, escort-cover, high-cover and top-cover wings. To avoid alerting the enemy's radar until the last moment, often the fighters assembled with the bombers below 500 feet off the Sussex coast. This was no easy task, let alone safe, as often the assembly would be during the early morning with sometimes heavy mist off locations such as Beachy Head or Selsey Bill. As some squadrons would circle to port and others to starboard as they waited for the bombers, inevitably there came a moment when they met head on! The Polish fighter formations were the most difficult as they arrived in strict formation as if expecting everyone else to move out of their way. It was never a moment too soon when the bomber leader arrived and the fighters could get into position and set off for the French coast.

The Channel was often crossed at low level and the fighters did not begin their climb to their assigned positions until the bombers started to climb to their bombing height, just in time to face the deadly German 88mm anti-aircraft guns on the coast, one of the best AA weapons of the war. The 'flak' was extremely effective in forcing the close-escort fighter pilots to climb another 1,000 feet or so, realising that a direct hit would be enough to shoot such a small aircraft out of the sky. This manoeuvre was not welcomed by the Blenheim pilots who had to struggle on and maintain their assigned height.

Once clear of the coast a fresh problem arose, as the fighters had difficulty keeping pace with the much slower bombers and could not reduce their speed as this would make it difficult to fend off a *Luftwaffe* fighter defence. To overcome this, the fighters weaved and twisted around the Blenheims in twos and fours so that they could remain in position, with one wit describing the manoeuvre as the 'beehive'. In addition to the escorts, other fighter squadrons carried out diversionary operations over enemy airfields, while some provided forward support and target support, and there was also cover for the withdrawal and even flank cover for the 'beehive'.

There was no question that these operations were successful in drawing the *Luftwaffe* into action. For the Blenheim, targets such as Lille and Tournai in northern France were long penetrations, and the fighter pilots recalled the air-to-air combat as some of the most intense they experienced throughout the war. Fighter sweeps were preferable to fighter escort for the bombers, not least because of the difficulty in identifying friend or foe when large numbers of pairs or fours were flying in close protection for the bombers.

The large number of fighters comprising the 'beehive' could be seen from some distance by the *Luftwaffe* Bf109s, helped by the flak bursts as the bombers and fighters made their way across France.

The advantage of surprise usually lay with the enemy, with the morning sun behind them so that often the first the escort knew was when the Bf109s attacked at high speed from six o'clock high. The irony was that the escort then had to move quickly, but instead of intercepting the German fighters, they had to get out of the way of the Spitfires flying top-cover as they screamed down to attack the Bf109s. 'It seemed to us that the risk of collision was far greater than the threat from a handful of Messerschmitts,' recalled one RAF pilot.

Not every *Luftwaffe* pilot favoured the direct attack, and some, aided by the cloud, infiltrated the 'beehive' as if they were additional escorts. This required skill and courage, especially as often as many as four Bf109s in formation would join the Spitfires. The usual tactic was to wait until the defending Bf109s dived before striking at the bombers. Other *Luftwaffe* fighters would wait in the cloud and appear below the bombers when everyone's attention was focussed on attack from above.

THE NOBLE ENEMY
The defence of occupied France included a number of *Luftwaffe* units, but the one that approximated most to the RAF's 11 Group was *JG* 26, '*Schlageter*' *Geschwader*, based on the Abbeville area with nine squadrons of Bf109s. At this stage of the war, it was under the command of the famous Adolph Galland, who claimed a grand total of seventy victories. One of the leading fighter aces of all times, he has been described as possessing a quiet dignity, combined with unshakeable confidence in the tactics he espoused.

One story told about him was that he was a chain smoker of cigars and had granted himself permission to smoke when on operations. He went so far as to fit his own Bf109 with an electric cigar lighter. When promoted to a senior rank, no less than five tobacco firms offered to provide him with free cigars for the rest of the war, each intending that they should have this as an exclusive right, but Galland, no doubt anxious not to disappoint anyone, happily accepted all five offers. He smoked twenty cigars a day and when captured by the Americans at the end of the war, still had sixty boxes.

His addiction incurred the displeasure of the Führer, Adolf Hitler, who forbade him to be photographed while holding, let alone smoking, a cigar as he was setting a bad example to the youth of the master race.

While attempts were made to use day fighters in the night role, as mentioned earlier during the Battle of Britain, and even attempts to make night fighters out of the Fairey Battle and, with slightly more success, the Bristol Blenheim, the first truly successful RAF night fighter was the Bristol Beaufighter, which saw action over North Africa and Italy as well as over the UK. Better still was the de Havilland Mosquito, fast and manoeuvrable. For the navigator/radar operator, the Mosquito also brought another advantage with more advanced radar, with just one screen instead of two.

DEFENDING LONDON
Night fighter crew were a closely-knit team with the navigator/radar operator every bit as important as the pilot, and often they were decorated together, as with Leslie Stephenson and Arthur Hall (mentioned later on page 138).

Flight Lieutenant John Hall and Flight Lieutenant John Cairns were another pilot and navigator/radar operator team, who came together when they joined No. 488 (New Zealand) Squadron in November 1943, which was based in Essex for the night defence of London. The squadron had Mosquitoes with the latest airborne interception (AI) radar.

On the night of 21/22 January 1944, the squadron was scrambled to intercept a major raid against London. Cairns acquired a target on his radar and directed Hall until they were within visual range, when they used night goggles and identified the target as a Dornier Do217. It was shot down by a short burst of fire. As they turned away they saw a Junkers Ju88 coned by searchlights, and chased it, forcing it into the sea.

Their success was seized upon by RAF public relations and they were brought to London to meet the press. Despite wartime shortages of newsprint, the *Sunday Express* published a centre spread with a large photograph of the two airmen and the headline 'The smile on the faces of the Flying Tigers'. 'We squirmed with embarrassment at the thought of the taunting of our peers,' Cairns later wrote. He was soon proved right as on their return they were offered raw meat at mealtimes until the novelty began to wear off.

Earlier, Cairns had worked with the Blind Approach Development Unit at Watchfield, and spent many hours flying and testing the equipment that would help bomber and night fighter crews land at airfields in bad weather. On one visit to a bomber airfield to explain the system, he encountered bad weather as bombers, many badly damaged or with seriously wounded crew onboard, approached. He was in the control tower. 'I watched these returning bombers attempt to land and listened to their radio transmissions,' he recalled. 'I do not want to hear another whingeing complaint about how stressful life is.'

Shooting down enemy aircraft does often have a serious downside, as the crippled aircraft has to come down somewhere. On one occasion, after shooting down a Ju88 on 21 March 1944, the wreckage landed on an airfield used by the USAAF, crashing amongst aircraft parked and armed and caused a massive explosion.

THE V-1 MENACE

Known as Hitler's 'revenge weapons', or *Vergeltunsgwaffen*, the V-1 and V-2 could be regarded as the predecessors of the cruise missile and ballistic missile, respectively. There was no defence against the V-2, but the V-1 could be countered by fighters.

Powered by a small pulse-jet engine, the V-1 was launched towards British cities, but its range was limited by its 150 gallons of fuel. It was pre-programmed so there were no radio guidance signals that could be jammed. Precise targeting was impossible and wind direction or wind speed could affect the point at which its motor cut out, at which those within hearing distance tried to make use of whatever cover was available. This was a contrast with the V-2, with the explosion as it hit the ground being the first indication of its presence.

V-1 missiles could be launched on an inclined ramp on the ground or air-launched from a bomber, which considerably extended their range. Developed at the test site established at Peenemunde on the Baltic, mass production started in 1943 and deployment was assigned to the *Luftwaffe*'s anti-aircraft arm.

First used against London on 13 June 1944, a total of 2,452 V-1s were launched by the end of the war. Roughly a third either crashed or were shot down by RAF fighters or AA fire before they reached the coast, while about the same proportion crashed or were shot down over southern England but outside the target area. Around 800 struck London, with the most serious incident being on 18 June, when one landed on the Guard's Chapel at Wellington Barracks during the morning service, killing 121 people, including 63 soldiers.

As the Allies advanced through Belgium and the Netherlands, the original launch sites were overrun and, because of this, and also to reach more distant targets such as Gloucester, a small percentage were launched from Heinkel He111s of the 3rd *Gruppe* of *Kampfgeschwader* 3 and, later, 53. Accuracy was much poorer with the air-launched versions, and so too was reliability, with as much as half of the air-launched missiles failing and crashing soon after launch.

Ernst Eberling was a German pilot with *Kampfgeschwader* 53.

Because there were no launch sites left in France and Belgium, the V-1 rockets were struggling to reach central London, so in October we began to fly with them. The main problem with them was the wind. If we didn't judge the wind right, we missed London. Also many of our V-1s got shot down by English flak. We had to climb to 500 metres before we could let go of the V-1, that is, if the English fighters didn't get us. It was dangerous for us because the light when we launched the V-1 would reveal the bomber. By the time the V-1 came in, we still had a little hope that we could win the war, but not much, as the Allied air power was so superior.[9]

In fact, at first, many of the V-1s disposed of by RAF fighters were not actually shot down. Instead, RAF fighter pilots would fly close alongside the V-1, and gently place their wing under that of the V-1, and tilt it until the V-1 changed course away from London, and sometimes upset the master gyro so that the missile went out of control. Fighter Command soon stopped this, instructing pilots to shoot down the V-1s as some exploded prematurely if their control mechanism was interfered with.

Notes
1. Cajus Bekker, *The Luftwaffe War Diaries*, Doubleday, New York, 1968.
2. Imperial War Museum Sound Archive.
3. *Front Line; The History Of The London Fire Brigade.*
4. Cajus Bekker, *The Luftwaffe War Diaries*, Doubleday, New York, 1968.
5. Imperial War Museum Sound Archive.
6. Cajus Bekker, *The Luftwaffe War Diaries*, Doubleday, New York, 1968
7. Imperial War Museum Sound Archive.
8. Imperial War Museum Sound Archive.
9. Imperial War Museum Sound Archive.

Chapter 6

The Siege of Malta

History could have been changed had the Second World War started in the Mediterranean after Italy's invasion of Abyssinia in 1935. The Italian action earned the disapproval of the League of Nations and saw plans for offensive action laid by the British armed forces, including a raid on the major Italian naval base of Taranto. While Britain's armed forces were not prepared for war at this time, those of Italy were not much better equipped, although they were well suited to the one-sided contest in Abyssinia, and by the simple expedient of closing the Suez Canal to Italian shipping, Italian forces would have been left without supplies. At the time, Germany was still far too weak and ill-equipped to have come to the aid of her ally.

As the 1930s continued, the Mediterranean was far from placid, as civil war broke out in Spain, with the flames fanned by German and Soviet intervention on opposing sides. German territorial ambitions in central Europe and those of Italy in North Africa have been well documented, but less well known was the Italian invasion of Albania at Easter, 1939.

The fall of France in June 1940 came as a double blow to British commanders in the Mediterranean theatre as it coincided with Italy's entry into the war. All at once, war was to be fought on two fronts against two well-armed Axis powers, while at the same time, Britain not only lost French forces, which in the 'Med' were stronger than her own, but also had much of North Africa in hostile hands. British forces were divided, even isolated, at Gibraltar, Malta and Alexandria, and to a lesser extent at Cyprus and in Palestine. South of the Suez Canal, there were also British forces in the Aden Protectorate, facing Italian forces in Somalia across the Red Sea.

Despite the importance of the area and every indication that the Italians would, sooner or later, ally themselves with Germany, in 1940, throughout the entire Middle East, the RAF had just 29 squadrons with 300 aircraft. Nine squadrons had Blenheims and another two, Sunderlands, while another two had Lysanders for army co-operation. These were the only truly up-to-date aircraft. Fighter support consisted of five squadrons of Gladiator biplanes.

Had Spain entered the war, Gibraltar would have become untenable, and the Mediterranean could have been closed to the Allies. It was fortunate that Spain remained neutral, exhausted after the civil war that had only ended months before the outbreak of the Second World War in Europe, and with armed forces that were ill-equipped while at that time Spain lacked the industrial base to develop and sustain substantial forces. At the outbreak of war, Gibraltar did not have a runway, but this was provided by the expedient of building one on the racecourse, close to the border with Spain.

In the middle of the Mediterranean, almost equidistant between Gibraltar and Alexandria, and again almost halfway between Sicily and Libya, Malta had been seen by both the War Office and the Air Ministry as being incapable of being defended. It was the Admiralty that insisted on Malta being defended and used as a base for offensive operations by submarines and light surface forces. The Admiralty got its way, and the other two services had to maintain a presence on the island so that it could continue as a base for the Royal Navy, even though the main part of the Mediterranean Fleet had to be pulled out to Alexandria.

Air, land and naval forces at Alexandria were there to protect the Suez Canal, and after French surrender faced threats on all sides. In North Africa, Italian forces invaded Egypt, while there remained the ever-present threat of the French territories of Syria and the Lebanon being used by the Axis as Vichy France was viewed as being hostile to the UK. The situation in the Balkans was perilous, and there remained, in 1940 and 1941, the very real threat that Turkey might join the Axis powers, having been a German ally and protégé during the First World War. Elsewhere, the situation was not easy, and there was an uprising in Iraq, while Iran had to be invaded to secure the southern flank of the Soviet Union and also to enable supplies to be shipped overland from the Gulf to the Soviet Union.

One feature of operations in the Mediterranean and North Africa was the integration of shore-based Fleet Air Arm activity with that of the RAF, with the FAA often providing support for ground forces during the desert campaign, while the RAF and FAA shared anti-shipping operations out of Malta, and No. 431 Flight, based on the island, flew Martin Baltimore bombers on reconnaissance over the Italian fleet at Taranto for the Royal Navy.

MALTA

Malta is not a single island but three inhabited and one uninhabited islands, with just 127 square miles in total. In 1940, Malta had a population of 270,000, and was a British colony. The RAF had three airfields on the island, at Luqa, Hal Far, which was also used by the Fleet Air Arm, and Ta Kali, and later also added an airfield at Safi, between Luqa and Hal Far.

There was also a flying boat base at Kalafrana, on the shore close to Hal Far. Given adequate naval and air power, its geographical position meant that whoever occupied Malta could control the Mediterranean, but it was just 80 miles from the air bases of the *Luftwaffe's Fliegerkorps* X in Sicily. Following the Fleet Air Arm's audacious attack on the Italian fleet at Taranto, *Fliegerkorps* X had been moved from Norway, where it had gained extensive experience in anti-shipping operations.

From Italy's entry into the war, Malta was under almost constant attack by the *Luftwaffe* and the Italian *Regia Aeronautica*. Once *Fliegerkorps* X arrived in Sicily at the very beginning of 1941, the situation changed for the worse, so that convoys to Malta came under unceasing aerial attack, with some losing all ships or others being forced to turn back. Malta could only feed itself for less than a third of the year and was dependent on regular supplies, but, by 1942, the population and the armed forces on Malta were starving and thirty-four per cent of babies did not live to see their first birthday. Relief did not come until the massive convoy, Operation Pedestal, of August 1942, and even that, regarded as a success, lost nine out of fourteen merchant ships, as well as an aircraft carrier, with two others badly damaged. Such was the intensity of the fighting that Malta convoys could not be protected by escort carriers, but needed the larger and faster fleet carriers.

In fact, Malta's plight was not really eased until the Allied landings in North Africa and the victory at El Alamein, followed by the landings in Sicily. While Malta-based aircraft played a small part in the latter, the limitations of the airfields meant that most of the airborne element was based in North Africa.

Despite this, the RAF and Royal Navy between them at one stage almost cut the supply lines between Italy and Axis forces in North Africa.

Military logic should have dictated that, on entering the war, the Italians should have sent their six battleships to bombard the main island, and followed this up by an invasion. This is what Hitler expected, with Operation Hercules, the invasion of Malta. After the German *Afrika Korps* arrived in North Africa, its leader, General Erwin Rommel, wanted Malta to be invaded. Nevertheless, Malta would have been difficult to invade, with small beaches with most having steep and narrow approaches that would have been easy to block, while glider-borne landings would have been difficult due to the small size of the fields, each bordered by drystone walls.

FIGHTER DEFENCE

The fighter defence of Malta in 1940 was non-existent, despite the threat from Italy. Anti-aircraft defences were also minimal, and primarily concerned with the defence of the main fleet base, Grand Harbour. Flying boat pilots from RAF Kalafrana flew three Gloster Sea Gladiators, the famous *Faith*, *Hope* and *Charity*, found in crates at Grand Harbour as the island's sole fighter defences in June 1940, although a fourth aircraft was shot down almost immediately. The meagre air defence was based on RAF Ta Kali. Someone at the Admiralty in London demanded to know why the RAF had been allowed to use naval equipment, to the annoyance of Admiral Sir Andrew 'ABC' Cunningham, commanding the Mediterranean Fleet!

'I wondered where the official responsible had been spending his war,' Cunningham remarked.

Reinforcements for the three Sea Gladiators arrived, but were then ordered to the Middle East. William Collins had been with a Hurricane squadron covering the British Expeditionary Force in France. Escaping south to Marseille, they were joined by the remnants of two other units, so that eventually there were two Bristol Blenheim bombers and ten Hawker Hurricanes. The French in Marseille cautioned them against their original plan to fly out via Ajaccio, in Corsica, where the local forces had thrown in their lot with Vichy, and suggested instead that they flew from Marseille to Tunis, a distance of 980 miles.

'We had overload tanks and we had approximately five hours thirty minutes' flying time,' Collins recalls. 'We set off and six of us made it and one of the Blenheims.'

On arrival in Tunis, they had been interned, although they were put up in a good hotel. Eventually they were released, told to refuel at a point in the desert, which they did, and then continued to Malta.

'But anyhow we went into Luqa in Malta on the day the Italians were bombing it. That's six Hurricanes and one Blenheim. And then for some unknown reason it was decided that the six Hurricanes would go on – should carry on with getting out to the Middle East.'[1]

The six Hurricanes would have been invaluable in the air defence of Malta at this early stage, within a fortnight of the start of the Italian air raids. It is not surprising that a later AOC Malta was to become notorious for hijacking aircraft and aircrew that caught his eye as they tried to use Malta as a transit point! Nevertheless, before leaving Malta on 24 June, William Collins had time to experience an Italian air raid.

I'd just landed and was having a bath when there was a terrible crunch, and the bath left the floor. And I was rolled out. But Malta was a marvellous place. You know, stone buildings and they had air raid shelters which were perfectly safe because the Italians only used at the maximum 250- or 500-pound bombs. So basically other than to the runway the damage was very small until, of course, the Germans came in ... later. And then Malta had trouble ... Had we left those six Hurricanes there instead of just the three Gladiators the defence of

Malta would have been more secure I think. You see they were never short of pilots in Malta. But they were short of aircraft.[2]

While the absence of substantial fighter defences for Malta was a serious weakness in British planning, the pressure on the United Kingdom itself was growing at this time, as the fall of France led immediately to the start of the Battle of Britain, the *Luftwaffe*'s concerted effort to destroy the Royal Air Force and its aircraft. It was fortunate that the Italians never mastered the art of the massed bombing raid, overwhelming the defences, while the Macchi C200, despite the manufacturer's experience in the Schneider Trophy races, was one of the poorest fighters of the Second World War, worse even than the Curtiss P-40, and probably only just superior to the Brewster Buffalo.

Despite the critical situation in the UK, on 12 August, a squadron of twelve Hurricanes was flown to Malta off the elderly aircraft carrier HMS *Argus*. Four additional Hurricanes reached Malta on 17 November, the only survivors of another fourteen flown off HMS *Argus*, with the remainder lost probably due to insufficient fuel since those that did make it to Hal Far arrived with very little in their tanks. Before the end of the year, a squadron of Hawker Hurricanes, No. 261, was flown into Hal Far.

Airfields were essential. Hal Far was in good condition, as was the new airfield at Ta Kali, originally intended as staging post for Imperial Airways. Luqa was newly completed. Kalafrana continued as a base for flying boats. None of these airfields had any protection against enemy bombing at the outset, showing that the impact that bombing would have on Malta was completely discounted. There were no protected dispersal bays for aircraft; no hardened hangars. At first, all that could be done in the way of AA protection of these airfields was to detail Lewis gun crews to each of them. Only later would they receive significant AA batteries.

The Royal Engineers and the Pioneer Corps were given the task of improving the airfields, often with drafts of manpower from the infantry battalions, so that at times as many as 3,000 men could be at work. During the next two years they were to construct 300 aircraft pens to provide some protection from bombing, saving aircraft from all but a direct hit. Between Hal Far and Luqa, an incredible 27 miles of dispersal area was provided, known as the Safi strip, from the nearby village, and, later, this was developed into a new airfield.

For most of the siege, the RAF had few ground staff in Malta, so the Manchester Regiment provided the manpower to keep Ta Kali operational, while the Royal West Kents did the same for Luqa and the Cheshire Regiment, the 'Buffs', looked after Hal Far. The Cheshire's 2nd Battalion of 1,000 men, more than fifty per cent more than the usual battalion strength, had arrived in February, 1941, with the 1st Battalion of the Hampshire Regiment. Given the confined space of Malta, and the barrier afforded by

72

the sea, there would in all probability have been little for these infantrymen to do otherwise.

For Malta, there was some relief at Easter 1941, when on Holy Saturday, 12 April, twenty Hurricane MkIIs were flown off the aircraft carrier *Ark Royal* to boost the depleted strength of No. 261 Squadron.

Attacks from the air, from the sea and from beneath it meant that, by October 1941, the Axis were losing more than sixty per cent of their supplies sent to North Africa, and, the following month, this rose to an incredible seventy-seven per cent. Rommel was prompted to make nightly signals complaining about the shortage of supplies, blaming this on the Italians and also criticising them for sending his supplies through Tripoli rather than Benghazi, and in so doing adding 500 miles to his already lengthy supply chain.

Throughout the summer and early autumn of 1941, more Hurricanes were delivered to Malta, so that by early autumn there were about seventy aircraft. These were day and night fighters and fighter-bombers, making offensive sweeps against Italian aircraft at their bases in Sicily, especially important as convoys approached Malta.

GETTING TO MALTA

Getting aircraft to Malta was hardly easy, especially for aircraft too large to be flown off an aircraft carrier. At Portreath, in Cornwall, the RAF had a unit tasked with despatching aircraft to the Middle East. Late in 1941, Air Marshal Sir Ivor Broom, then a sergeant pilot, found that with 230 hours' total flying time he was the most experienced pilot in a group of six, which he was asked to lead. They could not fly over occupied France, and so their journey started with a seven-hour flight from Cornwall to Gibraltar, where the runway built on the old racecourse was still quite short, and for the still inexperienced pilots there was the unnerving sight of wrecked aircraft that had failed to make a safe landing. The next stage of the journey from Gibraltar to Malta took seven hours, forty minutes. Flying a twin-engined Blenheim with a navigator was bad enough, since they hardly saw land between Gibraltar and Malta, so it is easy to understand the problems facing the solitary fighter pilots flying off from aircraft carriers, with limited navigational training and accustomed to fighting air battles within a radius of 50 miles or so from their home air station.

Promotion could be rapid, and because of Malta's isolation, what might be described as battlefield promotions were a necessity. Broom explains:

Now I was a sergeant pilot when I went to Malta. And we lost virtually all the officers, and we were left with a squadron leader who was due to go home, his tour expired. He was made acting wing commander until the new one came out. And I was commissioned in Malta. And one night I moved from the sergeants' mess to the officers'

73

mess and that was my commission. I ... bought myself a forage cap from Gieves ... and a few inches of pilot officer braid, and took the sergeant stripes off my uniform. Pinned on, sewed on, the pilot officer braid and that was commissioning in moving into the officers' mess.[3]

IMPROVING THE FIGHTER DEFENCES

Petty Officer Francis Smith of No. 828 Naval Air Squadron remembers that the big air raids had started in December 1941, and that the number of aircraft destroyed on the ground soared from this time.

> But the real shock of Malta came over the Easter weekend, 1942. The Germans and the Italians hammered *hell* out of us. And by this time, because of the raids between Christmas and Easter, what few fighters Malta had left had either been shot down or been shot up on the deck [naval slang for the ground]. And every month or so, the carriers used to come and fly off Hurricanes and Spitfires, from 600 miles away. Well those that got to the island got shot down when they got to the island, because the Mes were always waiting, all the time.
>
> So come Easter-time, 1942, we had practically no fighters left ... and there was practically no ack-ack ammunition left – that had all gone, because the convoys were not getting through. There was practically no food, there was no lights [sic], there was no beer ... there wasn't no anything. The island was really in an absolute desperate state, in May, 1942 ...[4]

Queenie Lee was the wife of a naval officer who lived in Malta for four years, two and a half of them under wartime conditions. She was involved with war work, but her main job was as a teacher at the Royal Naval Dockyard School.

> Our red letter day was Sunday, 10 May 1942: Spitfires had arrived ... 36 enemy machines were brought down in an hour.
>
> During these months fuel had become very scarce, and gas and electricity was cut off for five months.
>
> During this time, I was teaching at the Royal Naval Dockyard School ... one boy sometimes took 1½ to 2 hours to come to school, but come he did, and alone. They took the Oxford School Certificate and it took some time for the examination papers to arrive, but eventually they did, and they all passed.
>
> Only dire necessity forced us to use the shelters. Attacks were too exciting to miss. We groaned when our Hurricanes couldn't overtake the Messerschmitt 109; we cheered ourselves hoarse when gunners or fighters found their target, and blazing machines hurtled to earth followed by swaying parachutists.
>
> The Germans set up a steady timetable of raids, dawn, midday and dusk, sometimes with a few extras thrown in ...[5]

RADAR COMPROMISED

Even under these extreme pressures there could be examples of slow thinking and reluctance in adapting to changing times, and even changing needs and opportunities.

Reginald Townson recalls that the efficiency of the radar system was compromised by a still rank-conscious RAF. The controller had to be a senior officer, as no one below the rank of wing commander was regarded as being experienced enough to control aircraft. Yet, it simply was not done for a wing commander to speak into a microphone to an aircraft, so this was left to a signals officer. Thus the situation was that the wing commander would pass his instruction to the signals officer, who would pass them on to an aircraft, and then the signals officer would pass the reply to the wing commander!

This charade continued even after war broke out. In Malta, the original transportable radar station was soon joined by three more with a much improved capability for catching aircraft flying at lower altitudes, although it was not for many years later and the introduction of airborne early warning radar that the menace of very low-flying aircraft could be effectively countered. At operations control, the controllers and their staff worked on an ops table marked off with a map of the island with range rings and bearing lines, Townson believed at every ten degrees. Townson's station worked on range bearings. When the next stations were introduced, control didn't wish to change their table and replace it with one with a grid on it. This meant that the new stations had to pass their plots to the original station, which would convert them to its range and bearing and then, after this had been done, wasting precious time, pass them down to the ops room. This process would have taken minutes for every plot, and it was some time before control could be persuaded to have a grid.

The interception of incoming bomber waves while they were still over the sea some way off Malta, later in the war, would not have been possible using this system of passing plots through a central point for bearings to be allocated before passing these on to control.

This story puts the lie to anyone who believes that the RAF, as the most junior of the three services and the one most involved with the newest means of warfare, was the least bureaucratic and most flexible! You can't be either of these things commanding a small warship!

'SPEEDFIRES'

The arrival of the Spitfires had been cloaked in secrecy, or so the governor, Sir William Dobbie, had thought. He always made a point of visiting areas most seriously affected by the bombing raids. On 7 March 1941, he visited a small village close to Luqa. Despite the heavy damage to the village, most of the population had escaped, taking cover in the shelters. The nine fatalities had all come from the same family, who had their own private shelter beneath their house, but when this received a direct hit, the shelter collapsed into the cistern under the building, leaving those present to drown.

On this occasion, the Governor was in for a shock. Chatting with an elderly and very loyal Maltese, a veteran of the ill-starred Gallipoli campaign, he learnt that the man was expecting 'Speedfires' to be sent to the island soon: Dobbie had thought that only four or five people knew about the impending arrival of the Spitfires.

The man assured him that he had been told about the aircraft coming by the airmen at Luqa! Everyone knew about the aircraft, but no one knew when they would arrive.

As he moved on to his next visit, he was relieved not to hear the word Spitfire. He was soon to hear something else. As he left the shelter, shortly after 13.30, he heard the noise of aircraft engines, as aircraft raced in low, causing those around him to fear a German raid approaching beneath the radar coverage. People outside began to disperse and seek shelter, shouting warnings about the impending German attack. Suddenly, impervious to what seemed like imminent danger, a small boy shouted, 'Hurrah ... Spitfires.' Everyone turned, stared and started clapping, shouting hysterically, and offering prayers of thanks to the Almighty, Santa Marija (Saint Mary) and to the many favourite saints.

Fifteen Spitfires had been flown in from the deck of the veteran aircraft carrier HMS *Eagle*, some miles to the west, while south of the Balearic Islands.

That night, the fighter base at RAF Ta Kali was bombed, something that was all too painfully obvious to those sheltering under the towns of Rabat and Mosta close to the airfield.

On 10 March, the Spitfires saw action for the first time, climbing high before diving onto a small formation of three Ju88s escorted by Bf109s. Malta's AA gunners shot down one Ju88, before the Spitfires shot down a Bf109 and sent two others flying away trailing smoke. Once the score was tallied up later, it was found that the guns had accounted for one Junkers, with two definite and four probable Bf109s for the Spitfires, with another two probables for the Hurricanes.

It was not surprising that Rommel was so enthusiastic over the idea of invading Malta in early 1941, but, by June, the opportunity had gone following the debacle on Crete and the launch of Operation Barbarossa, Germany's invasion of the Soviet Union. It was Barbarossa that eased the *Luftwaffe's* pressure on Malta, just as it brought the blitz on British cities to a premature end. One of the objectives of Barbarossa was to secure oil supplies for the Axis; as it faltered and finally failed, the growing shortage of oil was to be felt most severely by Hitler's ally, Mussolini.

Francis Smith was with the Fleet Air Arm's No. 828 Squadron that had been sent to Malta ahead of its Fairey Albacore aircraft, pilots and observers, and was put to work with others to prepare for the safe arrival of the Spitfires.

> We knew they were coming. So what we did, we built pens of empty two-gallon petrol cans, filled up with sand, we built pens, and we organised everybody on the island – civilians, sailors, soldiers, everybody – into working parties, so many to an aircraft. All these aircraft came in, and I think about a third of them were left to use up their petrol in fighting the Mes, and the other two-thirds landed.
>
> Well as these aircraft landed they were grabbed by a duty crew of eight or nine people, they were refuelled and rearmed, and they got airborne. And it worked – they got airborne in time to let the others come down, those that stopped up in the air. And this shook the Germans something wicked, it did. Because they knew that week before we hadn't got any fighters ... so they got a nasty shock.[6]

The improvised aircraft shelters built in this way were sometimes known as 'sangers'. The ready availability of so many empty fuel cans was the result of having fuel brought in small quantities aboard submarines and the *Manxman* and *Welshman*, the two fast mine-laying cruisers. Ordinary merchantmen bound for Malta would also include some fuel amongst their cargo, although naturally this was nowhere near as efficient as using a tanker, but it did mean that some proportion of supplies got through if the tanker was sunk.

Good fortune accompanied the Maltese at this moment, since there was time to re-install the armament of the newly arrived Spitfires who went into battle on 9 May, when there were ten air raids and, between them, the fighters and the gunners accounted for thirty enemy aircraft.

No one could argue that the British were not trying. It was also clear that a cold calculation had been made. Malta could not unload so many big ships at once, so it was plain that not all were expected to reach the Grand Harbour.

One of the RAF's leading fighter aces, 'Laddie' Lucas, a former journalist with the *Daily Express*, was amongst those based at Ta Kali. Like the others, he had reached Malta having flown off an aircraft carrier. Lucas recalled some years after the war:

> We were then flying the Spitfires off the carriers, and we had some disasters with that. Mainly because they were sending pilots out who really weren't particularly well trained. If two pilots were asked to be sent out from a squadron, well, then, they sent people they didn't want, naturally. If you were a squadron commander and wanted to get rid of a couple of guys, send them out to Malta, so it was very rough on the people who were out there and surviving.

But anyway, then the American aircraft carrier *Wasp* was brought into play, which turned the battle in the middle of May – 9 and 10 May – for about ten days. It did two runs and it was fixed up by Churchill, with Roosevelt, special concession; it could take forty-eight Spitfires, whereas the *Eagle* could only take sixteen.

And the first run, I mean, it went off very well, but within forty-eight hours, of the forty-seven aircraft, there was one which didn't go ... they took off from a point about 60 miles north of Algiers, which was about 650 miles from the island, you couldn't get any closer, the Mediterranean Fleet wouldn't allow it. If the commander-in-chief said, 'That's quite close enough, you'll fly off from here with these 90 gallon tanks on,' which we did, it was a fairly rough assignment. We did our own navigation and all that. And when this first forty-eight were flown off the *Wasp*, loaded up in Glasgow and just sent through the Straits, after forty-eight hours of course the Germans had been monitoring this all the way, and these raids came in one after another. And of course they beat these planes up on the ground, and I think there were seven serviceable aircraft after forty-eight hours ...[7]

The USS *Wasp* had sailed from Glasgow with no less than forty-eight Spitfires for Malta, escorted by the battleship *Renown*, the anti-aircraft cruisers *Cairo* and *Charybdis* and a number of destroyers. Passing Gibraltar on 19 April, the ship launched her Spitfires towards Malta the following day. She had not entered port at Gibraltar to avoid any delay and hoping to give no clue to the Germans about her intentions, but the Germans also used radio intercepts, could track the course of the convoy by its signals, and guessed that the *Wasp* was ferrying aircraft to Malta. They also managed to ascertain just when the aircraft were launched. Just one aircraft failed to reach Malta, but after the remaining forty-seven landed, roughly half each at Ta Kali and Hal Far, a large air raid was mounted by Ju88s and Bf109s, catching the Spitfires on the ground, just twenty minutes after landing. Twenty of the aircraft were destroyed and another twelve damaged.

Churchill managed to persuade Roosevelt to allow the *Wasp* a second run, this time in partnership with the *Eagle*, so that sixty-four aircraft were sent to Malta. This was still not enough to satisfy the AOC, Air Vice-Marshal Hugh Lloyd. Lucas was amongst those who remembered Lloyd 'hijacking' aircraft intended for the Middle East.

Lloyd may have been something of a buccaneer, but he was also very practical. He ensured that a number of experienced fighter pilots were sent to Gibraltar so that they could lead in the aircraft from the carriers, keeping losses to the minimum. As for Lucas, he was so annoyed at the inaccurate coverage being given to the situation in Malta in his old newspaper that he managed to send a story to them, circumventing wartime censorship by sending it via a friend during a visit to Gibraltar. Perhaps Lucas held such a high opinion of Lloyd that when the AOC heard about the story, he correctly guessed the identity of the culprit, and contented himself with telling Lucas: 'Well, it's a good story, isn't it, but you know you're not allowed to do that.'

More important to anyone who has earned his living by writing, the newspaper sent Lucas a cheque for £50, which came in useful for a party in the officers' mess, and when the newspaper's proprietor heard about how much, or in his view, how little, had been sent, a further £50 followed!

Lucas had originally flown into Malta as a passenger in February 1942, aboard a flying boat from Gibraltar, landing at Kalafrana, alighting from the Short Sunderland just after dawn, and in time for the first air raid of the day.

> And suddenly one heard the throb of sort of Rolls-Royce engines, Merlin engines, and they sounded very rough I may say, and there were five old Hurricane IIs in an old fashioned vic formation which they'd given up in the Battle of Britain, just beginning to clamber up to gain height. And then about ... nothing more than a minute or a couple of minutes later, high up, and you could just see it as the dawn was breaking on the haze, a lovely spring morning, February, there were these, probably a *Staffel* I suppose, of 109s flying in that beautiful wide open nine abreast formation that they used to fly their Schwarms in. The Rot, the two aircraft was the ... basis of their flying. But then they used to put them together in fours. And they were flying high up, high and fast.[8]

Lucas found flying the Hurricane was a great experience before the Spitfires arrived, and made him realise what the Hurricane pilots had suffered in the Battle of France, whereas the Spitfire V and the Bf109 were fairly evenly matched, with many pilots feeling that perhaps the Spitfire had a slight edge on the Bf109, although the Fw190 when it arrived was a far more potent aircraft. The Hurricanes had been cannibalised just to keep a few aircraft airworthy. He came to admire those who had been battling against the Germans in the Hurricanes for five or six months, and was glad when his own time with the aircraft lasted just a fortnight.

Lucas considered the real architect of the fighter defence of Malta to be his commanding officer, the then Squadron Leader, later Group Captain, Stanley Turner, a Canadian in the RAF. During the Battle of Britain, Turner had flown with Bader in the Tangmere fighter wing. He scrapped the outdated vic formations, and taught the fighter pilots the technique known as 'finger fours'. The success of this technique was that the aircraft flew in line abreast, with the pilot on the right looking left and the one on the left looking right, covering the whole sky. It took Turner about a week to change No. 249 Squadron. Once the first Spitfires did arrive, Turner was rested from active flying, something that was long overdue as he had been flying in combat continuously from the start of the Battle of France in spring, 1940.

The other great contributor to the fighter defence of Malta was 'Woody' Woodhall, credited by Lucas as being the best fighter controller that the Royal Air Force had in the Second World War. This view was shared by the Italians, with a later post-war chief of the Italian Air Staff, Francesco Cavallera, who had been a fighter pilot based in Sicily during 1942, later remarking to Lucas that: 'Your great advantage was that you had the radar and we didn't in Sicily and this made it very difficult.'

The role of the fighter controller was crucial to success. Watching the enemy aircraft assemble over their airfields in Sicily was simply the easy part of the job; the real skill lay in knowing when to order the fighters to take off. Too early, and they could run short of fuel during prolonged combat. Too late, and they would not have time to get into position. It was also important to note the direction of any attack, as sometimes the attackers would try to work around the island and approach from a different direction hoping to catch the defenders off guard. It was important that the fighters should try to position themselves between the sun and the attacking force to maintain an element of surprise. Lucas recalls the German tactics:

> These German raids used to come in like a railway timetable. They used to come in at breakfast, lunch and dinner, just before dinner, sort of high tea time. And just occasionally they'd put in four but normally it was three [raids per day]. And so if it was a morning raid old Woody'd get us up very high, twenty-five, twenty-six, twenty-seven thousand feet, south of the island. And then he'd start to bring us in and he would say, 'Now, the big jobs with a lot of little jobs about and it's about eighty plus, approaching St Paul's Bay now. Suggest you come in now and come in fast.'[9]

The fighters would dive down through the Messerschmitt Bf109s and straight into the bombers, but the shortage of fighters in Malta meant that these successes in breaking up the bombers had to be offset by the losses amongst the fighter squadrons after they had landed to refuel, when the Bf109s would come in fast and low in a strafing attack.

Many attacks by aircraft based in Malta were beyond the range at which fighter protection could be provided, but whenever fighters were available and an attack was within range, an escort would be provided. On one occasion, Lucas led a fighter escort for the Swordfish on a strike against two Italian cruisers off the coast of Tunisia near Cape Bon. Three Swordfish were flying very low. Staying high himself, Lucas sent a section of four aircraft down lower, as he watched the Swordfish start their attack. He saw two of the Swordfish hit by AA fire before they could release their torpedoes, but the third aircraft managed to torpedo an Italian cruiser.

One point at which relations between the British and the Maltese came under some strain was when the Maltese found RAF pilots off duty in Valletta during air raids – they didn't realise that there weren't enough aircraft to go round!

When Lucas crash-landed in a field where Maltese women were packing potatoes into sacks, the three elderly ladies promptly emptied the sacks and filled them with earth before climbing onto the wing of his Spitfire and spreading the sacks on top of the smoking engine cowling.

'I have no doubt at all that the women had the most remarkable courage there.'

EASTER 1942

Francis Smith has already mentioned the heavy attacks of Easter 1942. These were the heaviest raids since the peak of the *Illustrious* blitz on 16 January 1941, when the *Luftwaffe* tried to destroy the aircraft carrier as she lay alongside in Grand Harbour being repaired after the heavy damage suffered earlier in the month as she waited for the handover of the convoy code-named 'Excess'.

The lack of accommodation at RAF Ta Kali, which was unfinished at the outbreak of war, meant that many of the pilots slept in tents erected in an olive grove. On 21 April 1942, these included the pilots of No. 603 (City of Edinburgh) Squadron, a unit that had started life as an Auxiliary Air Force Squadron. They were new arrivals on the island and still learning what their CO, Squadron Leader David Douglas-Hamilton, called the 'Malta form' from the more experienced pilots of No. 249 Squadron. That morning they were roused by the sound of cannon fire as Bf109s strafed the airfield.

As they made their way to the officers' mess, they saw a smoking Hurricane flying at around 800 feet. The pilot climbed out of his cockpit and jumped, but his parachute streamed and failed to open. One of the officers, Flying Officer Tony Holland, later wrote:

> We knew that many people had also witnessed this tragedy and knowing the inevitable outcome, none of us saw any point in demoralising ourselves by going to where he had struck the ground. There was nothing we could do apart from saying a short prayer for him.[10]

Squadron Leader Douglas-Hamilton and his three flight lieutenants next encountered an unexploded 1,000lb bomb near the dispersal hut, and watched while it was defused, before searching for serviceable aircraft. They found six. The Spitfires flown to Malta off the USS *Wasp* had either been destroyed by direct hits or badly damaged from shrapnel. He recalls that they put their kit into the available aircraft and waited.

> We were told the first raid generally came over at 8.00am. We would fly in a pair formation line abreast, crossing over in turn, and then dive on the bombers as they came in to bomb.
>
> I got a few more tips from Johnny Plagis, an old hand, who told me how in March they had been attacking very large enemy raids with only four and six Spitfires. One day he had had to do this four times, and on each occasion had been shot at by Hun fighters whenever he tried to land. He said, 'I don't believe the Battle of Britain had anything over Malta!'
>
> Suddenly the telephone bell rang. 'Stand to,' we were told. This meant climbing into the cockpit and getting strapped in, all ready ... We had not long to wait. 'Scramble!' Up we climbed to about 30,000 feet, joining up with another party of Spitfires and Hurricanes from the other aerodromes. From that height Malta looked about the size of a large penny ... Sicily, however, seemed very large ... For the rest, there was nothing but miles of unfriendly sea all around.[11]

The first indication that the enemy bombers were approaching came when they saw the bursts of AA shells below them. Not knowing the 'Malta form', Douglas-Hamilton and another pilot from his squadron dived down in the wrong direction and missed the bombers. They then attempted to chase some Bf109s, but couldn't catch them. This was the only time that they failed to get a shot at an enemy aircraft.

As they landed, other fighters lingered in the air to stop Bf109s sweeping down and attacking the aircraft when they were at their most vulnerable. Back on the ground, the bomber raid was followed by a strafing raid by the German fighters. They learned that two Junkers Ju88s and a Bf109 had been shot down and several more damaged. Next came a bombing raid, while they sought refuge in an air raid shelter. Many of those present thought that they would rather be in the air again.

The following morning one pilot from No. 601 (County of London) Squadron was shot down over the sea after seriously damaging or shooting down a Ju88, but succeeded in baling out and paddled back the 5 miles to Malta. Far less fortunate was Luqa-based Pilot Officer Frank Jemmet, whose aircraft was shot up and he died from injuries incurred when his aircraft crash-landed. He might have lived had he baled out, but a Maltese had stolen his parachute. When Wing Commander Gracie heard of this, he erected a gallows on the airfield as a warning to anyone else who might try to steal a fighter pilot's parachute.

That day, 22 April, saw just six Spitfires operational out of forty-seven flown to the island. Others were being repaired, but as soon as an aircraft was repaired, others were badly damaged either in combat, shrapnel or running into bomb craters, while inevitably others were either damaged beyond repair or shot down. The aircraft flown ashore from the USS *Wasp* had been attacked by the *Luftwaffe* less than ninety minutes after landing, and within three days the airfields at Luqa and Ta Kali had more than 500 tons of bombs dropped on them. The net result was that, at any one time, the defending forces would have just six to eight Spitfires ready.

While Churchill sent HMS *Eagle* on further fighter delivery trips, although she could manage just sixteen aircraft at a time, Churchill pressed President Roosevelt to allow a second trip by the *Wasp*.

In the meantime, 25 April 1941 was another busy day. There were three raids, each of around a hundred German aircraft. Compared to the Battle of Britain and the blitz on British cities, this might seem a small number, but the target was also that much smaller and more concentrated. Johnnie Johnson had arrived in Malta by this time, and when chasing a Ju88, he was suddenly pounced on by no less than six Bf109s, which he managed to evade with difficulty, but when clear he found himself utterly exhausted. When called upon to cover the landing of a damaged Spitfire at Ta Kali he was at first too exhausted to reply, but eventually recovered realising that a fighter pilot, even when driven to the limit of human endurance, was still expected to do more when dire necessity demanded it of him.

Late afternoon, at 17.41, there were just six Hurricanes and three Spitfires available when a force of fifty-seven Ju88s and twenty-seven Ju87 Stuka dive-bombers, covered by a large escort of Bf109s, approached Malta. This saw No. 603 Squadron's first confirmed kill. Pilot Officer Paul Brennan DFC, an Australian serving with No. 249 Squadron, recalls the action:

> About 500 yards away, and dead in front of us, was an 88 ... More 109s were coming down on me, but they were still out of range. I decided to take a chance and try to deal with my 88 before the 109s were on me. As I closed in the 88's rear gunner opened fire ... I was so excited and so keen to get the 88 before the 109s forced me to break away that I was unaware that his bullets were hitting my aircraft.
>
> I continued diving straight at him, until I was only 250 yards behind him. Then I opened fire with all four cannon. The rear gunner stopped firing. I concentrated my fire now against the 88's two motors and the pilot's glasshouse. I could see my shells crashing into him, and in a few seconds he started to smoke. I was acutely conscious of the 109s diving on me, and knew that if I waited to check my aim, I would be cold meat for them ... I kept on firing ... He caught fire and started to disintegrate.[12]

After this exciting and fruitful encounter, his aircraft was rocked by the blast from bombs exploding below as the Spitfire came into land, and he only managed to pull his aircraft up before a fresh bomb crater. On leaving his aircraft, he discovered ten bullet holes, one of which was through the propeller, and another, six inches from his head!

This high tempo of operations continued to the end of April, and during the month Malta's defences had accounted for at least 150 enemy aircraft, apportioned roughly 100 for AA fire and 50 for fighters, although once probables were added to the score, the total may have been in excess of 200. Nevertheless, the pressure and the inability of the Allies to get convoys through to the beleaguered island meant that ammunition was running low. The fighters were also running low, so that by 7 May, the day that General Lord Gort arrived to relieve General Sir William Dobbie as governor, there were just six Spitfires left.

More Spitfires were on the way, but it was essential that they should not be wasted and Ta Kali's CO, Wing Commander Gracie, when briefing his pilots that more Spitfires would arrive on 9 May, warned them that the aircraft must be refuelled and re-armed and be back in the air within fifteen minutes to save them from being destroyed on the ground by the *Luftwaffe* and *Regia Aeronautica*. Before long it was agreed that turning the aircraft round would also have army assistance. Preparations were made, with every blast pen having fuel and ammunition for its aircraft, while others were allocated to fill bomb craters in the runways or to drive Bren gun carriers that would pull damaged aircraft out of the way. Most important of all, the remaining six Spitfires were to be saved so that they could provide cover for the new arrivals.

Nevertheless, post-war revelations have shown that luck was an important part in the island's survival. Rommel wanted the island to be invaded, and Field Marshal Kesselring admitted that it would have been easy to seize the island at this time. Rommel was convinced that both Greece and Crete should have been left alone as a terrible waste of resources and Malta invaded instead. Short of food, fuel, ammunition, everything, in fact, Malta was at its lowest ebb. Troops were even put on 'sleep parades' to save energy. As summer approached, the Germans were so confident that Malta was on the brink of collapse, but the costly invasion of Greece and then what had almost amounted to a disastrous failure when invading Crete, had undermined the confidence of the German high command, while Hitler had forbidden any further parachute assaults because the casualties had been so high at Crete. It is also possible that the *Luftwaffe*'s control of the German parachute division played a part in the failure to invade. The German Army recognised that Malta was the key to the control of the Mediterranean and even access to the oil supplies of the Middle East; the *Luftwaffe* refused to accept that invasion was the only means of ensuring this.

Responding to demands elsewhere and confident that Malta had been neutralised by the constant air attacks, plans were laid to transfer forty-five fighters and forty dive-bombers to North Africa, while a bomber group and fighter group were sent to the Eastern Front ready for the renewal of operations after the Russian winter.

NIGHT FIGHTERS

As Malta's defences improved, the risk of being shot down by Malta's Hurricanes, and the heavy AA fire amassed around the Grand Harbour and other key objectives, meant that increasingly major raids took place at night. A Malta Night Fighter Unit was established during the summer of 1941, initially using Hurricanes, although these aircraft were not at all well suited for their new role. The aircraft were guided onto their targets by searchlights and Malta's air defence radar. It was not until later that radar-equipped aircraft, initially Bristol Beaufighters and then de Havilland Mosquitoes, were to reach Malta, arriving in November, 1942, after the real need for them had passed. The operation of the air defences over Malta at this time has been described as a 'three-dimensional chess game'. It was not just a question of attackers and defenders, since, as often as possible, the RAF and Fleet Air Arm would mount operational sorties against targets in Italy, Sicily and North Africa, and at sea, and often these aircraft would return badly damaged and unable to make the necessary man-oeuvres expected of them. Added to this, there were night flights from both Gibraltar and Alexandria, flown usually by either BOAC or the RAF, and usually these pilots were complete strangers to the Mediterranean air war, and even those who were familiar with the situation could find that changes had been made in the light of operational demands. Communication with incoming aircraft was difficult, since it could only be made *en clair*, and therefore could reveal too much to the enemy.

To make use of the Hurricanes, the island was divided into two air defence zones, with a Hurricane patrolling each, and with Valletta as the dividing line. The two Hurricanes were kept informed of the course, speed and altitude of the bombers as they approached, until the attackers were some 15 miles off Malta, when the Hurricanes would take a converging course to approach the targets on either side. The objective was to have the Hurricanes ready and waiting just as the bombers entered the searchlight zone. Experience showed that the defences had to be layered, with the Hurricanes responsible for aircraft above a certain height, and the AA gunners for all aircraft below that height. The system was ramshackle, but it worked, with subsequent analysis showing that out of every seven raiders flying over Malta, five were picked up by the searchlights, and of these, three would be attacked, of which two would be shot down. This meant that the *Regia Aeronautica* was suffering a far higher attrition rate than the RAF on its raids over Germany by this time. It was good, but not good enough, as a proportion of raiders continued to reach the airfields and the Grand Harbour, including one that sank the destroyer *Maori* with a direct hit.

Anti-aircraft fire was only effective up to 12,000–15,000 feet, so the Italian and German bombers flew above that level. This was where the night fighters lurked, with the assurance that they were not at risk from their own AA fire. From early summer 1942 onwards, radar-equipped Beaufighters were ready. The Beaufighter pilots served three months on duty in Malta at a time. While their role was less dangerous than that of the Spitfire pilot on day duty, considerable skill was required, not least when landing on a bombed airfield with only two directional lights at either end of the runway. That summer, the Beaufighter crews became so adept that even the night attacks were lessened.

Later, de Havilland Mosquito night fighters took over, but by this time, with Sicily in Allied hands and the war in the Western Desert over, the air battles over Malta had all but gone.

THE GLORIOUS 10 MAY

At first light on 9 May, Spitfires flew off from the decks of the *Wasp* and the *Eagle*. Four of the forty-seven flown off the *Wasp* failed to make it, with one crashing on take-off, another ditching and a third crashing on the African coast. A fourth jettisoned its auxiliary fuel tank by mistake and landed back on the carrier, which was no mean achievement given the lack of an arrester hook and the fact that the pilot had never made a carrier landing before. He wanted to continue to Malta but permission was refused as the carriers were now steaming back to Gibraltar. He eventually reached the island as a passenger aboard a Consolidated Liberator bomber, carrying supplies, within a few days.

Despite these losses, an unprecedented fifty-nine Spitfires had succeeded in reaching the island, with the first landing at 10.00, escorted by two of the island Spitfires flown by Flying Officer Tony Holland and Pilot Officer Ken Mitchell, who had between them shot down a Bf109 they encountered as they waited for the incoming aircraft. Twenty-three aircraft landed at Ta Kali, and another thirty-six were divided between Luqa and Hal Far. The target for refuelling and rearming was fifteen minutes, but the preparations worked so well that everything was achieved within ten minutes. Within the hour, all fifty-nine aircraft had arrived and were back in the air.

Not everything went to plan. When Tony Holland took off on his second patrol of the day, his first problem was that his radio would not work, leaving him feeling both deaf and dumb, and unable to communicate. At 24,000 feet, he lost the rest of his section and, believing that they had dived, did the same, only to find that his airspeed built up so rapidly as the aircraft went into a near vertical dive that he found it hard to control, with the airspeed indicator off its marked readings. He managed to regain control with difficulty, but his relief at seeing three aircraft ahead was soon ended as he realised that they were three Bf109s. He swept in behind the nearest aircraft, making sure that the safety catch was off for his guns, and attempted to open fire with all four cannon, expecting his prey to explode, but all four guns jammed. He passed under the German formation and they saw him, but he managed to escape by diving in a spiral and returned to Ta Kali.

That afternoon, flying a well-serviced aircraft, he finally managed to get a Bf109 as he caught one circling Ta Kali before it could do any harm. Like all of the fighter pilots, he preferred to be in the air where he could fight rather than be caught on the ground during an air raid.

Malta could come as a shock to even the hardened Battle of Britain veteran, as a young Pilot Officer Ken Mitchell recalled his first day at Ta Kali:

> The tempo of life here is just indescribable. The morale of all is mag-
> nificent – pilots, ground crews, and army, but it is certainly tough. The
> bombing is continuous, on and off all day. One lives here only to
> destroy the Hun and hold him at bay; everything else, living con-
> ditions, sleep, food, and all the ordinary standards of life have gone by
> the board. It all makes the Battle of Britain and fighter sweeps seem
> like child's play in comparison, but it is certainly history in the
> making, and nowhere is there aerial warfare to compare with this.[13]

Despite having fewer aircraft than a fortnight earlier, Kesselring was determined to break the island's reinforced fighter defences. He planned to bomb Malta all night and mount an all-out effort the following day. The balance of power was tipping against him, and while convoys were still not getting through, the large, fast minelayer HMS *Welshman* succeeding in reaching the Grand Harbour at 05.35 loaded with ammunition for the anti-aircraft guns, after a night when few got any sleep after constant raids by Ju87s and Ju88s. Nevertheless, on taking to the air at 05.00 to cover the approach of the *Welshman*, the defenders of Malta were relieved to see that, despite the noise and the bombing, there was relatively little fresh damage.

There was a lull in the bombing for much of the morning and it was not until 11.00 that a major raid was mounted, with the Germans clearly intent on tackling the *Welshman* as she lay under a heavy smokescreen in the Grand Harbour. The *Luftwaffe* sent ten Ju88s and twenty Ju87s, with a substantial Bf109 escort, but for once the numbers were evenly balanced. David Douglas-Hamilton was in the air leading No. 603 Squadron, and wrote about how impressive the harbour AA barrage was when seen from the air.

> It was a stupendous sight, and put to shame all other efforts at 'flak'
> which anyone had seen over Malta or France. An almost solid cone of
> AA burst over the harbour from ground level to about 7,000 feet. Into
> this the Huns were diving. Into it, too, the Spitfires dived, chasing the

Huns. It never occurred to any of us that we might just as easily get hurt. In fact, it was with some irritation that I watched an 87 I was making for in front of me blown to pieces by a direct hit. Afterwards it turned out that two of the squadron's pilots, Tony Holland and Johnny Hurst, received slight gashes in their machines from shrapnel, and a pilot in another squadron had to bale out.

We passed out of the barrage, chasing the 87s. I picked out my victim. It was a 109 crossing my front, he was in my sights now. Right! Quarter deflection and press the button. Brr! About five shots came out from each gun but no more. The 109 saw me and did the one thing a fighter pilot should never do – he turned away, leaving me a dead astern shot. I pressed the button again, but nothing happened. Cursing my luck, I went back and had another try, this time at an 87, but all four cannon had jammed ... I was very angry ... had almost reached the aerodrome when suddenly I heard the unmistakable sound of very close cannon fire above the noise of the engine ... a 109 passed overhead. He had been firing at me ... must have been a very bad shot, for I had not a scratch on my aeroplane.[14]

The rest of the squadron had been far luckier, with Bill Douglas having two 87s as probables and Johnny Hurst had one, while many more had been damaged, with Tony Holland catching no less than four.

The raid had seen some 40 tons of bombs dropped, with one just missing the *Welshman*. The RAF had been able to put thirty-seven Spitfires and thirteen Hurricanes into the air. The next raid, early in the afternoon, saw No. 603 remain on the ground in reserve, so its next scramble was not until the fourth raid of the day. In the meantime, he saw Spitfires shoot down three out of a group of five Italian bombers. Once again, his scramble was frustrated by a defect, with his radio failing to transmit, but he landed and the problem was fixed. Airborne again, he noticed many parachutes coming down and thought at first that the Germans were baling out, until he saw one of their aircraft blow up as it encountered a parachute mine projected into the air by the AA defences.

His wingman was Pilot Officer Mitchell, the new arrival.

We flew three times to and fro in the barrage, trusting to luck to avoid the flak. Then I spotted a Ju87 climbing out at the fringe of the barrage and I turned and chased him. I gave him a one-second burst of cannon and he broke off sharply to the left.

At that moment another Ju87 came up in front of my nose and I turned into him and let him have it. His engine started to pour out black smoke and he started to weave. I kept the tit pushed hard, and after a further two- to three-second burst with the one cannon I had left, the other having jammed, he heeled over at 1,500 feet and went into the drink.

I then spotted a 109 firing at me from behind and pulled the kite round to port, and after one and a half turns got on his tail. Before I could fire, another 109 cut across my bows from the port side, and I turned straight on his tail and fired till my cannon stopped due to lack of ammo. He was hit and his engine poured out black smoke, but I had to beat it as I was now defenceless.[15]

Defenceless indeed, as two more Bf109s were attacking him, and it took five minutes of violent manoeuvring to throw them off. This was a great day for No. 603, however, as the squadron had destroyed or probably destroyed six Axis aircraft and damaged another six. Overall, as many as forty Axis aircraft had been destroyed or probably destroyed by the Spitfires, and another twenty damaged. A radio broadcast from Rome that night was remarkably frank, saying that thirty-seven Axis aircraft had failed to return, but frankness had its limits as the broadcast went on to say that forty-seven Spitfires had been shot down while an attack was made on a strong British naval force in Grand Harbour. The truth was that three Spitfires had been shot down with the loss of one pilot, and the strong naval force, HMS *Welshman*, got away unscathed that night.

For the first time since June 1940, the Royal Air Force had regained aerial superiority over Malta. On 11 May, the headline of the *Times of Malta*, the main English-language newspaper read:

BATTLE OF MALTA: AXIS HEAVY LOSSES
'SPITFIRES' SLAUGHTER 'STUKAS'
BRILLIANT TEAM WORK OF AA GUNNERS AND RAF
63 Enemy Aircraft Destroyed or damaged over Malta yesterday.

No less to the point, Kesselring reported:

The British fighter pilots deserve recognition for their bravery and manoeuvring skill, especially in the perfect handling of their aircraft when diving from a high altitude (30,000–40,000 feet) through the middle of closed bomber formations.

Over the next few days, there were further raids, but after 14 May, it was some time before JU88s appeared over Malta and the Ju87 seemed to have disappeared completely, leaving fighter sweeps by Bf109s, many acting in the fighter-bomber role, as the main threat, but such aircraft could not carry heavy bombs. Even so, there was much to be done and all that had been achieved could be lost if a convoy did not reach Malta in time.

BACK TO THE OFFENSIVE

There were further reinforcements of Spitfires by the *Eagle* later that month, and, in June, two ships out of six arriving from Gibraltar, while a convoy from Alexandria was forced to turn back. The RAF continued to enjoy air superiority over Malta. This was helped by the arrival of sixteen Bristol Beaufighters, providing both night fighter cover and also possessing the ability to provide air cover some miles out to sea for approaching convoys. For the June convoys, a number of Spitfires were also fitted with auxiliary tanks to extend their range over the sea to protect the convoys.

For the fighter squadrons, June was a relatively quiet month, which was just as well as many of the pilots of No. 603 Squadron at Ta Kali went down with 'Malta Dog', an unpleasant form of dysentery, and were not available for duty for some time. Morale was shaken on 20 June by the fall of Tobruk, but, even worse, in Malta the Governor had been forced to set a 'target date', the date when the island could no longer survive due to a shortage of food, fuel and ammunition. Food was especially difficult as the island could in normal times only produce enough food to feed its population for about four months of the year.

One of the Malta squadrons, No. 249, which was there longer than any other, amassed the highest score of enemy kills of any RAF squadron during the war.

Perhaps part of the success of No. 249 was the squadron commander's luck in choosing the right pilots. David Douglas-Hamilton of No. 603 and Laddie Lucas of No. 249 tossed to go first to start their selection of newly arrived pilots. Lucas won, and picked George 'Screwball' Beurling, a man whom some initially considered to be a line-shooter. They were soon proved wrong as Screwball disposed of eight German aircraft in a very short time. Later, he shot down three enemy aircraft in a single day on at least two occasions, and one day he shot down four, when on 27 July a group of Ju88s were being escorted by around forty fighters. A master of deflection shooting, he fired ahead of a Macchi that flew into his cannon shells and crashed, before firing at another Macchi, which disintegrated, and then attacking a Bf109, which he hit in the fuel tank so that it went down in flames. Landing to refuel and rearm, he set off again, and found a Bf109, which he attacked and sent it diving into the sea.

On 14 July, the AOC Malta changed when AVM Sir Hugh Lloyd was replaced by AVM Sir Keith Park, who had commanded 11 Group during the Battle of Britain. Having aerial superiority over Malta was not enough for Park, who wanted the Malta Spitfires to become more aggressive, shooting down enemy bombers before they reached the islands, and attacking enemy airfields at the first opportunity.

On 1 August, No. 603 Squadron was to be disbanded and become the basis of a reformed No. 229 Squadron as 603 had lost many pilots over the past two months, and also was without its ground crew as their convoy had been unable to reach Malta, but were stuck a thousand miles to the east in Cyprus.

First, Squadron Leader David Douglas-Hamilton was sent on compulsory rest leave to an RAF rest camp in St Paul's Bay, his first leave since arriving in Malta.

August was the month that the great siege of Malta was lifted. This was due to Operation Pedestal, known to the Maltese as the 'Santa Marija' convoy as it arrived on the feast day of the Virgin Mary. The convoy included fresh Spitfires, mainly flown off HMS *Furious*, while HMS *Eagle* was torpedoed and sunk on 11 August, and the other two carriers, *Indomitable* and *Victorious*, were both badly damaged. Just five out of fourteen merchantmen succeeded in reaching the Grand Harbour, with the fast tanker *Ohio* strapped between two destroyers and arriving on 15 August, eventually sinking after her precious cargo of fuel had been unloaded.

With adequate supplies of fuel after the safe arrival of the tanker *Ohio*, the summer of 1942 saw Malta-based aircraft move to an all-out offensive, with the need for defensive sorties very much reduced as the *Luftwaffe* and *Regia Aeronautica* came under pressure. Air raids were renewed in July as soon as the RAF and the Fleet Air Arm resumed their attacks on shipping. The July bombing raids were less severe than those earlier, largely because these were intercepted before they reached Malta. The priority throughout this period was to keep the airfields in Malta operational, filling craters and continuing to work, even when unexploded bombs or landmines made this hazardous.

The plight of Rommel's forces in North Africa resulting from the success of the aircraft based in Malta provoked another attempt to neutralise the island's airfields and squadrons in October, with Malta's Spitfires being scrambled up to six times a day. This final attempt was short-lived as the *Luftwaffe* and *Regia Aeronautica* losses were too heavy to be sustained. Finally, in October, the 8th Army's victory at El Alamein, followed soon after by the Allied landings in North Africa in November, marked the turning of the tide.

Nevertheless, in the meantime, the struggle to survive continued in Malta. Malta-based aircraft could not taxi, but had to be manhandled to and from the runway by ground crews, often made up of soldiers. Engines would be switched off as soon as an aircraft landed. If an aircraft blocked Luqa's only runway, the one surviving Crusader tank would push or pull it out of the way, as it was judged expedient to clear the runway even if the aircraft was not damaged beyond repair as a result than to keep other aircraft in the air, wasting fuel, as they waited for their turn to land.

The tempo of offensive operations was slow to build up due to the fuel shortages. There were a few fighter sweeps over Sicily, on one of which Wing Commander Arthur Donaldson joined two of his pilots in the destruction of a Macchi 202 over the island. On another sortie, he suffered engine failure over Comiso, but managed to glide back to Ta Kali. After fitting an elementary bomb sight to his Spitfire, Donaldson practised dropping 250lb bombs on the uninhabited island of Filfla, and on a number of occasions these were dropped in earnest on airfields in Sicily. On 11 October, after dropping his bombs on Filfla, he noticed No. 229 Squadron's aircraft taking off and joined them, not realising that Kesselring had started a new offensive with aircraft that had returned from the Eastern Front. Within minutes they were facing three Ju88s escorted by upwards of twenty Bf109s. Attacking head-on, Donaldson shot down one of the bombers.

The offensive continued on 12 October, when Donaldson's wing surprised eight Ju88s and up to seventy Bf109s off Sicily. This time two Ju88s and a Bf109 were shot down by Donaldson, with another Ju88 and a Bf109 as probables. This was an incredible performance, as he recalled:

> It was the most spectacular sight I have ever seen. The whole sky was filled with enemy aircraft in severe trouble! I saw three flaming Ju88s and another three flaming Bf109s, and counted no less than ten parachutes descending slowly, three of them from a Ju88 I had shot down. Two of my victims, a Ju88 and a Bf109, both burst into flames.
>
> This practice of forward interception did not prevent eighty people being killed on Malta and more than 400 buildings being destroyed, but as a result a large number of Axis aircraft flying towards Malta never reached their destination. This required good controlling and accurate shooting at close range.[16]

The following day, he was much less successful, again confronting three Ju88s with escorts, but his aircraft was badly damaged and the most he could do was force the Germans to jettison their bombs.

Beurling nevertheless had a successful sortie that day, shooting down two Bf109s before turning his attention to a Ju88 with equally deadly effect.

On 14 October, Beurling was airborne just after noon when he found a formation of Ju88s escorted by some fifty Bf109s. He shot down a Ju88 with a short burst, and then turned to the leader of no less than eight Bf109s all chasing a solitary Spitfire, shooting the Bf109 down, and was about to shoot down a second Bf109 when machine-gun fire from a bomber wounded him in the arm and hand. He climbed away, only to find another Spitfire being threatened by a Bf109, so he dived and came up from below to shoot off its wing. His luck ran out as he then made what was for himself a rare mistake, watching the Bf109 crash downwards into the sea, only to find his aircraft being torn apart by cannon shells from another Bf109, which also wounded him in the leg and arm. He baled out, only to find the Bf109 pilot then firing at his parachute until chased off by another Spitfire.

Falling into the sea, he was picked up by the Malta air-sea rescue launch. He was soon in hospital, but in just a few weeks he had accounted for twenty-eight German and Italian aircraft, most of them fighters.

At 06.30 on 15 October, the *Luftwaffe* mounted one of the heaviest attacks for some months. First to be scrambled was the Luqa Spitfire Wing, but no contact was made with the enemy. Donaldson was then sent up, but could only muster a flight of four Spitfires to face eight Ju88s and up to seventy Bf109s. He led his flight in a head-on attack, breaking up the bomber formation and then turning his attention to a Ju88 bomber, which burst into flames. All this done while his own rear was unattended as the other, less experienced, Spitfire pilots had been unable to follow him. No sooner had he finished with the Ju88 than his own aircraft was riddled with cannon shells and the engine failed. As he glanced down, he could see blood everywhere and petrol leaking into the cockpit, while two fingers from his shattered left hand were lying on his lap.

Fortunately, the controls still responded and with his good hand he rolled his aircraft over and dived. He decided not to bale out for fear of drowning through loss of blood, and instead started to glide back to Ta Kali. Fortunately, the Bf109s did not follow. He made a wheels-up belly landing at the airfield, which was covered with delayed action incendiary bombs, but, regardless of the dangers, the fire-tender was with him almost as soon as his aircraft ground to a halt and he was pulled out of the aircraft and taken to the army hospital at Mtarfa for treatment. His reward for outstanding airmanship and bravery was to receive a visit from AVM Sir Keith Park to tell him that he had been awarded the Distinguished Service Order, making him one of the only three brothers in any of the armed services to have all won the DSO. All had been RAF squadron commanders.

The German attacks continued over the next few days, but it was soon clear that the RAF still had the upper hand and was inflicting greater losses on the *Luftwaffe* than it suffered. Nevertheless, in Sicily, Kesselring still had greater numbers of aircraft.

During the evening of 19 October, the *Luftwaffe* sent fighter-bombers that were met by the RAF over the sea, but this was a feint as the *Luftwaffe* immediately sent in three bomber formations, which approached Malta from the north, the east and the west. A squadron of Spitfires intercepted those approaching from the west, breaking up the formation, before flying back over Malta to intercept the bombers from the east, shooting many of them down. The bomber formation from the north then flew into a squadron of night fighters, which ensured that most of the Ju88s did not reach Malta.

Expecting this to be the start of a major air offensive, Malta's defences were on alert the next day, waiting for the next heavy air raid, but only a few light 'hit-and-run' raids ensued. The waiting continued the next day, but the truth began to dawn that they had won the air battle. Between 11 and 19 October 1942, no less than 131 German and Italian aircraft had been shot down for the cost of 34 RAF aircraft and 13 pilots. Kesselring had been forced to call off the attacks as the German losses were too high.

Throughout the attacks, all of Malta's airfields had remained operational and, while the fighters defended Malta, bombers based on the island carried out their attacks on Axis shipping every night but one. The fact was that while the RAF pilots had gained in experience, because of losses on the Eastern Front and over Malta, those of the *Luftwaffe* were increasingly less experienced pilots, often straight from the flying schools.

It was just a few days later, on 23 October, that the British 8th Army took El Alamein. A week later, on 30 October, Operation Supercharge captured the airfields at Matruba so that they would be available to provide air cover for the next convoy to Malta.

Notes

1. Imperial War Museum Sound Archive.
2. Imperial War Museum Sound Archive.
3. Imperial War Museum Sound Archive.
4. Imperial War Museum Sound Archive.
5. Imperial War Museum Sound Archive.
6. Imperial War Museum Sound Archive.
7. Laddie Lucas, *Five Up*, Sidgwick & Jackson, London, 1978.
8. Laddie Lucas, *Five Up*, Sidgwick & Jackson, London, 1978.
9. Laddie Lucas, *Five Up*, Sidgwick & Jackson, London, 1978.
10. Imperial War Museum Sound Acrhive.
11. *The Air Battle For Malta*, James Douglas-Hamilton, Mainstream, 1981.
12. Imperial War Museum Sound Archive.
13. Imperial War Museum Sound Archive.
14. James Douglas-Hamilton, *The Air Battle for Malta*, Mainstream, Edinburgh, 1981.
15. James Douglas-Hamilton, *The Air Battle for Malta*, Mainstream, Edinburgh, 1981.
16. Imperial War Museum Sound Archive.

Chapter 7

Greece and North Africa

The campaigns in Greece and North Africa are treated together because it was from North Africa that the RAF sent aircraft to support ground forces during the ill-starred Greek campaign. In fact, the Greek campaign was a serious impediment for both sides. For the Axis, it was a diversion that delayed the start of Operation Barbarossa, the invasion of the Soviet Union, and was one of the reasons why the German armies did not reach their key objectives before the onset of the Russian winter halted the advance. It also wasted Allied energies, which at the time were mainly those of the British Empire, at a time when resources were very short and the balance of power in the Mediterranean and in North Africa was most definitely not on their side. Defeat in Greece was almost inevitable and a further mistake was to try to defend Crete after the British and Greek forces had lost so much of their equipment in Greece, rather than simply using the island as a stepping stone for evacuation to Egypt.

At risk was control of the Suez Canal, the key objective for the Axis in North Africa, even though this was no longer the short cut it was intended to be for shipping between Europe and the Middle and Far East, and Australia, but with Italian and German forces dominating the Mediterranean, it was the main means of supply for British forces in North Africa, Cyprus and Palestine: just about the most roundabout route imaginable.

After the fall of France, initially the British hoped that Vichy forces in North Africa would fight against the Germans. They were soon disabused of this notion, and while Vichy forces did not ally themselves with the Germans, it was clear that they were hostile towards the Allies.

THE RAF IN THE MIDDLE EAST
On the outbreak of war on 3 September 1939, there was already an RAF Middle East Command, with ACM Sir William Mitchell as Air Officer Commanding. His command was in fact divided into four, and, somewhat confusingly, that part actually in Egypt was known as RAF Middle East, while there was also RAF Mediterranean, based on Malta, RAF Iraq, and RAF Aden. The latter enabled the UK to control the Red Sea approaches to

the Suez Canal and also to counter Italian influence on the other side of the Red Sea in Somalia, Abyssinia and Eritrea.

Early in May 1940, Mitchell handed over command to AVM Sir Arthur Longmore, a former RNAS pilot who had been transferred into the new RAF when it was formed on 1 April 1918. Despite the wide geographical spread and the fact that in the almost certain case of Italy entering the war on the side of Germany, RAF Middle East would be on the front line, when Italy finally entered the war in June 1940, Longmore had less than 300 aircraft in his twenty-nine squadrons. Worse still, many of the aircraft were obsolete, including Gloster Gladiator fighters, and Bristol Bombay and Vickers Valentia bomber transports – in effect, aircraft that could be used in either role but were poor at both.

At this time, priority was being given to the air defence of the UK, and it was inevitable that the RAF in the Middle East was not equipped with the most up-to-date aircraft. Initially, this was not a major problem as the Italian *Regia Aeronautica* was not as well equipped as the *Luftwaffe*.

The fighting in North Africa started with the Italian invasion of Egypt on 17 September 1940, from the newly created Italian colony of Libya, a merger of Tripolitania and Cyrenaica, colonised by Italy in 1912. This was a debacle for the Italians, who were only saved by the commitment to send British forces to defend Greece, which effectively reduced British air and ground forces to a dangerous level. Had not German assistance come to North Africa and had not British forces been fatally divided, the RAF could have countered the Italian opposition, even though outnumbered in North Africa and East Africa where the Italians had a total of 500 aircraft, but these were mainly obsolete. Before British forces were sent to Greece, the RAF had achieved equality in the air in North and East Africa, and was on its way towards air supremacy. The Greek campaign initially meant that four squadrons were transferred to the Balkans.

Nevertheless, the transfer of so much to Greece from North Africa meant that the RAF was left with just six squadrons with which to stem the initial advance by the *Afrika Korps* in May 1941, which quickly reversed the gains made by the 8th Army against Italian forces. In Greece, nine squadrons with less than 200 Blenheims, Gladiators, Hurricanes and Lysanders faced more than 1,200 *Luftwaffe* aircraft of the latest types. A good idea of the losses suffered by the RAF during the Greek campaign was that, after the withdrawal, just twenty-four aircraft were left to be evacuated to Crete, and when the *Luftwaffe* attacked, followed by an invasion led by German paratroops and glider-landed troops, just seven aircraft remained to be flown to Egypt.

This was a continuation of the succession of defeats suffered by British forces from the start of fighting in September 1940. There were a number of minor victories, with successes in Abyssinia, Eritrea and Somaliland, but these were areas in which Italian air power had been weak. Despite this, an

Italian air raid on Alexandria – the main base for the British Mediterranean Fleet after Malta became untenable – in June 1940 killed 650 civilians while there were also shortages of food and war *matériel*. A revolt in Iraq was put down by training aircraft. More significant was the invasion of Vichy French Syria, on 8 June 1941, by British and Free French forces to which the RAF committed Blenheims, Gladiators, Hurricanes and Tomahawks, augmented by Fleet Air Arm Fulmars. This did at least eliminate the threat of being caught in the middle had Vichy joined the Axis, which seemed to be a strong possibility.

With little else left to lose in the eastern Mediterranean other than the all-important Suez Canal and, secured by the invasion of Syria, the island of Cyprus, British forces concentrated on repelling the advance of the *Afrika Korps*. The experience was to stand all three services in good stead for the years ahead. This was for the most part a highly mobile war fought over vast distances, with a front line that moved some 1,500 miles. The exceptions to the mobile element were the siege of Tobruk and the Battle of El Alamein, the last victory gained by British arms alone. Essential to victory was close air support and re-supply of ground forces.

AIR WAR IN THE DESERT

Although outnumbered, the RAF did its best to conceal the fact from the Italians, and from the start took to the offensive so it was the numerically superior Italian forces who were put on the defensive. One ploy was to use a single Hawker Hurricane and switch this between landing grounds to give the impression that there was more than one aircraft. Real success included the shooting down of eight Savoia-Marchetti SM79 bombers on 17 August 1940 by Gloster Gladiator fighter biplanes without a single loss.

Nevertheless, despite being preoccupied by the Battle of Britain and then the Blitz, it was clear that the Mediterranean and the Middle East required reinforcement. This was no easy task, as the previous chapter has shown; the direct route across the Mediterranean was not available for as long as the Axis air forces held aerial superiority. Aircraft had to be flown or shipped to Takoradi on the Gold Coast (now Ghana) in West Africa, where those in crates were assembled, and then flown across Africa. The RAF in Egypt grew stronger during 1940 and by late November had been reinforced with two squadrons of Hurricanes, Nos. 73 and 274 Squadrons, and two squadrons of Vickers Wellington bombers, Nos. 37 and 38 Squadrons, although, of these, No. 37 had flown out via Malta and undertaken operational sorties from the island. An early sign that the force was to be more than just the RAF was the arrival of several squadrons from the South African Air Force.

The start of Operation Compass, the British counter-offensive against Italian forces, saw the RAF provide close support for ground forces in an operation that at times moved very quickly, with aircraft often landing after a sortie at a more advanced strip than that from which they had taken off.

Initially operations were carried out by 204 Group, under the command of Air Commodore Raymond Collishaw, with two squadrons of Hurricanes and one, No. 6, with Hurricanes and Lysanders. Another three squadrons, one of them RAAF, operated Blenheim bombers and two more had Martin Marylands. Command in North Africa passed on 30 July 1941 to AVM Arthur Coningham, Australian-born but brought up in New Zealand. Coningham set up his own HQ in that of the 8th Army, establishing a close relationship that was repeated right down to the operational squadrons. The operations in North Africa became a command in the full sense on 21 October 1941, when 204 Group became Air Headquarters Western Desert, although for two weeks in January 1942, it became Air Headquarters Libya before reverting to its original title. Initially, there were three wings, with 258 and 269 providing close support over the front line, while 262 defended the Nile Delta and Alexandria.

Not all of the units were from the RAF as Fleet Air Arm squadrons were deployed over the Western Desert from time to time. Stuart Jewers, later a lieutenant-commander, had trained on Sea Gladiators and once moved from operations over the Red Sea to the Western Desert he expected to find that his Fairey Fulmar monoplane would be an improvement. It was, but the Fulmar, burdened with a pilot and an observer, was still not fast enough and Jewers was frustrated as it could not even catch enemy bombers. In March 1942, he was transferred to No. 889 Naval Air Squadron just as it was re-equipping with Sea Hurricane IIs, which could at least catch the enemy bombers even if they could fall victim to a Bf109.

Sandstorms were a hazard for the aircrew, not only depriving them of visibility but the sand could block air intakes and lead to engine failure. One pilot recalled that it seemed to get everywhere. One pilot, Flight Lieutenant (later Group Captain) Mike Judd, of No. 238 Squadron, flew his Hurricane into a sandstorm, but managed to land and his aircraft was recovered and returned to service the following day. The Hurricane, when fitted with 20mm cannon, was a formidable anti-tank aircraft, but deliveries to the RAF of the Curtiss P-40 Kittyhawk provided a boost to capability, especially once fitted with long-range fuel tanks. By this time a squadron leader, Judd led No. 250 Squadron on sweeps against enemy supply dumps and airfields, destroying a Ju87 Stuka dive-bomber and damaging another.

The outstanding *Luftwaffe* fighter ace in North Africa was *Oberleutnant* Hans-Joachim Marseille, just twenty-two years old in 1942. His initial flying career was ruined by reports of his poor flying discipline. He soon proved to be an inspired fighter pilot and was eventually to achieve 158 victories. In fact, he scored the first victory for his squadron, 3/JG 27, shooting down a Hurricane over Tobruk. Nevertheless, his daredevil tactics often meant that his aircraft returned to base badly shot up. When he finally crash-landed on his own base, his *Gruppenkommandeur* decided to give the young man some timely advice.

'You are only alive,' he was told, 'because you have more luck than sense. But don't imagine that it will continue indefinitely. One can over-strain one's luck like one can an aeroplane.'[1]

On 1 September 1942, he set a record that has never been equalled, with seventeen victories in a single day. On 3 September, he was awarded the Diamonds of the Knight's Cross, Germany's highest decoration. A little over three weeks later, on 26 September, he only outmatched an RAF Spitfire with difficulty, taking a quarter of an hour to dispose of the British aircraft. It was his last victory.

On 30 September, he was leading high cover for a force of Ju87 Stuka dive-bombers, without making contact with the Allies. On his return, his cockpit was filled with smoke as his engine caught fire. He could not see. He called his comrades and his old No. 2, Poettgen, gave him directions, and then started to count down as they approached territory held by the Axis. At this point, Marseille called: 'I've got to get out.' He rolled the aircraft onto its back, and the cockpit canopy was jettisoned, followed by his body. His comrades watched in horror as he plummeted to earth, his parachute failing to open.

Another squadron commander immediately set off to find his remains and bring them back for burial, but on examination they found that he had not pulled the ripcord. A wide scar across his chest showed that he had been struck by the fin of his aircraft, knocking him unconscious.

On 12 May 1942, radio intercepts alerted the Allies to a German plan to send transport aircraft from Crete to Libya. Judd's No. 250 Squadron were sent to escort a Beaufighter squadron and intercepted twelve Ju52 troop carriers some 50 miles off the coast. He shot down two of the aircraft and his pilots accounted for another eight, with just two aircraft managing to escape.

In the run-up to the Battle of El Alamein, Judd returned to attacking supply and fuel dumps, and motor transport. He damaged two enemy fighters and, on 22 October, destroyed a Bf109.

A little over a year after the formation became known as Air Head-quarters Western Desert, the force was organised and renamed as the Western Desert Air Force on 27 October 1942. It was under the overall control of General Headquarters, RAF Middle East, but operated ever more closely with the ground forces, whose needs were paramount. It was a truly international organisation, including operational control of the US Desert Air Task Force, itself part of the US Middle East Air Force, with the exception of the 81st Bombardment Squadron.

Amongst the units were the South African Air Force's 3 Bomber Wing with three squadrons of Baltimores and Bostons, while No. 232 Bomber Wing included two RAF Baltimore and three USAAF Mitchell squadrons. The main roles were fighter, tactical reconnaissance, fighter-bomber and anti-tank operations, with 285 Reconnaissance Wing, a joint RAF and SAAF formation of four squadrons and one Baltimore flight, operating Spitfire VBs on photo-reconnaissance in No. 2 PRU Squadron RAF, and Marylands in No. 60 Survey Squadron SAAF. Hawker Hurricanes provided tactical reconnaissance in No. 40 Squadron SAAF and No. 208 Squadron RAF. Another mixed formation was 211 Group, with 233, 239 and 244 Wings, with a total of sixteen squadrons, three each with Hurricanes and Spitfires, while another four operated P-20F Warhawks, one with Tomahawks, and no less than seven with Kittyhawks, with eight RAF squadrons, five SAAF squadrons, an RAAF squadron and three from the USAAF. Far less varied was 212 Group, with 243 and 7 Wings, with a total of eight RAF squadrons and all operating Hurricane IIbs or IIcs.

None of this was easy. Squadron Leader Fred Rosier, with No. 229 Squadron, recalls:

> Life in the Western Desert was tough and demanding. We had to put up with the extremes of heat and cold – the sandstorms which got worse and, even more depressing as time went on, the flies (particularly where the Italians had been), the shortage of water, the monotony of the daily diet of bully beef and hard biscuits – and the fear … that feeling in the pit of your stomach before going on operations.[2]

The harsh reality was, of course, that the distances were vast and the terrain inhospitable. Flying boots were not ideal for desert conditions. In such circumstances unusual measures were taken out of humanity for a fellow pilot, but even these did not always succeed, as Rosier later recalled, by which time he was a wing commander leading the RAF's 262 Wing.

> It was the time when preparations were in hand for a new offensive – Operation Crusader. The fighter force moved forward to new landing grounds at Maddalena and the operation started on 18 November [1942]. Four days later I was ordered to go to Tobruk to organise the operation of fighters from there. I set off that afternoon in a Hurricane in which I had put all my worldly goods. Two squadrons of Tomahawks escorted me. We were well on our way when we were intercepted by 109s and the fight started. When I saw a Tomahawk diving down, streaming with smoke and then landing, I decided to try to rescue him. I went down and landed close to him; he ran across and sat in my cockpit. I discarded my parachute, sat on top of him, opened the throttle and then – disaster. As we started to move, a tyre burst,

the wheel dug in and we came to a full stop . . . I faced the prospect of a long walk. This time it would be through hostile territory, and I would be with an Australian pilot, Sergeant Burney.

My first thought was to avoid capture, for I had noticed several trucks not far away. Quickly we removed my possessions from the Hurricane and hid them under some brushwood. Then we ran to a nearby wadi, where we hid behind rocks. They spread out to search and soon found all my stuff – which included my wife's picture and a silver tankard given to me by the CO of No. 73 Squadron. It must have been the fading light that saved us. They came to within just a few yards of where we were hiding.

I decided it would be safer to walk towards the east rather than try the shorter route to Tobruk. We started later that night, using the North Pole star for navigation. In the early hours of the third day, we began to see odd shapes around us. They were enemy tanks and trucks. There was nothing else we could do other than to continue as silently as possible. Once we thought we had been spotted for some lights came on and we heard shouts in German. We lay motionless, and soon the lights went out and there was silence. We were making little progress. It would soon be dawn, and I was worried. But once again the fates were with us. We saw a ring of brushwood ahead. It was around a dried-up abandoned well, and we hid there.

Later that morning – I think we had been sleeping – we heard gunfire and the sound of shells passing over us. We could see the guns and thought we could hear shouting in English. Anyway, we decided to make for them. We were pretty exhausted, and Sergeant Burney's feet were in a terrible state, but we just ran and ran. At last we were safe. At first the gunners were suspicious, but then we were taken to a guards unit who passed us on to a brigade HQ. We were then driven back to Maddalena to find we'd been given up for lost.[3]

The Western Desert Air Force soon became known for its mobility and it set a fine example of what co-operation between air power and ground forces should be. This was a highly mobile war except for the battles at Tobruk and, later, El Alamein. Inevitably, it seems, at the start the WDAF was ill equipped and lacked aircraft capable of tackling the Bf109 once the Germans arrived in the theatre to support the Italians after their advance was reversed, with one squadron commander losing 120 per cent of his pilot strength in just six months. These units had started to assemble during the preceding summer, when the arrival of Spitfire Vs, followed shortly afterwards by three USAAF Warhawk squadrons, provided aircraft capable of meeting the Bf109. After this, the balance of air power began to shift in favour of the WDAF. Within a year, the WDAF comprised twenty-nine squadrons, of which nine were from the SAAF, flying

Hurricane, Spitfire, Kittyhawk, Tomahawk and Warhawk fighters and fighter-bombers, and Boston, Baltimore and Mitchell bombers. The US fighter-bombers were ideally suited to close air support, but so too were the Hurricanes fitted with four 20mm cannon or tank-busting rockets.

OPERATION TORCH – THE LANDINGS IN NORTH AFRICA

In North Africa, the British 8th Army inflicted a major defeat on the German *Afrika Korps* at the Battle of El Alamein, which lasted from 23 October to 5 November 1942. This was to be the first major British victory on land, although the Japanese were to be held in Burma, but it was also the last in which Britain fought alone.

By this time, even before El Alamein, the Allies had planned landings in North Africa, to squeeze the Germans between British and American forces. The North African landings were known as Operation Torch, and involved landing almost 100,000 men in Vichy French territory, on the Atlantic coast of French Morocco and in Algeria. In between these two large areas of Vichy territory was neutral Spanish Morocco. Responsibility for the operation was divided between the British, with the Eastern Task Force, and Americans, with the Western Task Force. The Allies now had General Dwight Eisenhower as Supreme Commander while Admiral Sir Andrew Cunningham was Allied Naval Commander. Force H, under Vice-Admiral Syfret, with the aircraft carriers *Victorious* and *Formidable*, and three battleships, including the new *Duke of York*, defended the eastern flanks of the invasion force from the Italian fleet and German U-boats. The Eastern Task Force, under the command of Rear Admiral Sir Harrold Burrough, with three cruisers, sixteen destroyers and the elderly aircraft carriers *Argus* and *Furious*, with two escort carriers, was to cover the sixteen transports and seventeen landing craft tasked with putting ashore Major-General Ryder's 33,000 British and American troops near Algiers. The landings to the north and south of Casablanca in French Morocco were covered by a Western Task Force, TF34, from the United States, which had twenty-three transports to land 34,000 troops commanded by Major-General Patton, protected by three American battleships, seven cruisers and thirty-eight destroyers, with air support provided by the USS *Ranger* and four American escort carriers.

In between these two major task forces was a Centre Task Force that had sailed from England under the command of Commodore Troubridge, with two escort carriers, three cruisers and thirteen destroyers escorting twenty-eight transports and nineteen landing craft to put 39,000 men ashore at Oran in Algeria under the command of Major-General Frendall.

Landings started at around 01.00 on 8 November at Oran, and then a little later at Algiers, while those in Morocco started at 04.30, with further landings at Safi, almost 200 miles to the south of Casablanca. Despite the size of the operation, almost complete surprise was gained.

While the battleships and cruisers attacked French ships and shore installations, the aircraft from the carriers were sent to attack airfields. Lieutenant (later, Captain) George Baldwin who was senior pilot, or second in command, of No. 807 Naval Air Squadron, flying Supermarine Seafire L.2s.

We thought that we had taken the French Air Force by surprise as we caught their bombers on the ground, and this was just before the sun came up over the horizon. It was just light enough to see targets for strafing and we went in rather over-confidently. I certainly made at least three strafing runs, which was later a forbidden ... tactic ... it became doctrine that you only ever made one run on a strafing attack because the danger rose so rapidly after the first run. I was sure that I had done very heavy damage to three bombers.

After pulling out of the ... attack, I was horrified to see a French Dewoitine fighter coming straight at me head on at about 1,000 feet. I managed to evade him and turn in behind him, and give two bursts of machine-gun fire, because all my cannon ammunition had been used in the strafing. Saw hits and his undercarriage fell down.

I then decided it was time to get home as quickly as possible ... but just as I was making my way back to the coast, I saw a second Dewoitine at right angles to me on my port side. And as I saw him, I saw machine-gun fire coming underneath me, and this was followed ... by a huge explosion behind my seat, and I expected the aircraft to go out of control, but curiously nothing seemed to happen ...[4]

He was soon to discover that his aircraft's radio wasn't working as he attempted to return to *Furious*, and this was followed by the realisation that the pneumatic system had also failed. He flew past the ship, signalling that he would have to land without flaps, meaning a faster than usual approach onto the elderly carrier's short flight deck. Fortunately, his undercarriage worked. On landing, he found that he was the centre of attention for a large number of aircrew and naval ratings who surrounded his aircraft. It was not until he climbed down from the cockpit that he discovered why – there was a large hole about 2 feet in diameter on the port side immediately behind his seat and inside he could see that the fuselage was full of acid as a result of the accumulator blowing up. His radio was in pieces. Potentially most serious of all, only one of the control wires to the rudder had not been severed, and this had got him back safely, otherwise he would have been in trouble, losing control at just 1,000 feet. Indeed, he could see that his Seafire had looked after him very well, as the armour plate behind his seat had been peppered with shrapnel and yet he escaped unscathed.

Baldwin's squadron commanding officer was the only person shot down from the squadrons aboard *Furious*, and was taken prisoner by the Vichy French. He sat in a French general's office while they decided what to do with him, and, when they eventually surrendered, he was returned, going aboard the carrier just two days after being shot down and one of the shortest spells as a prisoner of war on record!

Vichy resistance in North Africa ended on 9 November in Oran.

MEDITERRANEAN AIR COMMAND

After the invasion of North Africa and the subsequent defeat of German forces, the Allies created a new organisation, the Mediterranean Air Command, on 18 February 1943, under the overall command of ACM Sir Arthur Tedder. This was a reversal of the earlier structure as RAF Middle East Command, led by ACM Sir Sholto Douglas, became one of MAC's subordinate commands, as did Air HQ Malta, under AVM Sir Keith Park, and the Northwest African Air Forces (NAAF) led by Major General Carl Spaatz of the USAAF.

The decision to implement this reorganisation was taken at the Casablanca Conference the previous month, attended by Winston Churchill and the US President, Franklin Roosevelt.

Further down, the structure became more complicated. NAAF was the major sub-command and it in turn was divided into three. Major General Jimmy Doolittle commanded the North West African Strategic Air Force (NASAF) while the North West African Coastal Air Force (NACAF) was initially led by Group Captain G.G. Barrett, although he was soon relieved by AVM Sir Hugh Lloyd, and the North West African Tactical Air Force (NATAF) was commanded by Acting Air Marshal Sir Arthur Coningham. It was this latter command that took over the Western Desert Air Force, commanded by AVM Harry Broadhurst. There was also a tactical bomber sub-command within NATAF. On 21 July, the Western Desert Air Force became the Desert Air Force, but by this time its role in North Africa was ending and, despite its designation, it participated in the Salerno and Anzio landings, although in the former the distance from airfields in Sicily meant that close air support was initially provided by the Fleet Air Arm from escort carriers offshore. It then remained in Italy for the remainder of the war, developing new close-support bombing techniques and joining the Balkan Air Force in supporting Italian and Yugoslav partisans.

Notes

1. Cajus Bekker, *The Luftwaffe War Diaries*, Doubleday, New York, 1968.
2. Imperial War Museum Sound Archive.
3. Imperial War Museum Sound Archive.
4. Imperial War Museum Sound Archive.

Chapter 8

Taking the War back to the Enemy

Operation Torch, the Allied landings in North Africa, simply represented a liberation of territory that, although not occupied by the Germans, was in fact that of Vichy France, whose attempts at an alliance with the Germans had been spurned, possibly because the German leadership wanted to drive home the harsh facts of French defeat, but also because many of the Vichy leadership had in turn wanted an alliance on equal terms, outraging the Germans still more.

The next move was to carry the war to the enemy by invading and seizing territory. The Germans and the Italians were not unaware of this possibility, although in the Mediterranean they seemed to consider Sardinia as a more likely possibility than Sicily, but then it was also the case that Hitler believed that the Allies might return to the mainland of Europe by way of Norway.

The Italian campaign started with the invasion of Sicily on 10 July 1943 – Operation Husky. It was seen by Churchill as the start of an advance northwards through Austria to Germany itself, but this was overtaken by events elsewhere and also by the determination of the German resistance, even after Italy formally surrendered. Given the nature of the terrain to be covered, Italy was probably not the ideal route into Germany. On the other hand, the invasion of Italy had one immense benefit in that it re-opened the Mediterranean to Allied shipping and naval forces, enabling the Suez Canal to be used for the very purpose for which it had been built. Some estimates suggest that allowing supplies for the Middle East, India and Australia to use the Mediterranean and the Suez Canal was equivalent to giving the Allies another million tons of merchant shipping, a not unsubstantial benefit at a time when shipbuilding capacity was under pressure.

The limitations of the airfields in Malta meant that most of the air support required for the invasion was provided by the Desert Air Force in North Africa, with the Malta fighter squadrons providing escorts and top cover for the bombers and transports over Sicily. Less than a third of the

120 squadrons needed by the RAF alone could be based on the island's airfields. In total, the Allies were able to assemble a force of almost 4,000 aircraft of all types, against a combined Axis force of around 1,400. The total number of Allied troops was around 160,000 men, faced with 230,000 Italian and 40,000 German personnel.

Husky was not the first Allied assault to use paratroops and air-landed troops as these had been used during Operation Torch, but it was the first to depend heavily on paratroops and glider-landed troops. Despite the time of year, a storm threatened the success of the mission with paratroops being blown away from their planned landing zones, while many gliders crashed into the sea as the inexperienced glider tug pilots released their charges too early, with some 250 troops drowning, although others were rescued by some of the 3,000 ships in the seaborne assault force. Nevertheless, the poor weather and strong winds also meant that the Allies had the advantage of surprise as the Axis defenders assumed that no one would attempt landings in such conditions.

After the invasion, the US 9th Air Force's medium bombers and Curtiss P-40 fighters attached to the Northwest African Air Force under the command of Air Marshal Sir Arthur Coningham were moved to southern airfields on Sicily as soon they were secured. The 9th Air Force was a sub-command of RAF Middle East Command under Air Chief Marshal Sir Sholto Douglas. Middle East Command, like NAAF and Air H.Q. Malta, were sub-commands of MAC under Tedder, who reported to Eisenhower for NAAF operations but to the British Chiefs of Staff for Air H.Q. Malta and Middle East Command operations.

Hard fighting ensued on the ground, but the Allies were unable to stop the bulk of the German and Italian troops being evacuated across the Straits of Messina to mainland Italy to continue the war, although around 132,000 Italians were either killed, wounded or taken prisoner.

SALERNO

With airfields in Libya and Tunisia as well as those in Malta, carrier-borne aircraft had not been essential for the invasion of Sicily, but they were vital for the next stage, the invasion of mainland Italy, with landings at Salerno. Although Salerno was within range of bombers operating from airfields in Sicily, it was only just within range for fighter aircraft, leaving a Spitfire with just enough fuel for twenty minutes on patrol above the beachheads, and far less if engaging enemy aircraft. The obvious solution was to station aircraft carriers off the coast to provide fighter cover. The only Sicily-based fighters used to any extent over Salerno were USAAF Lockheed P-38 Lightnings, long-range twin-engined and twin-boom fighters that could spend an hour over the operational area.

Salerno was an attempt to shorten the war in Italy, but it was unsuccessful for reasons that could not have been fully foreseen at the time. It was meant not only to cut off the Axis forces fighting further south but also to enable the Allies to seize the important port of Naples. Operation Baytown had already seen Montgomery's 8th Army cross the Straits of Messina into Calabria on 3 September 1943, a relatively easy operation but one that left them at the very tip of the 'toe' of Italy, with some considerable distance to move through hilly terrain fighting German and Italian rear-guard actions. Salerno was some 200 miles further north. The prospects at first were extremely bright, for on the same day that Montgomery moved into Calabria, an armistice was signed in secret at Syracuse by Marshal Badoglio's new Italian government, formed after Mussolini had been deposed in July. Negotiations for the armistice had been prolonged as at first the Allies were suspicious of Italian objectives, but this did at least give the Allies time to plan their assaults on Salerno and Taranto, fully recognising that the Germans were likely to continue to resist whatever the Italians decided. This was another reason for choosing Salerno: the hope that a substantial number of German troops would be cut off and unable to withdraw. The armistice was announced on 8 September, on the eve of the Salerno landings, but it might have been as well to have waited another twenty-four hours as the Germans moved quickly to seize Italian airfields, although the Italians at least managed to move most of their fleet to prevent it falling into German hands. Had the Germans not known about the armistice in advance, the landings at Salerno could have been easier.

While in Sicily, two separate armies had been involved – the British 8th Army and the US 7th Army. For Operation Avalanche there was to be a combined British and US single army, designated as the US 5th Army, consisting of the US VI Corps and the British X Corps. A quick build-up of tactical air support operating from the beachhead was important to the operation. The USAAF official record states:

> It was planned to fly in not later than six days after D-Day a total of twelve squadrons of USAAF Mustangs and Kittyhawks, eight squadrons of RAF Spitfires, half a squadron of RAF Beaufighter night fighters and elements of one American Mustang and one RAF Spitfire tactical reconnaissance squadron. Once established ashore this force would come under the control of US 64th Fighter Wing.

The landings at Salerno, Operation Avalanche, on 9 September 1943, were co-ordinated with a British airborne landing at Taranto to seize the port and enable enemy shipping there to escape to Malta. Vice-Admiral Henry Hewitt USN landed Lieutenant-General Mark Clark's US 5th Army in a landing fleet covered by an Independence-class light fleet carrier and four escort carriers, as well as eleven cruisers and forty-three destroyers, while Force H, still under Vice-Admiral Willis, had the battleships *Nelson* and *Rodney*, and the aircraft carriers *Illustrious* and *Formidable*, as well as Force V with the maintenance carrier *Unicorn* operating in the combat role with another four escort carriers, known in the Royal Navy as auxiliary carriers, *Attacker*, *Battler*, *Hunter* and *Stalker*. Force V was under the command of Rear Admiral Sir Philip Vian. While the two large armoured carriers were intended to defend the fleet and look for enemy shipping, the carriers in Force V were solely concerned with providing fighter support, with each escort carrier carrying a single squadron of thirty Supermarine Seafire L.C2s, with their engines tuned to provide maximum power at 5,000 feet instead of the usual 15,000 feet, making it a very different aircraft from those at the North African landings almost a year earlier. *Unicorn* carried two squadrons with a total of sixty Seafires. As in the North African landings, the aircraft would be used to provide air cover and also to provide ground attack against German troops and airfields.

The Seafire was a big improvement in performance over anything that the Fleet Air Arm had operated before, being faster than the Sea Hurricane, although less manoeuvrable and more difficult to repair, and it had folding wings. The modifications necessary for carrier operation meant that it was slightly heavier than the Spitfire, from which it was derived, and so slightly slower. George Baldwin was one of the fighter pilots involved and was a former naval test pilot himself, having flown with the Naval Air Fighting Unit at RNAS Yeovilton. He visited the RAF to discover the latest in fighter tactics and up-to-date intelligence on German aircraft. The RAF personnel were helpful, but this couldn't disguise bad news. The latest versions of the Messerschmitt Bf109 and the new Focke-Wulf Fw190 were indeed formidable opponents, with the latter aircraft also having the manoeuvrability that the Bf109 lacked. Anxious to squeeze the last ounce of performance out of the aircraft, a programme of 'local modifications' was put in hand. The exhaust manifolds were removed and replaced with exhaust stubs to reduce drag and increase the thrust from the exhaust. The knobs for catapult (known at the time as 'accelerators') operation from carriers were also removed as the escort carriers lacked catapults, further reducing drag. Good quality furniture polish was somehow obtained, despite wartime rationing and restrictions on production of quality materials, and everyone, pilots included, spent hours polishing the leading edges of the wings to make the aircraft more slippery. Introduced between May and June 1943, in time for the invasion of Sicily, these changes gave the aircraft another 15 knots' maximum speed. The Seafire suffered from two shortcomings. The first was that, in common with many British fighters early in the war, it was short on range. The second was its tendency to pitch forward on landing, at best damaging the propeller, at worst the aircraft could be damaged beyond repair.

The British carriers made a feint towards Taranto after leaving Malta, although the assault on Taranto was covered by six battleships from Force H and the Mediterranean Fleet, and by aircraft from Malta. The announcement of the armistice saw the Italian Navy leave its ports of

La Spezia, Genoa, Castellamare and Taranto and steam towards Malta, being escorted by four of the Royal Navy's Mediterranean battleships, leaving the other two to accompany *Illustrious* and *Formidable* to Salerno. Despite the escort, the *Luftwaffe* mounted a heavy aerial attack against the Italian ships, sinking the new battleship *Roma* and damaging the *Italia*.

The aircrew aboard the carriers of Force V were awakened at 04.30 on the morning of 9 September. Several of those present recalled not having had much sleep and few had any appetite for the breakfast of eggs and bacon put before them in the wardroom. Amongst the first into the air before dawn were eight Seafires drawn from *Unicorn's* 809 and 887 Naval Air Squadrons, with four aircraft providing high cover and another four low cover, looking out for enemy dive-bombers and torpedo-bombers respectively. The practice was for aircraft to carry extra fuel in drop tanks, extending their patrol time, and to use this first as the tanks would have to be dropped to reduce drag before engaging in aerial combat. That first day, there was little sign of the *Luftwaffe*, but the troops landing encountered fierce resistance. In the days following the invasion, a strong counter-attack was mounted by mainly German forces accompanied by heavy aerial attack by the *Luftwaffe*, so that the entire operation soon appeared to be in difficulty.

Life was difficult aboard the carriers, with Force V given a 'box' offshore in which to operate, flying off and recovering their aircraft. In practice, this box was far too small for the ships, giving the carrier commanders great difficulties as they charged from one end to the other, but the situation was even worse for those in the air; with large numbers of aircraft circling within a confined space, the danger of a mid-air collision was very real as they waited to land on ships steaming close to one another. At times a light haze added to the difficulties. In contrast to the landings on Sicily, the whole operation took place in conditions of complete calm, with little wind – never more than 3 knots – and the Seafire needed 25 knots of wind over the deck for a safe take-off or landing, but the escort carriers could only manage 17 knots. Arrester wires had to be kept even tighter than usual, as were the crash barriers two-thirds of the way along the flight decks.

'Judgement of speed over the water, and height above the water, on the approach to land was extremely difficult,' recalls George Baldwin, an acting lieutenant-commander with the role of Naval Air Wing Commander and responsible for the four squadrons embarked on the four British escort carriers. Baldwin was referring to the difficulties of judging height above calm water, especially the clear calm waters often found in the Mediterranean.

Looking at ways around the problems, Captain Henry McWilliams, commanding officer of the escort carrier HMS *Hunter*, asked Rear Admiral Vian for permission to saw 9 inches off the wooden propeller blades of the Seafires. Vian gave his permission. The modification was relatively easy for the ships' carpenters to do and had little effect on the performance of the aircraft, while propeller damage during landing was much reduced. After initial trials, the entire stock of replacement propellers aboard the carriers was also treated in the same way.

It often seemed to be a case of learning through trial and error. The casualty rate amongst the Seafire pilots seemed to be unduly high in the air, not just in landing, as many seemed to be unable to bale out quickly enough. Learning the hard way, it was soon discovered that the RAF-recommended method of escaping from a Spitfire, rolling the aircraft and opening the canopy before undoing their seat belts and 'ejecting' (in other words, falling out) from the aircraft, didn't work. Possibly this was due to the higher weight of the Seafire. Eventually pilots were advised to jump over the side of the aircraft, and the survival rate amongst those shot down improved immediately.

Turning their attention to the carriers, the *Luftwaffe* mounted intensive attacks during 11 September, forcing the carriers to operate at full speed even when not flying-off or landing aircraft, and fuel consumption increased considerably. For the first time, the Germans used glider-bombs, saving their aircraft from the intense AA fire put up by the fleet offshore. That evening, Vian was forced to signal Vice-Admiral Henry Kent Hewitt in overall command of the operation: 'My bolt will be shot this evening, probably earlier.'

Hewitt had just been briefed by Lieutenant-General Mark Clark on the situation ashore, and guessed that more air attacks were imminent. He signalled back: 'Air conditions here critical. Can your carrier force remain on station to provide earlier morning coverage tomorrow?'

'Will stay here if we have to row back to Sicily,' Vian confirmed.

Hewitt's guess proved to be right. He wasn't surprised to learn that the carriers were low on fuel, but he didn't realise that they were already on their emergency supplies. The reason for the difficulty was not so much the German attacks forcing the carriers to operate at maximum speed through-out the day, but that the planners had assumed that the Fleet Air Arm would be needed for two days, or three days at worst, if the invasion met stiff resistance. After that, it was expected that airfields ashore would have been taken and would be available. As so often happens in warfare, every-thing was not going to plan. The airfields were still not available that would allow the RAF and USAAF to bring aircraft forward from their bases in Sicily.

In the end, the carriers remained on station until 14 September, by which time the 180 Seafires had been reduced to just thirty, more by accident than the efforts of the *Luftwaffe*. One consequence of this was that many senior officers blamed the Seafire for the losses, rather than a combination of factors that had to include the difficulty in operating high performance aircraft off escort carriers with their short decks, lack of accelerators and low speed, in light wind conditions. The aircraft had its weaknesses, and, as one naval officer put it, 'was too genteel for the rough house of naval flying,' but it had its strengths, as Baldwin had discovered earlier during Operation Torch. It was also true that the naval air squadrons had carried out far more than the planned number of sorties, despite the high accident rate.

Even with land-based aircraft to support the ground forces, German resistance proved strong and was joined by a number of Italian units who had refused to surrender.

MEDITERRANEAN AIR FORCE

Shortly after the Salerno landings, on 10 December 1943, the Mediterranean Air Command was replaced by the Mediterranean Allied Air Force (MAAF), with Air Chief Marshal Sir Arthur Tedder as Air Commander-in-Chief Mediterranean, with Major General Carl Spaatz of the USAAF as his deputy. MAAF's main constituent commands were Mediterranean Allied Strategic Air Force (MASAF), Mediterranean Allied Tactical Air Force (MATAF), and Mediterranean Allied Coastal Air Force (MACAF).

On 12 January 1944, Lieutenant General Ira Eaker, previously commander of the US 8th Air Force, replaced Tedder. The primary missions of MAAF were to support the combined bomber offensive in the Mediterranean and to provide close air support for ground forces in the Italy campaign, while helping to keep the sea lanes open. Twelfth Air Force also reorganised during this period with Major General John Cannon assuming command on 21 December 1943. On 1 November 1943, Fifteenth Air Force was established to concentrate on the combined bomber offensive taking the six heavy bomber groups and two long-range fighter groups from the Twelfth Air Force, which increasingly became a tactical air force.

ANZIO

Disappointed by the slowness of the northward advance after the Salerno landings, the Allies were forced once again to make landings closer to Rome, at Anzio, code-named Operation Shingle. Nevertheless, by this time sufficient bases were occupied ashore for carrier-borne air support not to be needed. Shingle had three phases, of which the first, from 1 to 13 January 1944, concentrated on attacking communication targets in northern Italy to mislead the Germans into expecting an assault against Civitavecchia. The second phase saw air strikes against airfields and communications targets, aiming to isolate the beachhead and this continued until the landings on 22 January. During this phase, MAAF aircraft flew 9,876 sorties, dropped 6,461 tons of bombs, and destroyed over fifty enemy aircraft. In addition, the US Twelfth Air Force was reinforced with seven squadrons from the Desert Air Force, flew 3,340 sorties during the week prior to the landings and another 5,500 or so afterwards. Airfield runways were cratered with 500lb bombs, trapping aircraft on the ground to be destroyed with 20lb fragmentation bombs. Finally, the third phase was the provision of air cover over the beachhead and invasion fleet, as well as close air support to the assault forces.

The Allied planners estimated that the Germans had some 270 combat aircraft in Italy, 95 in southern France, and 190 in Greece and the Aegean, but MAAF, with more than 2,600 aircraft, overwhelmed the Germans. Aircraft of MASAF and MATAF flew 12,974 sorties, dropped 5,777 tons of bombs, and destroyed over ninety enemy aircraft.

The attacks on the airfields employed subterfuge to fool the German defences. First, Boeing B–17 Fortresses and Consolidated B–24 Liberators were escorted by Lockheed P–38s, flown at normal altitudes to be picked up by radar. They were followed by Republic P–47 Thunderbolts, which flew below enemy radar and overtook the bombers before climbing to a higher altitude as they approached the target area. The result was that the Mustangs arrived over the enemy fighter stations fifteen minutes early and caught the *Luftwaffe* fighters scrambling to intercept the bombers. Taking them by surprise, the Thunderbolts destroyed the fighters, leaving the bombers to continue towards their target and drop their bombs without interference from the fighters.

The deception worked brilliantly, so that when the landings at Anzio followed on 22 January, there was minimal resistance. The invasion was supported by more than 360 Allied ships. While Allied airmen flew more than 1,200 sorties, the *Luftwaffe* managed just 140. Twelfth Air Force covered the assault force and the US 5th Army, while the Desert Air Force supported the British 8th Army.

To enhance co-operation between the ground and air commanders, 5th Army and Twelfth Air Force personnel met nightly to review the day's operations and plan for the next. Targets were identified and priorities were agreed, improving co-ordination between the air and ground forces and identifying potential problems. An innovation in a highly mobile war was a system known as 'call targets', which only required a telephone call from 5th Army to Twelfth Air Force when emergency air support was needed, with a squadron designated to stand by to attack.

Lessons had been learned from Avalanche, including the differences in spotting procedures between the USAAF and the USN. USAAF North American P–51 Mustangs were used to spot for the ground forces while RAF Spitfires spotted for the Navy. Another innovation over the front line was to have fighter-bomber squadrons assigned as 'rover' units, which used a system known as the 'cab rank', with aircraft in the cab rank arriving over the front every half-hour, waiting up to twenty minutes to be called upon to attack a target, and then, if not needed, moving on to attack a previously assigned alternative target. As these squadrons often had difficulty locating targets threatening the infantry, a forward control light aircraft, usually an L-5, was flown at 6,000 feet over the front line or up to 5 miles behind it with an army observer aboard so that it could direct aircraft to designated targets.

THE GERMAN COUNTER-ATTACK
On 4 February, Field Marshal Albert Kesselring launched a vigorous counter-attack that lasted until early March. The most intensive fighting took place between 16 and 22 February. At one point the Germans penetrated the Allied lines and advanced to within a few miles of the landing site. On 15 February, Twelfth Air Force, augmented by the Fifteenth, committed 813 bombers and fighter-bombers, which dropped over 970 tons of bombs. Again, on 29 February, the Germans attacked and the MAAF flew 796 sorties and dropped over 600 tons of bombs to help Allied ground forces stop the offensive. Despite this effort, it took almost three months before the Allies could finally breach the Gustav Line and advance on Rome.

SUPPORTING THE ARMY
Bill Bundock was posted to a Desert Air Force squadron operating in Italy. At this stage in the war, it entailed spending six weeks in a transit camp just outside Naples before his posting to No. 87 Squadron came through. This was after two years of training in what was then Rhodesia. The training, as part of the Empire Air Training Scheme, did not consist solely of flying and bombing practice using North American Harvards as it included the role of bombing supervisor, which entailed spending two weeks at a time in a vehicle located in a forward position giving instructions on targets to the other pilots flying their aircraft. This meant that they soon understood the problems of forward control and once in Italy it proved invaluable as the Army had people performing a similar role in small cars or jeeps known as 'rovers', who could direct aircraft onto a target at very short notice, often no more than a few minutes, and when possible used a smoke marker to identify the target.

Not having known the operational role of the squadron, he joined No. 87 at Foggia airfield only to find that it was a fully mobile unit, with accommodation for the personnel in six large tents with another three marquees as messes. The squadron operated Spitfire Vs and the next day it was flown north to a base just outside the small hill town of Perugia. He was impressed at the speed at which the tents came down after breakfast, but soon realised that this was done so efficiently because it had been done so often. With his comrades, he had to wait for the lorries carrying the tents to catch up with the aircraft once they had landed at Perugia, but after an hour everything arrived and the first priority was to erect the mess tents so that the cooks could prepare lunch.

In some cases, abandoned *Luftwaffe* or *Regia Aeronautica* airfields were used, but often the Royal Engineers constructed landing strips using perforated steel planking, known as PSP, which consisted of interlocking steel strips. This provided good all-weather runways, although it had the disconcerting habit of producing a rattle when the aircraft first touched down, so that pilots not used to this type of runway found themselves worrying that part of their aircraft had fallen off.

Apparently the official rations were not that good and were either dehydrated or tinned. The pilots spent some time visiting local farms and managed to buy poultry and vegetables as well as some demijohns of local wine. Currency came from their monthly ration of four cans of beer, a bottle of scotch, fifty cigarettes and a bar of chocolate. On one occasion, they used a bottle of scotch to 'buy' a jeep from the US Army. The jeep had a puncture, and, rather than repair it, the Americans simply abandoned it and got another one. The squadron motor transport sergeant quickly repaired the puncture!

While accommodation was erected and taken down quickly, washing facilities were primitive, with men using their steel helmets as basins for washing and shaving. A mobile bath or shower unit appeared just once a month, by which time it was very welcome, especially during the hot Italian summers.

The priority the next morning was a sector reconnaissance so that the pilots would become familiar with the countryside surrounding the airfield. On this occasion they stayed away from the front line. Their first sortie was to escort bombers, but as the Spitfire had a short range, they flew to a forward landing strip to refuel before joining the bombers. Soon afterwards, they switched to the fighter-bomber role, finding that the Spitfire V was not a stable platform when carrying a 500lb bomb, but after a week received the Spitfire IX, which was far superior in this role. With some experience, the squadron's pilots soon found that they could bomb with considerable accuracy.

They spent a month at Perugia before moving to keep close to the front line.

One of his best sorties was when they were asked to attack a control tower at an airfield still in German hands.

It was while flying from this airfield that I had one of the most satisfying sorties. We were airborne and waiting for a call from our Rover control, when he came on the air and asked us to go to a small airfield right on the front line. Our controller described the situation to us. Our troops were around the perimeter of the airfield but were pinned down by gunfire being directed from the control tower. He

114

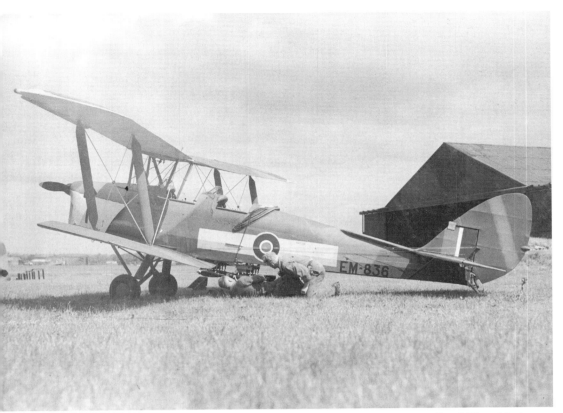

1. The beginning for many RAF and other British Empire pilots was the de Havilland Tiger Moth, one of the great training biplanes. (*BAE Systems*)

2. The age of the monoplane had arrived, yet RAF Fighter Command still fielded the Gloster Gladiator biplane, its first aircraft to have a covered cockpit, but outclassed in 1939. (*BAE Systems*)

3. The Westland Whirlwind equipped just two fighter squadrons as single-engined fighters tended to be much more manoeuvrable. As a single-seat aircraft, it would not have been suitable for development as a night fighter. (*IWM*)

4. Winston Churchill believed that all fighters should have a rear gunner, as with many in the First World War, but the Boulton-Paul Defiant lost speed and manoeuvrability as a result, while German fighter pilots soon realised that there was a rear gunner and attacked from below. (*Dowty*)

5. Usually, there was little in the way of flying gear other than a leather helmet, goggles, flying boots and a Mae West, so uniforms could and did get very badly worn in the confines of a fighter cockpit. (*IWM*)

6. Not much room, or comfort, for the pilot – a Spitfire cockpit. (*IWM*)

7. The burden of the Battle of Britain was taken by the Hawker Hurricane. Although slower than the Spitfire, it was easier to repair and had a tighter turning circle. (*IWM*)

8. Ground crew sit on the tail of a Spitfire while its guns are tested. During the Battle of Britain, the Spitfire, while a match for the *Luftwaffe*, nevertheless suffered from poor guns, with either eight machine guns, which lacked the punch of a cannon shell, or twin cannon, which proved to be unreliable. (*IWM*)

9. Another shot of a Hawker Hurricane. The Hurricane pilots tried to concentrate on the bombers during the early years of the war, but later, fitted with cannon, proved effective tank-busters in North Africa. (*USAF Archive*)

10. The main opposition, not just during the Battle of Britain, was the Messerschmitt Bf109, which appeared in many guises, each usually more formidable than the one it replaced. Although not available on early versions, the fitting of a cannon firing through the propeller hub made the aircraft even more effective. (*USAF Archive*)

11. When the Germans struck east in Operation Barbarossa, invading the Soviet Union, one of the more modern Russian aircraft encountered was the Yakovlev Yak-1, but for the most part the *Luftwaffe* encountered obsolete types. (*Yakovlev*)

12. In Malta, aerial bombardment was so heavy, especially over airfields, that stone 'sangers' were built to protect aircraft on three sides whilst on the ground. Army and Navy personnel often helped in the work of construction as there were few RAF ground personnel on the island. (*IWM*)

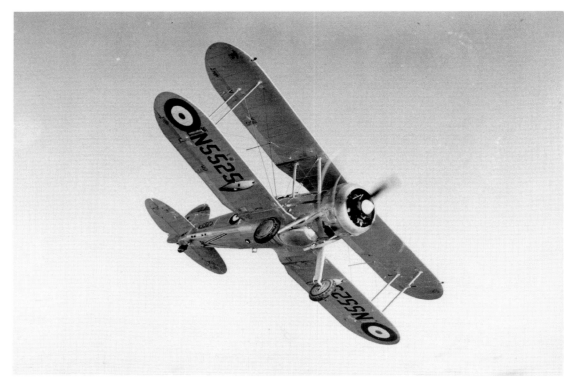

13. When Italy entered the war, the only fighter defence available for Malta was the Gloster Sea Gladiator, three of which became the famous trio of *Faith*, *Hope* and *Charity*. (*BAE Systems*)

14. A typical wartime shot, with a mobile AA gun to protect this Spitfire as it is serviced between sorties. (*IWM*)

15. Fighter pilots of No. 213 Hurricane Squadron being debriefed after a sortie at a base in the Western Desert. (*IWM*)

16. Supermarine Spitfire wearing desert markings. Aircraft camouflage had to be changed as the theatre of operations changed. (*BAE Systems*)

17. A more effective fighter than the Bf109 was the Focke-Wulf Fw190, seen here lined up. It was not available in time for the Battle of Britain or for the invasion of the USSR. (*IWM*)

18. Not all fighters had a base to return to or even an aircraft carrier, such as this Sea Hurricane, which belonged to the RAF's Merchant Service Fighter Unit, whose aircraft were catapulted off CAM-ships (catapult-armed merchant ships). They made a single sortie and the pilot then had to bale out and hope to be picked up. (*IWM*)

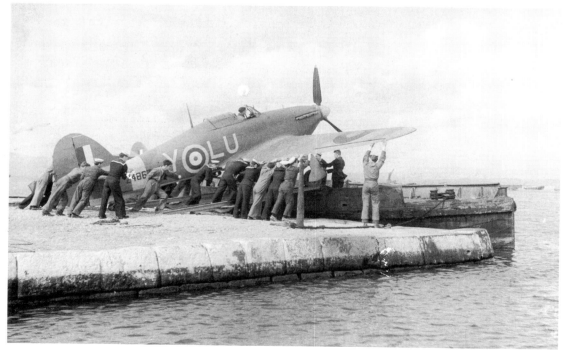

19. The solution to the heavy night bombing was the night fighter, once airborne radar could be provided – first on the Bristol Beaufighter and then later on the de Havilland Mosquito, one of which is seen here. (*BAE Systems*)

20. The Messerschmitt Me110 was originally used at the outset of the Battle of Britain as a long-range escort fighter, but it was no match for the Spitfire and was soon switched to other duties. Later, it did become an effective night fighter. (*USAF Archive*)

21. The USAAF's arrival in Britain soon brought long-range escort fighters to the skies over occupied Europe. One of these was the North American P-51 (later F-51) Mustang, seen here with 'invasion stripes'. These are early versions without the later bubble canopy and licence-built Merlin engine. (*USAF Archive*)

22. The Mustang as most people recall it, as a much more handsome aircraft with a bubble canopy. (*USAF Archive*)

23. The twin-boom fuselage of the Lockheed P-38 (later F-38) was distinctive. This was one of the most successful long-range escorts. (*USAF Archive*)

24. Despite its rotund appearance, the Republic P-47 (later F-47) Thunderbolt was an effective fighter, albeit one that seems to have been prone to burst into flames, if Heinz Knoke's accounts are typical of aerial combat with this aircraft. (*USAF Archive*)

25. The cockpit of a Thunderbolt – roomier than that of a Spitfire. (*USAF Archive*)

26. A Mosquito night fighter lands after a sortie. The steel strip used for runways and taxiways can be clearly seen. (*USAF Archive*)

27. Experience in North Africa had shown that cannon and rocket-armed fighters were highly effective against ground targets, even including armour. This was one role for the Hawker Typhoon, one of which is seen here at Gatwick. Another role was disposing of the V-1 missiles, or 'Doodlebugs'. (*BAE Systems*)

28. Despite almost five years of war before the Allied landings in Normandy, aircraft recognition remained poor, hence the use of black and wh   'sion' stripes on aircraft, while this was another attempt to draw attention to the disti   ng features of the Typhoon.

29. The Messerschmitt Me262 should have been the world's first jet fighter, but Hitler insisted that it be used as a bomber until Adolph Galland insisted to Goering that the policy be changed. (*Author's collection*)

30. An Me262 on the ground. Once used as a fighter, the aircraft had a devastating effect on USAAF day bomber formations, and might have prolonged the conflict for a short period had it been deployed earlier to fighter squadrons. (*USAF Archive*)

asked us to attack the tower in order to eliminate this observation post. We carried out our normal bombing run starting at 10,000 feet and going into a dive of about 80 degrees. This allowed us to keep a sight of our target right up to the moment when we started to pull out of the dive at about 3,000 feet. We didn't have a bomb sight but dropped our bombs by judgement; as we started to pull out, the target disappeared under our noses, we then released our bomb, which was a 500-pounder. By this time having been in a steep dive for some 7,000 feet we were travelling very fast and the aircraft had to be very carefully handled or you could bend the wings by exerting too much 'G' force. It always surprised me that we could achieve any accuracy bombing in this way but our results were consistently good and in this particular sortie our own troops were only about 250 yards from our target, so obviously our Rover control had faith in our accuracy.

Having finished our bombing run we regained height whilst our Rover control was getting very excited saying that we had successfully destroyed the observation post and that the Germans were abandoning the place. He asked us if we could come in again for a strafing run as the Germans were all easily seen and without cover. We then made a low level attack, being guided by the controller and as we came in we could see the Germans running through an olive grove. We went in turn, firing our 2mm cannon and 0.50 machine guns, each of us making several attacks until all our ammunition was expended.[1]

OPERATION DRAGOON

By August 1944, the entire strategic situation in Europe had been transformed. Not only had German resistance been broken and Rome liberated, but Allied forces had landed in Normandy in June. This had been another major operation without carrier air cover, but on this occasion the reasons had been simple: it wasn't necessary. The Normandy beachheads were within range of airfields in the south of England and the sheer size of the invasion force and the constant stream of vessels across the English Channel meant that there would have been no room for carriers to operate their aircraft. A number of Fleet Air Arm aircraft had flown from shore bases in the south of England in support of the landings and the bridgehead, while naval aircraft also flew reconnaissance sorties and operated in the spotter role for the heavy guns of the battleships and cruisers covering the landings. The Italian campaign was maintained throughout this period because it forced the Germans to divert ground and air forces from the Normandy campaign.

Landings in the south of France were an easier option than landing in Normandy, although logistically it would have been difficult to have put the same quantities of men and *matériel* into such an operation as had been achieved in the Normandy landings, which had even included the construction of two ports to keep the invaders supplied. Serious consideration had been given to an invasion of the south of France as early as August 1943, but the British had objected, declaring that it would divert resources from the advance through Italy, which they believed would lead to an invasion of Germany through Austria – a highly optimistic assumption given the intervening terrain! The south of France had then slipped down the Allied order of priorities as attention focussed on the invasion of Normandy, through which France and the Low Countries could be liberated and meanwhile further landings in Italy at Anzio had proved necessary. The original name for the invasion was Operation Anvil, but this was later changed to Dragoon.

The south of France was seen as being easier than Normandy as the Germans had not taken Vichy territory until late 1942, and, not only did they not have the time to build anything on the scale of the famous 'Atlantic Wall' fortifications along the English Channel coastline, but the resources were also becoming increasingly scarce. By this stage in the war, as well, interference from enemy naval forces could also be discounted. As a consequence, the fast armoured carriers of the Royal Navy were sent to the Pacific to join the United States Navy in taking the war ever closer to Japan, and instead the entire air defence and ground attack needs of the landing force was entrusted to the two navies using nine escort carriers, with the five British ships carrying Supermarine Seafire L2Cs again, and the four American ships carrying the new Grumman Hellcat, a true carrier fighter aircraft. Heavy fire support was provided by three US battleships plus one each from France and the UK, while the USN also provided three heavy cruisers.

The overall invasion fleet was under the command again of Vice-Admiral Henry Hewitt who was to land Lieutenant-General A.M. Patch's US Seventh Army and General de Lattre de Tassingny's II Free French Corps along the French Rivieras between Baie de Cavalaire to Calanque d'Anthéor. Rear Admiral Tom Troubridge commanded the British carriers and Rear Admiral Durgin the US ships.

Landing on 15 August, more than 56,000 troops were landed on the first day, and, by 28 August, the key naval base of Toulon had been surrendered as well as the major port of Marseilles. The most notable feature of these landings was the limited effort from the *Luftwaffe*, leaving the naval airmen to provide support for the ground forces. One pilot recalled having a good relationship with the US Army commanders who made good use of naval aerial reconnaissance.

The lessons of the Salerno landings had been learnt, with more aircraft carriers and adequate room to manoeuvre, while the carriers were able to retire to Corsica for replenishment and new aircraft, so there were none of the fuel shortages that had so nearly placed the Salerno operation in jeopardy. It was also fortunate that the weather conditions were ideal for carrier operations with a breeze and gentle swell offshore.

For many of the American carrier pilots, it was their first experience of operational flying, and much attention was paid to minimising their casualties during the vital first sorties. One British naval fighter pilot who witnessed the early misadventures of the Americans was Lieutenant-Commander George Baldwin.

> We were very worried about the Americans. They were . . . unblooded. They had come straight from the United States and never seen any kind of action before. So they had been given a very considerable briefing by some of our air staff on the sort of things they needed to know about the German opposition . . . type of anti-aircraft fire and what not to do . . . The poor chaps, they flew a flight of four aircraft over Marseilles the first morning in formation in a straight line and the first salvo from the 88mm guns knocked two of the four aircraft out of the sky. Sad loss . . .[2]

The Americans had been warned that aircraft should never fly in formation or in a straight line, but instead be well spaced to allow weaving and only to fly between 9,000 and 11,000 feet when climbing or ascending since the German 88mm AA guns were very accurate between these heights. Sound advice, but it had either not been passed down to the squadrons or had been ignored.

Despite being under pressure in the east and in Italy, as well as in the north of France, the *Luftwaffe* was still able to deploy fighters over the south of France, although the force was being withdrawn. One of the German fighter pilots was Horst Rippert, who was later acknowledged to be the man who shot down Antoine de Saint-Exupery, the celebrated French author and pioneering pilot on 31 July 1944. Saint-Exupery was flying a Lockheed P-38 Lightning from Borgo in Corsica when he was discovered over Toulouse, flying too low. As it happened, the German, flying a Bf109, was an ardent admirer of the Frenchman, and when he later discovered that he had shot down his hero, he was distressed.

> If I had known, I wouldn't have fired. I did not target a man I knew. I fired at an enemy aircraft which was shot down . . . His works inspired many among us to become aviators.
>
> Like me, he was over the sea and flying towards the mainland. The pilot was flying carelessly, as if enjoying himself, at a vulnerable 6,000 feet. I said to myself: 'My boy, if you don't get lost, I'm going to shoot you.' I dived in his direction and I fired, not at the fuselage, but at the wings. I hit him. The plane crashed into the sea. No one jumped.
>
> I did not see the pilot and even so, it would have been impossible for me to tell that it was Saint-Exubery. In our youth at school we had all

read him, we loved his books. I loved his personality. If I had known, I wouldn't have fired. Not at him.[3]

A noble sentiment, but in aerial warfare, it is almost invariably a case of kill or be killed.

The landings in the south of France were successful, putting additional pressure on German forces and providing yet another front on which German troops had to fight. They were followed soon afterwards in September and October by British naval forces, using nothing heavier than cruisers and escort carriers, cutting the German evacuation routes across the Aegean from Greece and destroying the remaining German naval units in the Aegean.

THE BALKANS

General, later Field Marshal, Bernard Montgomery famously warned '... never get involved in the Balkans.' The Germans and the Italians had learnt the truth of this the hard way, but as the end of the war in Europe came in sight, the Allied experience of the Balkans was better than most.

Yugoslav partisans had been active throughout the war, and even before the Allies had gained a foothold on the Italian mainland, RAF squadrons, including Nos 37, 70 and 178, started to drop supplies to partisan groups. In June 1944, the Balkan Air Force (BAF) was formed at the Italian port of Bari under Air Vice-Marshal Elliott. This was a relatively small organisation, with just eight squadrons and one flight of aircraft. In addition to dropping supplies, whenever possible the squadrons that comprised the BAF had also been providing air support for the partisans from late 1943. Other units mounted anti-shipping strikes over the Adriatic, and mined ports and the River Danube, often with the participation of the Desert Air Force, as mentioned above.

The BAF's area of operations extended well beyond anything implied in its designation, and included missions as far north as Poland, often operating on behalf of the British Special Operations Executive and the American Office of Strategic Services. Balkan Air Force personnel came from no less than eight nations, and as many as fifteen different types of aircraft were used at various times between its creation in June 1944 and May 1945. During this period, it flew 38,340 sorties, dropped 6,650 tons of bombs and 16,440 tons of supplies. Some 2,500 people were flown into Yugoslavia, and 19,000, mainly wounded, were flown out.

In late August 1944, German forces began to withdraw from the islands in the Aegean and the Ionean seas, and, on 1 September, the BAF and naval forces started a concentrated effort to stop this traffic, while the BAF and partisans mounted 'Rat Week' to stop all German traffic through Yugoslavia and between garrisons within the country. This was invaluable in preventing German attempts to consolidate their forces against the advancing Allies in Italy and the advancing Soviet forces coming from the east.

Nevertheless, despite operating from Yugoslavia during the final days of the war, it soon became clear that the main partisan groups, those led by General Tito, did not intend co-operation to continue after German defeat. A similar situation in Greece was only avoided by the despatch of British troops who could be ill spared from the Italian campaign in late 1944.

Notes
1. BBC *People's War Archive.*
2. Imperial War Museum Sound Archive.
3. *The Scotsman,* 17 March 2008.

Chapter 9

The Eastern Front

After being badly delayed by the need to complete the invasion of Yugoslavia and Greece, started by the Italians, Operation Barbarossa, the German invasion of the Soviet Union, began on Sunday, 22 June 1941, starting at 03.15, attacking along a line drawn from the Baltic in the north to the Carpathian Mountains in the south. The attack was not unexpected, and Stalin had ordered that all units were to be decentralised and camouflaged, but this message was received too late for the various headquarters to pass the message on to all units in time. The USSR had some 18,000 aircraft, although only a fifth of these could be regarded as modern, and many of the pilots were still undergoing training. Half of the aircraft were deployed in the west. Against this figure of around 9,000 Soviet aircraft, the *Luftwaffe* had 1,945 aircraft, with 1,400 immediately ready for combat, including 510 bombers, 290 dive-bombers, 440 fighters, forty fighter-destroyers (fighter-bombers) and 120 long range reconnaissance aircraft. This force was in three air fleets: *Luftflotte* 1 under General Keller was assigned to Army Group North; *Luftflotte* 2 under Field Marshal Kesselring was assigned to Army Group Central; and *Luftflotte* 4 under General Lohr was assigned to Army Group South. The total *Luftwaffe* strength was augmented by that of Germany's allies, giving another 1,000 aircraft. Rumania sent 423 aircraft, while Finland, still recovering from its Winter War with the Soviet Union, sent 317, although only 41 of these were bombers. The Italian *Regia Aeronautica* sent 100 aircraft to operate in the southern zone, operating as the *Comando Aviazione*, the air command of the Italian Expeditionary Force, but these didn't arrive until late July! *Luftflotte* 4 also had the Hungarian Express Corps with a fighter and a bomber squadron, as well as some reconnaissance units, and the Croatian Air Legion, with a fighter group and a bomber group, another fifty or sixty aircraft.

Many Germans were surprised by the attack as a treaty had been agreed with the Soviet Union in August 1939 and the USSR had been Germany's partner in the invasion of Poland, which had been effectively partitioned between the two states. One of those surprised when he received his orders was a *Luftwaffe* general.

'Impossible!' retorted General Alfred Keller, when told to strike at Leningrad. 'We've got a treaty with the Russians!'

'Don't worry your head about politics,' replied Hitler's Air Minister, Hermann Goering. 'Leave that to the Führer.'[1]

Goering was in fact one of Hitler's close circle who had tried to persuade Hitler not to start Operation Barbarossa, mainly because he realised that Germany could not fight a war on two fronts. The *Luftwaffe*'s Quarter-master General, von Seidel, warned that the service could not cope.

INVASION

In the air and on the ground, the initial assault went well, even better than expected. The *Luftwaffe* caught most of the Soviet airfields by surprise, in a carefully co-ordinated attack by no more than thirty bombers with specially trained crews with just three bombers assigned to attack each Russian fighter airfield, dropping small fragmentation bombs to cause the maximum damage and confusion. Later, a second wave was launched as the main attack, with 637 bombers and 231 fighters attacking 31 Soviet air-fields. Before noon this was followed by 400 bombers striking at a further 35 Soviet airfields. Altogether, these 66 airfields accounted for seventy per cent of the Red Air Force's strength in the west. One Red Air Force officer, Lieutenant General Kopets, lost 600 aircraft without making any impact on the Germans, and committed suicide the following day. Almost half the Red Air Force aircraft were believed to have been non-operational on the first day of the invasion.

After weeks of ignoring warnings from the Allies, Stalin had tried to alert his forces to the likelihood of a German attack at 01.30 that Sunday morning, but it was too late and most of the units did not get the message in time. The commanding officer of the 23rd Air Division, Colonel Vanyushkin, later explained what had happened.

> It was early on Sunday morning, and many of the men were out on a leave pass. Our airfields lay far too close to the frontier, and their positions were perfectly well known to the Germans. Furthermore, many airfields were just re-equipping with new types of aircraft, even on operational airfields. With proverbial Russian negligence both old and new types stood all about in uncamouflaged rows ...[2]

Vanyushkin was later taken prisoner by the Germans.

The *Luftwaffe* commanders couldn't believe their good fortune. Hans von Hahn, in command of I/JG3, part of V Air Corps, operating around Lvov, recalled:

> We hardly believed our eyes. Row after row of reconnaissance planes, bombers and fighters stood lined up as if on parade. We were amazed at the number of airfields and aircraft the Russians had ranged against us.[3]

The initial attacks were designed to gain air superiority, and once again the *Luftwaffe* would then switch to providing close support for ground forces so that an air-ground *blitzkrieg* could roll across Russia. To cripple the Soviet air forces on the ground, small SD2 fragmentation bombs were used, each weighing just 4lbs; they were known as 'Devil's eggs'. They could explode either on the ground or just above it, sending 50 small and 250 very small shrapnel particles over a radius of as much as 40 feet. Originally developed as an anti-personnel weapon, a direct hit was needed to knock out an aircraft.

The SD2s were dropped by bombers and from Bf109s with all the aircraft in *JG* 27 fitted with bomb cages beneath the fuselage able to carry ninety-six bombs. The trouble was that air pressure often led the first row to remain hung up, unknown to the pilot, and could drop as the aircraft was landing, either exploding behind the aircraft or lying unexploded on the runway, a threat to any aircraft following and to the ground personnel who had to clear them. After their success in the opening stages of Barbarossa, the SD2 was quietly abandoned, not just because of its poor reliability, but also because effective Russian AA fire forced aircraft to fly higher.

The Russian tactics as the German advance got under way showed considerable desperation. When 2nd Lieutenant S.Y. Sdorovzev found that, despite scoring hits on a He111 bomber, the aircraft continued to fly, he approached the bomber from the rear, and inserted his propeller into the He111's elevator. He tried again, and this time managed to get the He111 to crash, before flying back to his base, a distance of almost 50 miles, with a damaged propeller.

Sdorovzev was lucky. A fellow officer, 2nd Lieutenant D.V. Kokorev of the 124th Fighter Regiment, was in conflict with an Me110 when the guns of his I-16 Rata fighter failed. He pulled his aircraft round and rammed his opponent, sending both aircraft crashing to the ground.

The Russian fighters, which included I-15 biplanes as well as monoplanes such as the Rata, were more manoeuvrable than the Bf109, although much slower. The tactic was to wait until the German fighter was ready to open fire and then turn, so that the opposing aircraft were facing each other head on. This often led to the Germans wasting their ammunition. On a fighter sweep over Grodno, Major Wolfgang Schellman, leading *JG* 27, did manage to shoot down a Rata, which exploded and his own aircraft with its superior speed flew into the burning particles, forcing him to bale out.

Nevertheless, despite a Russian bomber attack on the German airfields later on that first day, this was the most decisive victory ever experienced by one air force against another. Major Graf Schonborn's *Stukageschwader* 77 had landed after striking at targets along the River Bug, when six twin-engined bombers were spotted. They arrived as three Bf109s sped to defend the airfield. Herbert Pabst remembers what happened next.

As the first one fired, thin threads of smoke seemed to join it to the bomber. Turning ponderously to the side, the big bird flashed silver, then plunged vertically downwards with its engines screaming. As it crashed a huge sheet of flame shot upwards. The second bomber became a glare of red, exploded as it dived, and only the bits came floating down like great autumnal leaves. The third turned over backwards on fire. A similar fate befell the rest, the last falling in a village and burning for an hour. Six columns of smoke rose from the horizon. All six had been shot down![4]

The Russians lost 1,811 aircraft while the *Luftwaffe* lost only 35. Of the Soviet losses, 322 were due to fighters or AA defences, while no less than 1,489 were destroyed on the ground. Goering couldn't believe the figures and insisted that they be checked. By the time the Russian airfields were overrun, he sent staff officers to count the wrecks, and they counted more than 2,000 aircraft destroyed.

In the first few months of the air campaign in support of Barbarossa, the *Luftwaffe* came across large marching columns of Russian troops and substantial troop concentrations, with the ground on either side of the roads, baked hard in the summer heat, also being used as a roadway, so that often the roads were as much as 100 yards wide. Yet, because of a shortage of bombs of the right types, the *Luftwaffe* was unable to press home all of the advantages that aerial supremacy had granted it. There is little doubt that the inability to disrupt these troop concentrations was a contributory factor at Moscow and Stalingrad.

As the German advance drew closer to the great cities, intense anti-aircraft fire was encountered, and at Leningrad German pilots reported that it was far more intense than anything experienced over London during 1940-41.

It has often been said that Russia's greatest defender was 'General Winter', and the *Luftwaffe* was soon to discover this. Indeed, the German reputation for being meticulous in preparation does not seem to have been in evidence during Barbarossa. This was partly due to the Russian winter weather not being fully understood, but the failure to achieve the German's objectives before the worst of the winter caught the armies exposed on the steppes was another factor.

There were other factors. In the battle of Kiev, the *Luftwaffe* was expected to stop Russian supplies and reinforcements reaching the battlefield, yet lacked the munitions necessary to destroy railway junctions and bridges. The *Luftwaffe* simply did not have the heavy bombs, and especially the blockbuster types used by the RAF, and it did not have aircraft suitable for their delivery. The *Luftwaffe* was at its best when fighters, fighter-bombers, light bombers and dive-bombers were required. It was not until some time into the war that it received heavy bombers, but only in small numbers and too late to make a difference.

A good idea of the extent to which the *Luftwaffe* was facing serious operational difficulties during the Russian winter comes in extracts from a report written by Lieutenant General H.J. Rieckoff. This refers to the *Luftwaffe*'s experience during the winter of 1941–42, when the temperatures in the theatre stayed between minus 30 and minus 50 degrees centigrade for periods of several weeks, relieved only by those occasions when temperatures plunged to minus 70 degrees! The General commented that, for the most part, the problems were at their most serious when aircraft were on the ground, being prepared for operations. He noted:

> ... extensive icing of wings and tail assemblies ... cannot be removed manually ... Canvas covers are used to protect smaller aircraft ... a completely inadequate measure because the covers themselves freeze stiff and are then almost impossible to handle, especially when ... there is a violent wind. Closed ... hangars are rarely available. The attempt to prevent ice forming ... with water repellent oils has failed due to the shortage of lubricant supplies ... Snow-skid landing gear has proved ineffective except for the Fieseler Storch ... which can be kept ready under any snow conditions by this method.

The report also noted that the cold affected engines when they were started up, requiring precise observation of the instructions for a successful cold start, which was done by feeding a lubricant diluted with gasoline to the engine while starting. It took some twenty minutes of flying time for the gasoline additive to evaporate and for the engine to run at normal oil temperature. Often, the problems were encountered with equipment used to start the engines as oil froze in the pipes of the equipment rather than with the engines themselves. To improve matters, sometimes fires were started under aircraft and start-up equipment. Great care was needed as the starters' shafts sometimes broke if engaged abruptly. Propellers sometimes iced up during flight, and on occasion damage occurred to aircraft, and injuries amongst their crews, from flying chunks of dislodged ice.

The report was comprehensive. The instruments of the aircraft seemed to cope very well with the cold, as did the communications equipment, although this did suffer badly from the effects of moisture. Aircraft guns, on the other hand, didn't like the cold, usually because the oil lacked resistance to the cold, while electrically-guided weapons suffered from the effects of condensation. Given a depth of snow of 3 feet or more, short-fused bombs, whether high-explosive or fragmentation, were much less effective as the snow muffled the effects of the explosion. It was also noted that up to seventy-five per cent of the detonators on fragmentation bombs failed to work in deep snow, although they remained active and acted as land mines! Frozen hard ground shattered high-explosive bombs without them exploding.

The Germans used one- or two-piece sheepskin flying suits, which proved to be cumbersome if the wearer had to walk any distance, such as after an emergency landing. Thermal suits, apparently, were worse, requiring attention in regulating temperatures, while they were so fragile that they could be damaged in an emergency landing, after which, of course, they provided the wearer with little protection against the cold. The suggestion was made that lightweight fur or camel-hair clothing, with waterproof linings, should be provided, but nothing of leather (a material that the Germans loved to wear normally). The Russian felt boots were regarded as more suitable, especially on a long walk, than the German fur boots, which did not fit tightly enough, and good anti-skid soles were also required.

Between the start of Operation Barbarossa and mid-May 1942, the *Luftwaffe* lost almost 3,000 aircraft and another 2,000 were badly damaged. Of the losses, 1,026 were bombers and another 762 were fighters. Meanwhile, the Russians had gathered 3,164 aircraft on the Soviet Western Front, of which more than 2,100 were of modern design. A new commanding officer, General A.A. Novikov, took command of Red Air Force units on the front. A further indication of the way the tide was turning came from the battles around Kharkov in mid-May, when the Germans had just 1,500 aircraft, and the Soviets twice as many!

On 28 June 1942, the Germans started their second summer offensive on the Eastern Front, supported by the *Luftwaffe*'s VIII Air Corps under General Fiebig. General von Weichs moved his troops out from Kursk against Soviet troops at Bryansk under General Golikov.

It was not just aircraft that the United States and United Kingdom sent to the Soviet Union. A Free French fighter group, *GC-3 Normandie* (*Groupe de Chasse*-3, Normandy), was despatched to Russia, and instead of flying the Hurricanes and Spitfires supplied from the UK, were given Yakovlev Yak-3 fighters. One of the pilots was the Marquis de Saint Phalle, who shot down a Focke-Wulf Fw190 fighter, while overall the squadron accounted for 273 German aircraft between March 1943 and May 1945. As the Germans regarded France as being defeated and occupied, Field Marshal Wilhelm Keitel decreed that 'any French pilot captured should be immediately executed.'

The Normandie pilots were volunteers. One of the pilots was Marcel Albert, who had flown with the Vichy air force after the fall of France before making his way to the UK and joining the RAF, flying Spitfires, initially from Scotland but then on fighter sweeps over France. After flying with No. 340 *Ile de France* Squadron, he volunteered to join the *Normandie* Group in late 1942, and early 1943 they were sent to the Soviet Union. After training on the Yak-1, the first Soviet fighter capable of confronting a Bf109, he too moved on to the Yak-3. His first victory was a Focke-Wulf Fw190 on 16 June 1943. In September, he was promoted and became commander of the 1st *Escadrille* (squadron). He scored a further seven kills in the fighting over Niemen in Lithuania in October, for which he received the Gold Star and was proclaimed a Hero of the Soviet Union, a great honour for a non-Russian. He later also was awarded the Order of Lenin, before returning to France.

Such was the reputation of the squadron that Stalin suggested it be renamed *GC-3 Normandie-Niemen*, recognising the role it played in the battles to cross the Niemen River in what is now Belarus.

While service on the Eastern Front has sometimes been portrayed as a 'punishment' posting for German personnel, in fact, many of the Reich's most able personnel found themselves embroiled in a war that they knew they could not win. One of these was the leading fighter ace of any combatant air force during the Second World War, with no less than 352 kills, Colonel Erich Hartmann of the *Luftwaffe*. He not only faced the pilots flying with the Red Air Force, but also, when based in Romania during the German fighting withdrawal back to the Reich, found himself on more than one occasion facing USAAF P-51 Mustangs. Fair-haired and blue-eyed, he was known as the 'Blond Knight'. He recalls his technique.

My only tactics were to wait until I had the chance to attack the enemy and then close in at high speed. I opened fire only when the whole windshield was black with the enemy. Then not a single shot went wide. I hit the enemy with all my guns and he went down.[5]

Nevertheless, he was also lucky and cunning. On the one occasion when his Bf109 was shot down over the front, he was arrested by Soviet soldiers. He was lucky not to have been shot on the spot. Instead, he feigned injury and was put in the back of a lorry in a stretcher. Once the lorry left the soldiers behind, he sprang up and threw his guard against the back of the cab before jumping out and dodging shots before disappearing into a field of tall sunflowers. Sleeping by day and walking by night, he eventually found the German lines and was soon reunited with his unit, *JG 52*.

He became a favourite of Adolph Hitler, and for his victories was awarded the Knight's Cross, to which were added in quick succession the Oak Leaves, Swords and finally Diamonds. The award of the Diamonds to the Knight's Cross came after the failed assassination attempt on the Führer in July 1944. Hartmann was told to disarm himself before meeting Hitler. 'No pistol,' he retorted, 'no Diamonds – unless I am trusted.' Having made his point, he surrendered his pistol before entering the Führer's presence. On another occasion, he arrived to meet Hitler while much the worse for drink, and the Führer's aides had to stop him from juggling with Hitler's uniform cap.

For the most part, by June, 1943, the *Luftwaffe* units on the Eastern Front were confined to tactical operations in support of the increasingly beleaguered ground forces. The intensity of the Allied bombing campaign had forced the *Luftwaffe* to deploy its best fighter aircraft to protect German cities, so on the Eastern Front the mainstay of the German defences was the Bf109, while the Russians were receiving new equipment, much of it from the United States and the United Kingdom, who sent the Russians 18,000 aircraft during the period from June, 1941, onwards.

It was to no avail. On 12 July 1943, Soviet forces mounted a massive counteroffensive. From this time onwards, the Germans were on the defensive. Hitler had other priorities by this time, following the Allied invasion of Sicily two days earlier; he transferred important elements of the *Luftwaffe* from the Eastern Front to Italy, doubtless to the immense pleasure and relief of those involved.

Operation Barbarossa was delayed because of the German armed forces' heavy commitments in Yugoslavia and Greece, where they had to take over after the Italians failed to occupy these two countries. Some commentators also believe that the operation could not have started much earlier because of the time needed for the ground to harden, having been too soft for tanks and other heavy vehicles after the winter snow had thawed. Nevertheless, the late start meant that the Germans were overtaken by the harsh winter before they had met their objectives. That such a supposedly efficient nation should have allowed their armed forces to advance so far into Russia without adequate precautions for the winter months almost beggars belief. The many omissions in the planning and execution of Barbarossa are all the more difficult to understand because one of the compelling reasons for mounting the campaign was to secure vital strategic supplies that had been provided by the Russians.

Notes

1. Cajus Bekker, *The Luftwaffe War Diaries*, Doubleday, New York, 1968.
2. Imperial War Museum Sound Archive.
3. Cajus Bekker, *The Luftwaffe War Diaries*, Doubleday, New York, 1968.
4. Cajus Bekker, *The Luftwaffe War Diaries*, Doubleday, New York, 1968.
5. Cajus Bekker, *The Luftwaffe War Diaries*, Doubleday, New York, 1968.

Chapter 10

Action over Normandy

The Allied invasion of Normandy, Operation Overlord, is often seen through the eyes of the invading ground forces, including the glider-landed troops and paratroops as well as those in the amphibious assault, or of the bomber crews who provided support for ground forces by making it difficult for the Germans to move their forces into position to repel the invader. Nevertheless, before, during and after the landings, a vital role was played by fighter and fighter-bomber units who had already shown in North Africa and Italy that they could co-ordinate well with ground forces and respond quickly and effectively to calls for help from army commanders.

While Stalin kept demanding a 'second front' from the USA and UK, and the Americans wanted an invasion of France in 1943, the British leader, Winston Churchill, felt that the time was not right and that the Allies were not ready. He was almost certainly right. The Mediterranean campaigns were the way forward given the situation at the time and the equipment and experience available. Winning in North Africa safeguarded the Mediterranean and also eased the pressure on the Allied navies and on merchant shipping. The successive invasions of Italy, apart from the original at Sicily, which contributed to the improved situation in the 'Med', were of moderate importance and failed to achieve Allied expectations. Far more important was the invasion of the south of France.

In any event, while the Allies were engaged in the Battle of the Atlantic, fighting in North Africa and across the Mediterranean, as well as the various different theatres in the Far East, they did not have to look for a 'second front' as they had enough 'fronts' already.

Such an undertaking as the Normandy landings did indeed require substantial preparation over and above building up massive forces. For the RAF, planning began in 1943. Preparation meant two things. First, a structure had to be prepared for command and control of the units assigned to support the landings and the advance across Europe that would follow. Second, the process of softening up the German defences had to begin.

The first steps were taken in reorganisation on 1 June 1943. Bomber Command's No. 2 Group, the main light and medium bomber force, was put under the control of Fighter Command. Nevertheless, this was not to be the structure planned for the invasion, which required a new command of its own, but simply a reflection of the fact that the new command would require squadrons from a number of different commands in order to have the right balance of capabilities. The Allied Expeditionary Force was already in formation, and on 13 November 1943, the next step, the Allied Expeditionary Air Force (AEAF) was established under the command of ACM Sir Trafford Leigh-Mallory.

AEAF was another international command. It included the US 9th Air Force, an existing formation, and on 15 November its other two major sub-commands were formed. The first of these was the Second Allied Tactical Air Force (2nd TAF) and the second was the revival of the Air Defence of Great Britain (ADGB). This latter organisation was substantially weakened by the creation of 2nd TAF, which had no less than thirty-two of Fighter Command's squadrons transferred to it, leaving ADGB with ten day and eleven night fighter squadrons. In effect, Fighter Command no longer existed, with ADGB taking over its duties and commanded by AM Roderick Hill. The new organisation was not permanent, however, and on 15 October 1944, ADGB became RAF Fighter Command once more.

In the meantime, 2nd TAF became a substantial organisation in its own right.

DIEPPE
Well before preparations for the invasion had started, the previous year it was decided to test the defences of the French Channel port of Dieppe by mounting a raid, predominantly with Canadian forces after the country's government pressed for its troops to have a more active part in the war.

Initially codenamed as Operation Rutter, the raid was to be led by Major-General J.H. Roberts, commanding officer of 2nd Canadian Division, at the time part of the then Lieutenant-General Bernard Montgomery's South Eastern Command. As planning progressed, the raid developed into a full frontal assault, but without a heavy preliminary air and naval bombard-ment. Originally planned for 7 July 1942, bad weather caused its cancel-lation. Montgomery strongly recommended that this should be 'for all time' before leaving to take command of the British 8th Army. His view was not shared by the Chief of Combined Operations, Vice-Admiral Mountbatten, who resurrected the raid as Operation Jubilee. A new date was fixed, 19 August 1942. Montgomery's opinion was influenced by the fact that secrecy had been lost before the original raid was cancelled, as the Canadian troops aboard the ships had been briefed and their ships had been discovered and attacked while anchored in Yarmouth Roads, off the Isle of Wight.

Another problem, no doubt as Montgomery had suspected, was that the resources to support the raid were not available. The Air Ministry would not allow bombers to be diverted from the strategic air offensive against Germany, so out of seventy-four squadrons drawn from nine nations, sixty-six were fighter squadrons under the overall command of AVM Sir Trafford Leigh-Mallory. The fighters were there to provide support and also in the hope that the *Luftwaffe* could be brought to battle, which it was.

Johnnie Johnson was in one of the RAF squadrons whose unit was designated for the RAF's part of the operation. This was No. 610 Squadron flying the Spitfire Mk 6, a rare version with a pressurised cockpit, which no one liked as hot air was blown over the pilot, and, as fighter cockpits of the day were much like greenhouses, this made conditions even hotter and sweatier than usual. Instead of a sliding canopy, which most pilots preferred to have open during take-off and landing, the canopy was dropped over the cockpit before take-off and locked into position by four clamping levers. Overall, the cockpit felt like a cross between a Turkish bath and a glass coffin. He recalled on hearing of the Dieppe raid that the experience of RAF pilots was that it was heavily defended, in contrast to the view of British intelligence.

German air defences had also been boosted by a new arrival, the Focke-Wulf Fw190 fighter, which was far more manoeuvrable than the Bf109.

Although photographic reconnaissance had shown many of the German positions, too little was known about the location of command posts while the beach gradients were calculated from holiday postcards. The assault force was spotted at 03.48 by a small German convoy, and so surprise was lost. The main assault followed at 05.20 after preliminary landings, under cover of smokescreens laid by aircraft. The assault was soon halted and only one unit reached all of its objectives, with withdrawal beginning at 11.00 under heavy fire and completed by 14.00. British Army casualties were 275 and those of the Royal Navy were 550, while a destroyer was lost along with 33 landing craft, but the Canadians suffered most, losing 3,367 men out of a total force of 4,963, although the numbers killed were 807 men. German casualties in the raid were 591. In the air, the RAF lost 106 aircraft against the *Luftwaffe*'s 48 out of 945 deployed.

Despite what had amounted to a postponement because of bad weather, conditions were not good when the raid actually took place in August. Johnson recalled flying low across the choppy English Channel before climbing to their assigned altitude of 10,000 feet when they were 10 miles off Dieppe. He was with the group providing top cover. A heavy pall of black smoke hung over the port and they could hear another wing leader ordering his pilots to fight their way out, but to watch for the Fw190s at six o'clock high.

Ahead of us Spitfires, Messerschmitts and Focke-Wulfs milled about the sky. It was too early to search for an opening, since the 190s had the height on us, and my task was to keep the squadron together as long as possible and guard the two squadrons below. Crow [his CO] called a break and we swung round to find the 190s at our level in pairs and fours seemingly baffled by our move. A 190 pulled up in front of my own section and I gave him a long burst from the maximum range. Surprisingly it began to smoke, the wheels dropped and it fell away to the sea, and Crow said, 'Good shooting, Johnnie.'

The Messerschmitts and Focke-Wulfs came down on us from astern and the flanks. They were full of fight, and for the present we thought of nothing but evasion and staying alive. During a steep turn I caught a glimpse of a strong formation of enemy fighters heading towards Dieppe from inland and I called the wing leader: 'Jamie, strong enemy reinforcements coming in, about fifty-plus. Over.'[1]

The wing leader called for assistance from 11 Group. Meanwhile, Johnson's flight shot down another Messerschmitt, but three of the squadron's Spitfires were shot down. The air battle ranged from just above ground level to around 20,000 feet. Suddenly, Johnson found himself on his own, saw a solitary Fw190 and got into position to attack, but the enemy pilot noticed him. To Johnson's amazement, the aircraft had Italian markings, and they were soon whirling around in what he described as 'ever decreasing circles', before the Fw190 ended up on his tail. His only means of escaping the faster aircraft was to put the Spitfire into a near vertical dive, making a sharp turn at the bottom and racing low over Dieppe, deciding that the only way to escape was to race low over British warships off the coast – something they had been told not to do for fear of being shot down. He suddenly found himself between the flak and tracer from a destroyer and the tracer from the Fw190. Then he was through it and able to set a course for his base at West Malling, while the Fw190 had disappeared, either put off by the flak or shot down by it.

This was the first of four sorties by Johnson's squadron over Dieppe that day, but it was also the one that saw most air-to-air combat.

PREPARING FOR OVERLORD

After the Dieppe debacle, No. 610 was sent to Caithness, at the very north of the Scottish mainland, but returned south to Tangmere in January 1943. The squadron resumed operations over occupied France, often flying ram-rods but on other occasions providing close escort for light and medium bombers. On one occasion, with two other squadrons, escorting twelve Lockheed Ventura medium-bombers on a raid against Caen, they were pounced upon by a large number of Fw190s. As the fight developed, Johnson found his unit struggling to protect the rear of the bombers as they completed their mission and turned for home. Within a couple of minutes, three of his aircraft were either shot down or very badly damaged.

The only means of escape was to fly as close to the surface of the sea as possible, so that an Fw190 making a tight turn risked catching the inboard wingtip in a wave, which would cartwheel the aircraft into the water. It also made it difficult for enemy aircraft to dive at the Spitfires at high speed because of the need to pull up well above the waves to avoid crashing into them. As they flew back, he realised that he had just seven aircraft left, so where were the other two? Scanning the sky, he saw them, flying well above the rest of the squadron, with the lead pilot being an officer temporarily posted to the squadron before being moved on elsewhere and unaware of the best tactics for daylight sweeps over France. Johnson saw something else as well: a bunch of Fw190s racing after the two Spitfires. He shouted a warning and turned what was left of his unit towards them, but it was too late, for as they completed their turn towards the dogfight, he could see the two Spitfires plunging seawards, one of them pouring black smoke before bursting into flames.

Johnson and his pilots watched in horror, waiting for the pilot to bale out, but instead he appeared to panic and started to swear at his comrades over the radio, blaming them for the fact that he was on fire and that he was going to die. Johnson switched on his radio to jam his emissions. They saw the aircraft slam into the sea, but when they flew over the site, could not see wreckage or a dinghy.

While two of the three aircraft damaged in the main battle got home safely, in five days the squadron lost five pilots, an attrition rate that was unsustainable. The superiority of the Fw190 over the Spitfire was such that, when Johnson became the temporary wing leader, he did not lead the wing into combat unless the position of the sun and the altitude of his formation enabled them to make a surprise attack, known as the perfect 'bounce'.

He did not have long as a temporary wing leader as a few days later he was promoted to wing commander and put in command of a wing manned by Canadians at Kenley, flying the new Spitfire 9s. This was a feature of the wartime RAF, with squadrons manned by many different nationalities, not just by those from the British Empire but also from the free forces of occupied Europe. There were even three squadrons with Americans until the US entered the war and shortly afterwards they were transferred to the USAAF. Nevertheless, there were also squadrons with as many as half a dozen different nationalities, and the general view was that these were easier to lead and direct to a common purpose than those manned by a single nationality but with a wing leader who was British. The Canadians had a reputation for being tough and hard to handle.

One of the duties that fell to the 2nd TAF fighter squadrons was to escort bombers softening up targets in France. Johnnie Johnson, then a wing commander, was sent to liaise with an American bomber unit. He discovered that they did not want a close escort as they preferred to form their own defensive bomber boxes, and this suited Johnson well as it meant that his Spitfires had freedom for offensive search and action. The Americans made it clear that any aircraft that approached their defensive screen would be regarded as hostile. 'We gave the Fortress gunners a wide berth, for, like many others, they shot first and identified afterwards.'

Another RAF officer leading a wing of Canadian squadrons was the then Wing Commander Mike Judd. In the run up to D-Day, his Typhoons were tasked with attacking V-1 rocket-launching sites and coastal radar sites in the Pas de Calais region. On 1 June he was summoned to a meeting at 21st Army Group and given a detailed briefing on the plans for the Normandy landings, as a result of which he was not allowed to fly for several days in case he was shot down and captured. He recalled how frustrating he found it standing and watching his pilots taking off to strike at German gun positions.

The Typhoon was one of the most capable RAF fighters late in the war, fast enough to face an Fw190, heavily armed and capable of carrying a 1,000lb bomb under each wing. It was known affectionately by the RAF as the 'Tiffie'.

After a further day's delay because the invasion was postponed for twenty-four hours due to bad weather, at dawn on 6 June he took off from a Hampshire airfield leading two of his squadrons to destroy two German 88mm gun positions, each aircraft carrying two 1,000lb armour-piercing bombs. The German 88mm gun was one of their most effective weapons, devastating against tank armour or as an anti-aircraft weapon. Despite the low cloud base, the aircraft managed to find the targets and attack. As he pulled away, Judd caught a glimpse of the massive invasion fleet and later recalled: 'I knew that this was a historic moment I would never forget.'

Another officer on a sortie over Normandy on that fateful day was Squadron Leader Geoffrey Page of No. 132 Squadron. As always happens, the weather on D-Day, while better than the previous day, was still far from calm. He too was impressed by the sheer scale of the operation and recalls what he saw.

It was fascinating to see our troops and the Americans and the Canadians going into France again. I was sitting over the beaches at about 1,000 feet and I had a dress-circle view of the whole of the Normandy landing. We felt sorry for the troops who were coming across in the landing craft. There were thousands of vessels from big battleships down to landing craft, and the little landing craft were taking a tremendous pounding from the bad weather conditions. The Channel was rough. I should think a tremendous number of them were being ill from sea-sickness – and of course, to get out of a landing barge on a beach – to be fired at and to be a brave man and attack the enemy is not the easiest thing in the world. And of course, after I had been there for an hour, I'd fly back to England, and I'd tuck into breakfast and I'd be comfortable, while those poor chaps were still there on the beaches. That was our several-times-a-day routine, going back out over the beaches – and it became a little boring, in fact, after a while, because the Germans, I think, thought that the Normandy invasion was a dummy attack – they put up no air resistance at all. I believe two German fighters, which I never saw, came over once during the first fortnight.[2]

AFTER D-DAY

For the three weeks after D-Day, almost all of the fighter and fighter-bomber operations were from bases in the south of England. While *Luftwaffe* activity over the invasion forces was relatively low, there was intense anti-aircraft fire. On D-Day Plus One, Judd's aircraft was hit, with the hood disappearing and a large hole blown in one of the wings, so it was with difficulty that he managed to nurse the aircraft home to an emergency landing. It was not until 27 June that he and his comrades were moved to a temporary air strip in Normandy.

Targets were those identified by the Army, attacking transports and the bridges over the Orne and Odon as the Germans started to retreat eastwards. Later, after they moved to the Netherlands they attacked trains carrying the V-2 rockets to their launching sites.

Superstition runs high amongst aviators, especially military aviators in a war zone. The disappearance of a gold ring upset Flying Officer Ken Adam of 2nd TAF's 609 Squadron.

I had a gold ring made up of the wedding rings of my mother and father. Before I went on an op I would turn this ring three times. On one particular occasion we had to attack a Gestapo headquarters in the middle of Dunkirk. As I started my engine I went to turn my ring, but it wasn't there. I must have dislodged it when I went to grab my parachute. So I said to myself, 'Well, this is it.' I started to look for any reason to abort the mission. But the plane was behaving perfectly. I took off, and it was a particularly nasty attack in which we lost the squadron commander and three other pilots. I was hit several times, but managed to get back. As I climbed out the fitters were walking towards me, great grins on their faces, holding my ring, which they had been turning for me.[3]

The aircrew often met their fate with great stoicism, as Adam recalls.

There was a Canadian pilot called Piwi Williams who went to his death, fully aware that he was going to die. It was unbelievably touching.

We were flying an operation over France and I could see his aircraft gradually losing height and I called on my radio, 'Piwi, what are you doing?' He called back and said that he was hit and paralysed, and he went slowly down for several minutes. I never forgot his last words, just before he hit the ground. 'Order me a late tea.'[4]

While the Allies had aerial superiority, inevitably there were occasions when this was not enough. Wing Commander Basil Carroll was in command of three squadrons of rocket-armed Typhoons that had been savaging German armour and communications when enemy aircraft attacked their forward base at Coulombs between sorties. A fuel dump and two Typhoons were set on fire. Carroll saw that fire tenders were pressed into service, and the fire in one Typhoon was put out, but the other aircraft, already loaded with bombs, rockets and cannon shells, continued to burn. He realised that two of the rockets were pointing towards other aircraft. With Flight Lieutenant Wilfred Turner, Carroll grabbed asbestos gloves and crawled under the wing to release the rockets and roll away two 500lb bombs that were in danger of being engulfed in the blaze. Had the undercarriage collapsed or the plane blown up, both men would have been killed instantly.

FRIENDLY FIRE!

The relatively low naval casualties during the Normandy landings make a subsequent event a couple of months later all the more poignant. On 27 August, two of the Royal Navy's minesweepers were sunk and a third had its stern torn off after an attack by Hawker Typhoon fighter-bombers from Nos 263 and 266 Squadrons, Royal Air Force. Often friendly fire incidents are between units of different nationalities, but this was an entirely British affair.

The First Minesweeping Flotilla was operating off the French coast near Cape d'Antifer when it was decided to move it to a new area, and details of the change were sent by signal and circulated to all interested parties. Later that day, another naval officer came on duty and decided to send the flotilla back to its original area of operations, and again details were sent by signal, but due to an error these were not circulated to the area naval headquarters, so they in turn could not communicate the change to the Royal Air Force. So it happened that when Allied radar spotted three ships sweeping in line abreast formation at noon on 27 August, it was immediately assumed to be a German formation. Not having been told of the change, Flag Officer British Assault Area (FOBAA), on learning about the ships, agreed that they must be German. Two of the ships were quite substantial, with *Hussar* and *Britomart* having served as sloops on convoy escort duties, and of sufficient size given the difficulty in assessing size from the air to appear to be small German destroyers. A Polish airman flew over the ships in his Spitfire, mis-reported their position, but also reported that they seemed to be Allied ships. FOBAA then attempted to contact the officers controlling minesweeping, but telephone lines were down and so no confirmation could be made. Next, FOBAA called for an anti-shipping strike and sixteen Typhoons of the RAF's 263 and 266 Squadrons were ordered into the air. On approaching the flotilla, the strike leader was immediately suspicious and suspected that he could see Allied ships, so he radioed questioning his orders, only to be told to attack. He subsequently queried his orders twice.

The attack began at 13.30, with a classic attack out of the sun towards the first ship, HMS *Britomart*, strafing and firing anti-tank rockets that were deadly against the thin hulls of minor warships. Within two minutes, this ship had lost its bridge and was listing heavily, while another ship, *Hussar*, was on fire. The immediate reaction of those aboard the ships was to assume that the aircraft were from the *Luftwaffe*, with *Jason* signalling that she was being attacked by enemy aircraft, but as the aircraft roared away, the distinctive D-Day 'invasion stripe' markings could be seen, and another ship, *Salamander*, fired recognition flares, forcing the leader of the strike to query his orders for the fourth time. Once again, he was ordered back into the attack, and at 13.35 dived down towards the warships, hitting *Britomart* yet again and strafing *Jason* while rockets went into *Salamander* and *Colsay*. A third attack followed at 13.40, despite a large white ensign and a Union flag being draped over the stern of *Jason* as she fired further recognition flares, hitting *Hussar*, which exploded, and *Salamander*, whose stern was blown off by rocket strikes. As the stricken *Salamander* drifted towards the coast, a German artillery battery with 9.2-inch coastal guns opened up, forcing *Jason* to launch her small boats to tow *Salamander* out of danger.

The end result of the worst 'friendly fire' incident faced by the Royal Navy during the Second World War was that 117 officers and ratings were killed and 153 wounded. The whole sorry incident was covered up and only came to light when the papers were released by the then Public Record Office (now the National Archive) in 1994. The survivors from the crews of the two ships sunk were separated and ordered never to discuss or disclose details of the incident. At a subsequent court martial of three officers responsible for supervising the minesweepers and who had ordered them into the area without checking that details were circulated properly, one was severely reprimanded and another two were acquitted.

CLOSING THE FALAISE GAP
While landing in Normandy had caught the Germans by surprise, inland the terrain favoured the defenders, with miles of sunken roads and high hedgerows. Initially, the Allies broadened their grip on the court,

advancing to Brittany, taking Cherbourg on the way to provide a port, and then advancing to the Seine. The western districts of Caen were seized on 8 July after the city had been devastated by heavy bombing, while Operation Goodwood on 18/19 July had the city virtually surrounded, although with heavy losses in British armour. A serious loss to the Germans had come a day earlier when their commander in the field, none other than General Erwin Rommel, was badly wounded when his car was shot up by an RAF fighter.

Throughout the weeks after the Normandy landings, German defence was largely paralysed by fears that the Normandy landings might still be a diversion and that further landings might be made in the Pas de Calais. The railway network had been so badly damaged by Allied bombing that they had difficulty in moving Panzer divisions from the south of France. After the USAAF had devastated the German front with a massive bombardment, the Americans reached Avranches by the end of July. Hitler intervened and ordered the ten remaining Panzer divisions to counterattack, but they were easily held by the Allies. Montgomery was next to intervene, changing the original plan and ordering US General Patton to swing his army round so that they trapped the Germans, with the two Allied armies just 15 miles apart on each side of Falaise.

The new German commander, Kluge, was frank with the Führer, insisting that the only way of saving the remnants of some fifty divisions was to retreat immediately. On this occasion, Hitler agreed. The German withdrawal was aided by the sacrifice of the Twelfth SS Hitler Youth Division, which held open the route to allow the rest of the army to escape to the Seine. Although the bridges had been destroyed, the Germans were able to ferry their men and equipment across by 19 August.

With control of the skies, all this was done under intense Allied aerial attack, as Flight Sergeant Allen Billham of No. 609 Squadron recalled:

The Falaise Gap is difficult to explain. There are a lot of roads, valleys leading up to the exit to the gap like the little roads in the Yorkshire Dales. They were full of German petrol lorries, tanks and all sorts of supply vehicles. They had made their attack and got blunted. The Americans came round from the south and the British, Canadian and Polish came round from the north, and started nipping. The Germans just weren't allowed to retreat at first and when they were allowed to retreat, it was too late. During daylight hours, nothing moved, because if it moved it got shot at.

The Germans certainly fought their own corner during the week of the Falaise Gap. Whereas the British convoy would stretch over 2 miles and have the regulation 50 yards between each vehicle, the Germans believed in putting everything close together and having flak all the way round and in the middle of them. Everything joined in our attack – Spitfires, Mustangs, Thunderbolts, you name it. But our Typhoons had the rockets and the 20mm cannon, so we did most of the damage, certainly against the armoured vehicles. We never sensed in our attacks that we would not defeat the Germans. After all, they were just fighting a rearguard action.[5]

Aircrew rarely get to see the fruits of their labours at close hand. Nevertheless, Ken Adam had that doubtful privilege.

After Falaise Gap we managed to get some leave and we went to the area. The first thing you noticed was the smell, mainly of dead animals. It was incredible – all the horses or cattle were completely rigid. Then we started seeing the bodies of the Germans we had killed. I'll never forget them. The tanks in their retreat had driven across anything in their path and it was grotesque, ghastly. I actually managed to win a German Volkswagen, one of these staff cars, but I didn't have the courage to get the two bodies out of the car. I left that to a New Zealander to do. So we had a German VW with our flight for seven or eight months but we could never get rid of the smell – the sweet smell of death.[6]

The Allies had mounted night fighter patrols over the Falaise Gap, and these soon proved their worth as the Germans tried to air drop supplies to their beleaguered forces, as Ernst Eberling, a pilot with *Kampfgeschwader* 53, recalls:

On 19 August 1944, we had to fly from Paris to supply the trapped German troops in the Falaise Gap. We were supposed to drop our supplies between a triangle of three fires, but when we got there, there were fires all over, so the first night we didn't know what to do. However, the drop the next night was better. It was dangerous and we suffered many losses from the Allied night fighters.[7]

One of the units involved in night fighter patrols over Normandy was the RAF's No. 219 Squadron, which operated the de Havilland Mosquito Mk XXX. One of these was flown by Flight Lieutenant Leslie Stephenson, who was partnered with Flight Lieutenant Arthur Hall as navigator and radar operator. The two had flown together for several years, broken only by being rested in different training units in late 1943. The duo had each won the DFC (and later awarded a bar to the medal) for their single most successful sortie on the night of 23/24 May 1943, when they shot down three *Luftwaffe* aircraft over Sicily in their Beaufighter.

On the night of 15/16 August 1944, they shot down a Junkers Ju188 medium bomber over Caen with two bursts of cannon fire at 250 yards after the target had been acquired by Hall on radar at a range of 4 miles.

Notes

1. 'Johnnie' Johnson, *Wing Leader*, Chatto & Windus, London, 1956.
2. Imperial War Museum Sound Archive.
3. Imperial War Museum Sound Archive.
4. Imperial War Museum Sound Archive.
5. Imperial War Museum Sound Archive.
6. Imperial War Museum Sound Archive.
7. Cajus Bekker, *The Luftwaffe War Diaries*, Doubleday, New York, 1968.

Chapter 11

Over Occupied Territory

For the first few years of war, bomber operations over Germany were unescorted, simply because no fighter had the necessary endurance. This changed when aircraft such as the de Havilland Mosquito, Lockheed P-38 Lightning, the Republic P-47 Thunderbolt and North American P-51 Mustang appeared. Even on operations across the English Channel during the Battle of Britain and then the Blitz, it was difficult for the Bf109s to provide close support for the German bombers as they did not have the endurance, which is why the *Luftwaffe*, like the RAF, favoured night operations, especially when some distance over the other side's territory. Hit-and-run raids, sometimes called 'tip-and-run' on targets close to the coast, were, of course, a different matter.

Unlike the Allies, the Germans did not have the same success in developing long-distance fighters. The Junkers Ju88 and Messerschmitt Me110 were not as effective as the more agile Bf109, but this was always a problem with twin-engined piston aircraft. The Focke-Wulf Fw190 was deadly, but by the time it arrived in service the Germans were on the defensive. One US bomber squadron commander found the Fw190 with four cannon deadly, 'lighting up like a neon sign!' Ju88 and Me110 night fighters were of course able to cope with bombers, being much slower and more cumbersome than fighters, but even this began to change with the arrival of the Mosquito, probably the first truly multi-role aircraft, which was officially a light bomber, but one that could carry the warload of a medium bomber, and which was fast, especially once it had dropped its bombs. While Mosquitoes were used on raids against the prison at Amiens and Gestapo headquarters in The Hague, they are often best remembered for their role with the RAF's Pathfinder units.

THE GERMAN DEFENCES
Fewer Germans seem to have recorded their war experiences than their Allied counterparts, and this applies as much to the *Luftwaffe* compared to the RAF as it does to any other service. Some believe that this is because the British and Americans are more obsessed with war, but in fact the real reasons are partly down to the higher casualty rates that would have

affected the Germans and partly because they lost, and it is always easier to write from the point of view of the victor. In short, the Germans, Italians and Japanese are more likely to want to forget the war, while for the Allies this was a period of glory. At least the Germans don't overlook the fact that the war happened, while it is omitted from the history syllabus in Japanese schools.

One German fighter pilot who wrote at great length on his wartime experiences was Heinz Knoke, although towards the end of his book one gets the feeling that he did so not simply to provide an excellent war record, as he has done, but to distance himself and other German fighting men from the Nazis and the atrocities committed by them.

By late 1942, the Germans had learnt the hard way that good communication and direction between ground controllers and fighters was essential if the growing Allied bombing campaign, at this point still essentially an RAF campaign although the USAAF had mounted its first mission in July 1942, was to be countered. Not only had the RAF bombers increased in size and destructive power with the advent of the four-engined 'heavies', but the new fast light bomber, the Mosquito, was, as already noted, a menace to the Germans not only because of its speed and manoeuvrability, but the fact that its bomb load was really that of a medium bomber.

The Germans had introduced a new system, the 'Y' system, which provided vastly improved long-distance radio communications between the ground controllers and aircraft in flight. Control rooms were set up on an area basis as the territory occupied by Germany by late spring 1940 stretched from the North Cape to the Bay of Biscay. That for the Netherlands was typical of others, with a large bomb-proof shelter with a large map of the country on plate glass in the centre. As with the British control centres, which covered a smaller area, there was a raised platform at one side of the map, with *Luftwaffe* women personnel sitting with a battery of headphones and microphones. Reports were received from coastal radar stations as soon as they picked up approaching Allied formations and the changing position of the approaching force was moved by the girls projecting lights onto the 'map', in contrast to the British system of moving markers, while other personnel also marked the position of the *Luftwaffe* fighters.

On the other side of the map, on another raised platform, sat the ground-control officers, able to direct every fighter formation by ultra-short-wave radio telephone. All together, around a thousand personnel were needed for just one control centre.

In addition to the Dutch control centre, the *Luftwaffe* had other centres at Berlin, Stade, Metz, Munich and Vienna.

The latest mark of the Bf109 was the Bf109F, but by late 1942, this was superseded by the Bf109G, known to the *Luftwaffe* fighter pilots as the

'Gustav'. This was considerably faster than the then current production mark of the Spitfire. Nevertheless, confidence in this latest version of the aircraft was dented when Hans Joachim Marseille, Germany's top-scoring fighter ace who had shot down 158 Allied aircraft, 150 of them over North Africa, was killed as he baled out when his aircraft suddenly caught fire.

Based at Jever, only hours after hearing of Marseille's death, Knoke, then a lieutenant, was scrambled with another pilot, Sergeant Wenneckers, to intercept a Mosquito that was on reconnaissance over Oldenburg. Wenneckers started to fall behind, so Knoke called him on his radio, but received no reply. By the time he reached the altitude of the Mosquito, it had flown away so Knoke started to return, descending in three or four wide spirals to return to base, and he noticed the flaming wreckage of an aircraft on the road below. He was surprised on returning to base to find Wenneckers waiting for him – his Gustav had caught fire, but he had baled out successfully and was picked up and taken back to Jever. Nevertheless, reports soon began to come in of Bf109Gs catching fire.

Knoke and Wenneckers were the only two pilots in their unit capable of flying 'blind', but on 6 November 1942, with cloud base at just 100 feet and steady drizzle, and unable to see across the airfield, Knoke was telephoned by the fighter controller to see if he could fly. He explained the situation. The telephone rang a few minutes later. This time a colonel was on the line, insisting that he should take off as Goering was insisting that if two British Mosquitoes could fly over Berlin, the *Luftwaffe* could take off and shoot them down.

At 13.30, they took off.

I can see hardly anything ahead. This blasted rain! Keeping down low, we hurtle over the roof-tops, trees and power lines. Radio reception from the ground is good. Leutnant Kramer directs me.

The Tommies are heading north-west over the Bremen area. From past experience they may be expected to cross the East Friesian Islands.

I head for the coast. The weather over the sea is not any better ... I am unable to see anything at all ahead. It is maddening. Base calls: 'You should see them now. Try a little to the left.'

I do not answer. For a shadow suddenly looms out of the greyness ahead. It is a Mosquito.

He has spotted me also, and whips round to the left in a vertical bank, almost dipping his wing-tip in the sea. Now he twists around to the right. The he dodges to the left again.

'No, no, my friend, it is not such a simple matter to shake off Knoke.' Every time he turns I fire in front of his nose.

We are flying low, very low, heading out over the open sea now. My Tommy leaves a faint trail of smoke ... He moves at such a blasted high speed. But my good Gustav is just able to maintain the pace. I stay on his tail. Wenneckers gradually falls behind ... I want to fire at only the closest possible range ... I draw nearer to my opponent ... the range drops to 150 feet. He is squarely in my sights.

'Fire, Knoke, fire – NOW!!'

I press both firing buttons. The burst catches him in the left engine. The plane is constructed of wood. The wing goes up in flames at once and shears off at the root. A few seconds later one ... Mosquito vanishes into the green depths of the North Sea.[1]

This was Knoke's third kill. It seems that while he had a Bf109G, the Gustav, his wingman Wenneckers had an older aircraft, possibly a Bf109F.

THE ALLIES GAIN AN ADVANTAGE

Wartime was a constant race between those seeking to improve the air defences, whether over Germany or over Great Britain, and those seeking to overcome the air defences. One such device used by RAF Bomber Command was called 'Window'.

Window was one of the most successful aids used by Bomber Command in the ceaseless battle against German anti-aircraft defences. Early experiments in dropping aluminium strips to confuse enemy radar had seemed to have little effect, but experiments at the Telecommunications Research Establishment (TRE) found that oblong aluminium strips would be effective. This was known as early as April 1942, but the project was shelved after RAF Fighter Command objected, pointing out that Window had interfered with the radar on the RAF's night fighters, and if Bomber Command started to use it, the *Luftwaffe*'s bombers could be expected to do so as well.

Fighter Command continued to object even later in the year, when Air Scientific Intelligence reported that the Germans were aware of the principles behind Window and were expecting it to be used. Fighter Command wished the introduction to be delayed until they had effective counters to it. By April 1943, with losses beginning to mount again, Harris pressed hard for its introduction, but on this occasion he was overruled by the Allied Chiefs of Staff, who wished its introduction to be delayed until after the invasion of Sicily, set for 10 July. Even then, it took Churchill's personal intervention before Window could be introduced!

The irony of the situation was that the device had, despite secrecy and wartime censorship, been known outside the RAF for some time, even featuring in a *Daily Mirror* cartoon as early as July 1942!

The first use of Window was for a raid on Hamburg, Germany's second largest city, on the Baltic, and a major industrial centre and port, as well as a naval base. It was a tempting target, of immense strategic value, and, being on the coast, was ideally suited to the Pathfinder and heavy bombers' H2S radar location and targeting. On 27 May 1943, the operational order for the city's destruction was circulated to the Bomber Command groups. Given the title Operation Gomorrah, it was emphasised that the destruction of the city would be of significant value in shortening the war, but that it would take more than 'a single night'. The raid was scheduled for the night of 22/23 July, allowing the first use of a new device, Window, to disrupt the enemy radar at a minute past midnight! Unfortunately, the weather was too bad on the set night, and remained bad for the following night, so that eventually the first raid had to be postponed to the night of 24/25 July.

On the chosen night, diversionary raids were mounted to distract German attention for as long as possible. A mixed force of 791 bombers was assigned to the Hamburg raid, each aircraft having its own supply of Window. The bomber streams, with up to 200 from each group, would converge into a single stream of aircraft, about 10,000 feet deep, 5 miles wide and 50 miles long, all heading in the same direction. The crews were instructed to drop a bundle of Window at one-minute intervals starting at 60 miles from the target and continuing until they were 60 miles from the target on their homeward run. One wireless operator recalled that the foil strips being unloaded into the night sky were like 'a shoal of fish darting along in the murky water'. The Pathfinder aircraft were fitted with H2S, and used yellow, green, and red target incendiaries, while the main attack force dropped a mixture of high explosives and incendiaries.

Window caused much confusion. One of those flying on the operation recalled: 'We heard one German controller get fixed on a packet of this stuff which obviously was not an aircraft and telling it to waggle its wings and so forth, without any success. When another controller saw extra aircraft appearing where only one had been before, he burst into indignation over the radio, "The English bombers are propagating themselves."'

One can only assume that the reluctance of the Germans to use the same tactic was because of objections from their fighter leaders, but the opportunities to use a German version of Window would also have been much fewer. By this time, there were fewer major raids over Britain by the *Luftwaffe*, and while heavy bombers started to appear in the form of the Dornier Do177, they were relatively few in number. The smaller German bombers also had much smaller crews, and allocating someone to cast out strips of foil would have been difficult.

COUNTERING THE AMERICANS

The USAAF's policy of mounting heavy daylight raids has often been regarded as controversial given the RAF's experience earlier in the war. There were two good reasons for the USAAF having daylight raids. The first was that when massive raids were mounted, there was intense congestion in the airspace over airfields, and spreading operations over the twenty-four hours stopped this becoming worse, with the risk of aircraft colliding in mid-air. The second was that whenever a major target was selected, it became possible for a daylight raid to follow a night raid, so that not only was the damage intensified, but attempts to repair the damage were foiled.

The different bomber types used in the European theatre all had their strengths and weaknesses. The British Avro Lancaster was rugged and could carry the heaviest bomb load of the war, with modified versions able to carry a 22,000lb 'Grand Slam' earthquake bomb. The American Consolidated Liberator had the longest range, while the Boeing B-17 Fortress, or Flying Fortress, was heavily armed. Both these American aircraft were also high flying. Heavy defensive armament was essential for daylight bombing, and a force of 300 Liberators possessed a total of 4,800 heavy machine guns, usually firing tracer bullets. As one German fighter pilot put it: 'Even if only one in ten have a chance to fire that still means we run into quite a barrage.'

Heinz Knoke was amongst those who had to face the high-flying USAAF formations, with aircraft spaced so that their defensive fire protected each other. For him, 26 February 1943 was a memorable day.

We draw closer to the bomber formation. I must have opened the throttle subconsciously. I can distinguish the individual enemy aircraft now. Most of them are Liberators . . . I pick one out as my target.

I shall make a frontal attack. The Yank is focused in my sights. He grows rapidly larger. I reach for the firing button on the stick. Tracers come whizzing past my head. They have opened up on me!

Fire! I press both buttons, but my aim is poor. I can see only a few hits register in the right wing.

I almost scrape the fat belly as I dive past. Then I am caught in the slipstream, buffeted about so violently that for a moment I wonder if my tailplane has been shot away. I climb up steeply and break away to the left. Tracers pursue me, unpleasantly close.

I come in for a second frontal attack, this time from a little below. I keep on firing until I have to swerve to avoid a collision. My salvoes register this time.

I drop away below. As I swing round I turn my head. Flames are spreading along the bottom of the fuselage of my Liberator. It sheers away from the formation in a wide sweep to the right.

Twice more I come in to attack, this time diving from above the tail. I am met by heavy defensive fire. My plane shudders under the recoil from the two cannon and 13mm guns. I watch my cannon shell-bursts rake along the top of the fuselage and right wing, and I hang onto the stick with both hands.

145

The fire spreads along the right wing. The inside engine stops. Suddenly the wing breaks off altogether. The body of the stricken monster plunges vertically, spinning into the depths. A long black trail of smoke marks its descent.

One of the crew attempts to bale out. But his parachute is in flames. Poor devil! The body somersaults and falls to the ground like a stone.[2]

Knoke saw the aircraft explode at 3,000 feet, with the fuselage falling apart, leaving fragments of blazing wreckage to land on a farm close to an airfield, with the exploding fuel tanks setting the buildings ablaze. He landed on the airfield, diving out of the sky, and ran over to the site of the crash, where a crowd was trying to fight the fire in the farmhouse. He joined in, bringing out furniture and machinery as well as animals. He was blinded and choked by the smoke while his flying suit was scorched. They managed to save the farmhouse and the barn. All that was left of the Liberator lay in a field; the bodies of the crew, thrown out by the explosion, scattered around it.

Despite this success, the *Luftwaffe* was under pressure and the pilots knew this better than anyone. Knoke reflected on the possibility that his turn would come soon, and that they had much in common with the Americans, and that: 'Separated for the moment by the barrier of war, we shall one day be reunited by death in the air.'

Looking for a means of tackling the growing strength of the USAAF, one of his comrades, *Leutnant* Dieter Gerhard, had the idea of the Bf109s dropping small bombs on the close-flying USAAF bomber formations. Discussing the idea together, they decided that the bombs would have to be dropped from a flight of Bf109s in close formation above the bombers, and then be followed up by a conventional attack with cannon fire. The Bf109 could carry a single 500lb bomb or four 100lb bombs, or a rack of anti-personnel bomblets such as those used by the *Luftwaffe* against the Soviet armies. The fuses would have to be set for fifteen seconds, meaning that release would be 3,000 feet above the American formations.

After persuading his commanding officer that the idea was not a joke, he was sent to his divisional headquarters to explain the idea to a general and a colonel. They agreed that the idea deserved investigation and preparations were made for exercises using 100lb dummy bombs, while the squadron rehearsed its formation flying. A Junkers Ju88 with a target drogue was also provided, but the early results were far from satisfactory. It took some days before everything worked as planned.

The squadron was ready by 18 March, but was scrambled that day to confront another formation of Liberators in such a hurry that there was no time to 'bomb up' the aircraft. Nevertheless, Knoke managed to shoot down another Liberator, which also exploded in mid-air, by which time he was so close to the aircraft that he had difficulty avoiding being struck by the debris.

On both sides, it was common for fighter pilots to stick to a target aircraft until it was definitely destroyed. Attacking an aircraft, seeing it in flames or with an engine knocked out, was not enough as it could still dump its bombs and make its way back to base.

Looking for another victim, Knoke suddenly realised that his friend Dieter Gerhard had also shot down a Liberator, but was by this time in the middle of the American formation chasing the leader, while being shot at himself with guns on all sides of him. Determined to rescue Dieter, Knoke dived down firing indiscriminately at the bombers, only to see his friend's Bf109 suddenly dive steeply, emitting smoke from its engine. Dieter opened his canopy, and struggled out. Flying past him, Knoke saw that his friend was in pain and must be badly wounded. He followed him down, reported his position and saw Dieter scramble into his dinghy.

Later that night he received a telephone call to say that Dieter Gerhard was rescued, but died from stomach wounds. The pilots had agreed that each keeps a bottle of brandy in their lockers, to be drunk by their comrades on their death as a toast to the fallen.

BOMBING THE BOMBERS

The idea of dropping bombs onto bombers was not new and not unique to the *Luftwaffe* as the RAF had the same idea earlier in the war. The fundamental difference was in the techniques used. Knoke and Gerhard proposed using fighters, while the RAF had attempted to use obsolete bombers. The *Luftwaffe* planned formation bombing of the bombers, while the RAF had sent a solitary aircraft into the air. The *Luftwaffe* was countering day bombers and could formate its aircraft above the bomber streams, while the RAF had been operating at night and effectively 'blind'.

A further alert on 22 March also meant that there was no time to load the bombs onto the aircraft. Knoke's flight took off, expecting to encounter a USAAF bomber formation, but were ordered to land after just seven minutes as the Americans had turned west. On returning, the aircraft were refuelled immediately, to be prepared in case the Americans changed direction again. Knoke took the opportunity to have a 500lb bomb fitted under his aircraft, but before the work was finished, they were scrambled again. Determined not to take off without the bomb, he ordered Sergeant Wenneckers to take command. While he urged the ground crew to finish the job, news came that the Americans had already crossed the Dutch coast.

Once the work was finished, he had to taxi his aircraft so that it could take off into the wind with its heavy load, but, as he turned at the end of the runway, his aircraft suddenly listed to port as a tyre burst. He fired off a red signal flare. Twenty or thirty ground crew realised what had happened, and piled into a lorry and raced to his aid. Incredibly, most of them lifted the aircraft up on their backs while two others changed the wheel, even though the engine was still running. 'All clear', he called, and the men scattered while he opened the throttle and the Gustav started its take-off roll, with speed rising slowly because of its heavy load. It climbed away, by this time searching for the Americans who were on their way home having bombed Wilhelmshaven. It seemed that the Bf109 did not like the weight of the bomb, and, unlike some of the Allied fighters, proved poor in the fighter-bomber role. It took Knoke twenty-five minutes to reach 30,000 feet.

This time, he was tackling a formation of B-17 Fortresses. He flew over them taking fire from the bombers, and noticed two or three holes in his port wing.

> I fuse the bomb, take final aim, and press the release button on my stick. My bomb goes hurtling down. I watch it fall, and bank steeply as I break away.
>
> Then it explodes, exactly in the middle of a row of Fortresses. A wing breaks off one of them, and two others plunge away in alarm.[3]

The bomber crashed into the sea with no sign of fire. Knoke does not mention any survivors, but does record that the wing followed the bomber, fluttering down 'like an autumn leaf'.

His idea was a success, and he was ordered to report on landing to the *Kommodore* of his wing. The *Kommodore* had been flying that day and had seen for himself the end of the Fortress, and wanted the whole of Knoke's flight to use the same technique, which was, of course, the original idea. He received a telephone call from his colonel, who was also delighted. Next, he was awakened in the middle of the night by a telephone call from a major on Goering's staff. When asked on whose authority he had conducted the operation, he explained that he acted on his own initiative. This is received in silence, and he suddenly thinks that he could be in serious trouble as 'it occurs to me that I was never authorised to lay so much as an egg on the head of that wretched Yank, and so they might consider that I had acted in an exceedingly high-handed manner.'

The major came back on the line to tell Knoke that he was putting him through to the *Reichsmarschall*, giving Knoke what he claimed was the fright of his life. Instinctively, he sprung to attention even while lying horizontally in his bed!

'*Leutnant* Knoke here, No. 5 Flight Commander, No. 1 Fighter Wing.'

'I am delighted over the initiative you have displayed,' said Goering. 'I want personally to express to you my particular appreciation.'

That was that. Despite this, the following morning, General Kammhuber, the architect of Germany's fighter defences, phoned Knoke at 10.00, and gave him a strong reprimand for his high-handed action. Kammhuber, who Knoke described as a 'poisonous little twerp', known to the men as 'Wurzelsepp', was incoherent with rage. Kammhuber's tirade ended by him asking if Knoke had anything to say for himself. Inevitably, Knoke said that he had and explained that the Reichsmarschall had telephoned him last night to personally explain his appreciation of Knoke's initiative. Knoke then had the pleasure of hearing Kammhuber deflate with a gasp.

The technique was sufficiently exciting to the Luftwaffe for Colonel Lutzow, Inspector of the Fighter Command, to fly in to see Knoke that same afternoon for a debriefing. A popular figure amongst the fighter pilots and an ace himself, Lutzo decided that in addition to Knoke's flight, one of the flights in No. 26 Fighter Wing, based on the Channel coast, would use the same techniques. Knoke and Lutzow agree that the technique cannot be used for long once the Allies provide fighter top cover for the bombers.

'What an unholy flap there has been over that wretched egg, sir!' exclaimed Knoke. 'It makes me wish I had never dropped it!'

Lutzow laughed: 'Me too!'[4]

The first attempt at 'bombing the bombers' in flight strength was not until 17 April, while the Americans were over Bremen, but none of the bombs hit a bomber. The flight then attacked with cannon, and shot down three Fortresses.

On 14 May, they tried again over Kiel, but it seemed that the Americans were expecting them and were able to weave out of the way. Frustrated, especially after his formation was disorganised by accurate Kriegsmarine AA fire, he ordered the flight to attack individually. While his bomb failed to explode, three other members of the flight accounted for three bombers. He then attacked using cannon fire, but his aircraft was damaged. As the engine was undamaged and the aircraft responded to the controls, he attacked again, firing into the cockpit of a Fortress, which reared up out of control and then fell away, with a wing breaking off at 10,000 feet.

The flight's total reached fifty heavy bombers that day, as many as the rest of the squadron, earning them a visit from General Galland, the general commanding the German Fighter Command, who signed the visitors' book with good wishes and congratulations.

ROCKET ATTACK

In late June 1943, Knoke was badly wounded whilst shooting down another Fortress, his thirteenth victim, and had a finger amputated. Discharging himself from hospital, he was given leave and spent a week with his family before returning early to duty. A strap was put on the control column of his aircraft to make it easier for him to fly with his still-wounded hand. He had been promoted to Oberleutant and had completed more than 200 operational sorties.

On 15 August, his flight's aircraft were equipped with rocket-firing tubes, which the pilots called 'stovepipes', and were told that they were to fly at a range of 2,500 feet behind the Allied bomber formations and fire the rockets at them.

Early on 17 August, the flight was suddenly transferred to Rheine, 120 miles south, to defend central Germany from anticipated attacks by the USAAF. Before operational sorties began, they were transferred yet again, to Gilze Rijn, in the Netherlands.

The flight was scrambled at 13.15, and they encountered Fortresses escorted by Spitfires over Antwerp. This gave Knoke and his flight a dilemma, as he could not engage the Spitfires without first jettisoning the rocket tubes. He trailed the bombers, waiting for the Spitfires to have to return home as fuel ran low, but, as he prepared to attack, defensive fire from one of the bombers shot away a 'stovepipe', and the aircraft became unbalanced. He worried that the main spar might have been damaged, so realised that he could not make any sudden manoeuvres. No opportunity came for Knoke to fire his second rocket, but two of his pilots scored direct hits, shooting down two bombers.

On landing, he was told that the main spar of his port wing was broken, but the wing would be replaced overnight. Meanwhile, he explored his new base, and found that elements of many different fighter wings had been assigned to the base, but that many of the personnel were inexperienced and there were no formation leaders. While this was going on, a large USAAF bomber formation passed overhead on its way to the ball bearing factories at Schweinfurt, and this made Knoke determined to get back into the air despite his aircraft being unserviceable. He was warned against this action by the leader of the ground crew, but he ignored the advice and summoned together all of the pilots who had landed and told them that they were under his command.

The fighters took off in a large but compact group at 17.00, determined to catch the Americans as they flew homeward. Knoke had to handle his aircraft very carefully. Climbing to 22,000 feet, they soon saw around 250 Fortresses flying towards them. As the two formations closed, he sent the aircraft in to attack one by one, before choosing as his own target a solitary Fortress flying to the left of the main formation and slightly below it. At a range of 500 feet, he opened fire, and was met with a hail of tracer from the Fortress.

Suddenly my poor plane is literally caught in a hail of fire. There is a smell of burning cordite. The engine still seems to run smoothly, however. I bend double up behind it. It offers good enough cover. Closing up to within 300 feet, I take aim calmly at my victim.

Woomf! My fuselage is hit. The sound is more hollow than that made by the engine or wings [when hit].

My own shooting takes effect. By this time the Yank plane is in flames, swerving off to the left as it drops away below the formation. Four parachutes mushroom open.

Suddenly my aircraft is hit several times in succession and badly shaken. It sounds like a sack of potatoes being emptied over a barrel in which I am sitting. Flames come belching out at me from the engine. The smoke is choking me, and my eyes water.

I slide back the side windows because of the fumes. The smoke grows denser. Hot oil from the engine flows like treacle down my left wing-root.[5]

As he broke away from the enemy formation, Knoke saw the Fortress crash in flames in the Eiffel Mountains. He cut the ignition and fuel, as his oil and radiator temperatures were at boiling point. He feared that his left wing might break off at any moment. Nevertheless his action allowed the fire to burn itself out. He jettisoned his canopy and prepared to bale out. Still his badly damaged aircraft, full of holes, continued to fly. He feathered the airscrew and started to glide. At 10,000 feet, he decided that he was losing altitude too quickly, and might not reach the airfield near Bonn that he had selected, so Knoke attempted to start the engine. It started! The aircraft climbed gently to 12,000 feet, before starting to smoke and burn again. Once again, he cut fuel and ignition and continued to glide. By this time, Knoke realised that he could not reach his intended airfield and decided he must use a field. He started the engine again, but after a minute or two, it seized. He skimmed over the roofs of houses at 200mph, then just missed trees at 150mph, before hitting the ground at 100mph, crashing through fences, and braced himself. The plane crashed, followed by a deathly silence. He unfastened his seat belt and scrambled out. His aircraft was barely recognisable, with nothing intact except the tail-wheel, while blood oozed from his right sleeve.

The base had a rescue plane, a Weihe light aircraft, which it used to pick up downed pilots who had survived. The pilots showed their appreciation of its unstinting service by calling it the 'flying garbage truck'. Knoke was returned to his squadron the next day, but in the meantime the medical officer at Hangelar air base, his intended emergency destination, removed some shrapnel fragments from his upper right arm.

The *Luftwaffe* persisted with the rockets while also adding extra auxiliary fuel tanks to the Bf109Gs to extend their range. The end result was that this high-performance aircraft, faster than the Spitfire marks of the day, became sluggish. Quite why extra fuel tanks were considered a good idea for aircraft now confined to fighting over their own territory is not explained in Knoke's book. The time for such tanks would have been during the Battle of Britain and the Blitz, when the time a Bf109 could spend on the other side of the English Channel was limited.

151

When scrambled in a new aircraft on 27 September 1943, Knoke took his flight to 20,000 feet before ordering them to jettison their auxiliary tanks, even though these were still almost full. Freed of the weight, the formation turned quickly to begin a rocket attack on a large formation of Fortresses. The Fortresses broke up into groups of thirty or forty aircraft each, and began to zigzag. When his flight was 2,000 feet from the American bombers, Knoke ordered his pilots to fire their rockets. The two rockets from his aircraft hit a Fortress, which exploded into a solid ball of fire with its full load of bombs. Sergeant Wenneckers also scored a direct hit. Sergeant Reinhard, Knoke's wingman, also fired his rockets, which exploded close to a Fortress, damaging the fuselage and causing the aircraft to swerve away.

Although all seemed to be going well for the Germans, Knoke looked up and saw twin vapour trails from what seemed to be very fast aircraft, circling above. He noted that the planes looked peculiar, and suddenly realised that they were Lockheed P-38 Lightnings escorting the bombers. He climbed to take a closer look and confirm his suspicions. There were at least twelve and he could do little alone, so radioed a warning to his flight, and returned to attacking the Fortresses. He was interrupted by four single-engined fighters diving past him, and he realised that these were Republic F-47 Thunderbolts. He gave chase, seeing them after a Bf109 that was intent on shooting down a crippled Fortress. He called: 'Reinhard, Reinhard, wake up! Thunderbolts behind!' Reinhard gave no sign of hearing and continued to attack the Fortress. Knoke dived down and shot at the leading Thunderbolt, with a single burst sufficient for it to burst into flames and fall out of the sky.

Having saved Reinhard, Knoke felt a hammering noise in his aircraft, and realised that he had a Thunderbolt on his tail with two more ready to join it. He pushed his control column sharply forward, but his engine was already on fire and the heat was becoming unbearable.

Jettisoning the canopy, I pull the oxygen mask off my face. I unfasten the safety harness and, drawing up my legs, kick the stick forward with all my strength. I am shot clear out of the aircraft and somersault through the air in a great arc. I feel the flying-suit whipped against my body by the rush of wind.

Slowly I pull the rip-cord. The harness cuts in, and I am pulled up with a jerk as the parachute opens. After the terrific drop I seem to be standing on air. I swing gently from side to side. Overhead the broad, white silk parachute spreads out like a sun awning. The supporting shrouds make a reassuring 'whoosh'. I quite enjoy the experience. What a marvellous invention the parachute is, to be sure – always provided it opens![6]

152

Knoke looked at his watch after landing: just thirty-one minutes had passed since taking off. He was one of four pilots in his flight to have been shot down, but he was one of the lucky ones as one of the others had been killed and another wounded. The rest of the squadron had also suffered heavy losses, with the worst affected being No. 6 Flight, with nine of its twelve pilots killed, and the other three either had to bale out or crash-land. This was a high cost for twelve Allied aircraft shot down, of which no fewer than six were by Knoke's No. 5 Flight. No one had expected the USAAF to have provided an escort.

The main achievement of the squadron was that the bombers had failed to reach their objective and had been forced to turn back, except for a small formation that had dropped its bombs through a hole in the clouds on the town of Esens in East Friesia. Unfortunately, they hit a school and killed 120 children, a third of the town's child population.

In preparing the escorts for their bomber formations, the Americans had ideas of their own. Not only the heavy bomber formations but also the medium bomber formations had placed much importance on creating defensive 'boxes' so that the bombers' own guns defended each other and provided a deadly barrage to thwart any attacking *Luftwaffe* fighter. Despite changes and trials with different formations, this never worked as well as expected. An RAF officer, Tom Dalton-Morgan, who later became a group captain and was mentioned earlier, was seconded to give advice on bomber escorts. Already an ace, he chaffed at not being able to join the bombers and fly the new long-range fighter, the North American P-51 Mustang. The USAAF agreed to his joining the fighter escorts, and in more than seventy sorties between March and October 1944, Dalton-Morgan may well have doubled his score with the RAF, but his name did not appear on the official US 4th Fighter Group records at the time, even though he was awarded the US Bronze Star, but that was for his attachment. Unofficially, he was also awarded the Silver Star and the US Distinguished Flying Cross in the field. His tally did not feature in RAF records either as the service assumed that he was behaving as an officer in a ground appointment should!

In early October, Knoke and the rest of his squadron were moved to Marx, from where their first scramble was a failure after a formation of Fortresses turned back over the sea, and, in bad weather, one of his flight's Bf109s crashed with the loss of the pilot.

On 4 October 1943, in bright sunny weather, the squadron's pilots were all sitting in front of the hangar while the loudspeakers played music. The fighter pilots on both sides had much in common, especially trying to take their ease as far as possible between operational sorties. Like Johnnie Johnson, always a possible opponent, Knoke had a dog that he kept on the station. Unusually, his dog would always sit on the port wing as he prepared for take-off and stay there until blown off by the propeller slipstream. He would then chase the aircraft down the runway until it gained speed and left him behind.

One big difference between the *Luftwaffe* and the RAF was that, after the first year or so of war, all RAF aircrew were either senior NCOs, warrant officers or commissioned officers, largely to ensure better treatment if they were taken prisoner. The *Luftwaffe* right to the end of the war had many pilots who were ranked as corporals, as well as having sergeants, warrant officers and officers. A sergeant in the *Luftwaffe* could command a flight or section, although these were more usually commanded by a *leutnant*, or lieutenant, compared to a flight lieutenant in the RAF, who was one rank above the German, and squadrons were commanded by captains, as opposed to the squadron leader in the RAF, who was, of course, equivalent to a major.

As a flight commander, Knoke's time between sorties was not always relaxing, and he expressed his irritation when a senior warrant officer approached him with a large folder full of paper requiring his signature.

This placid scene was soon interrupted by the music being stopped by an alert, while the telephone rang and all flight commanders were summoned to see the squadron commander. At the briefing, the flight commanders were told that a large bomber formation was over the North Sea approaching the northernmost part of the Netherlands. The tactics for the day were to be different as for the first time the entire squadron would fly in close formation to attack the bombers head-on. This meant that the Americans would suddenly find themselves confronted by more than forty German fighters.

They took off flight by flight starting at 09.32. Instead of climbing to the prescribed altitude flight by flight, they circled the airfield until the entire squadron was airborne, then were given a course and started to climb to 22,000 feet with strict orders only to break radio silence when absolutely necessary. Knoke recalled the cold, with his breath freezing on the oxygen mask and having to slap his thighs vigorously to keep warm.

Eventually they spotted the USAAF formation, some 300 or 400 heavy bombers, and the squadron commander swung the formation round towards them. At a closing speed well in excess of 600 miles per hour, they were soon within range, with the Bf109s heading at full speed each towards a chosen Liberator, guns blazing. Knoke dived under his chosen aircraft to avoid a collision and turned to complete the job. He saw that it was dropping out of the formation and turning. Knoke waited until his target was clear of the protective firepower of the entire formation before closing in under the belly of the Liberator, and started to fire until the aircraft was in flames. He noted that the Liberator seemed to burn much faster than the more streamlined Fortress, and saw eight parachutes as the crew baled out. As the stricken bomber glided down, he drew alongside it, certain that everyone had left, but suddenly the guns in the dorsal turret opened up and his engine burst into flames and he found that his aircraft no longer responded to the controls. Once again he baled out, although this time he was thrown out as the aircraft stalled and then lurched to port. On this occasion, he did not remember pulling the rip-cord.

Landing in the cold sea, Knoke's life-jacket inflated and he struggled for breath as breakers burst over him. Nevertheless, while his rubber dinghy inflated automatically, he had some difficulty getting into it in the choppy seas. He opened a packet of dye to colour the sea to make his position easier to spot.

While he realised that his comrades would have reported his position, all was not well. His rough ejection from the fighter meant that his clothing was torn so he lost not only his emergency rations but also his Very pistol. Fortunately, a rescue aircraft soon appeared – a Weihe – and he was spotted and a life raft dropped. The Weihe circled overhead as he swam through the seas to the life raft, and, once boarded, Knoke collapsed exhausted. In another two hours, he was discovered by a rescue boat and taken to Heligoland, from whence he was flown back to his base in another Weihe.

Baling out was never an easy option and carried many risks. Getting out could be difficult and, as we saw earlier in the case of Marseille, being struck by the tailplane was a hazard even before the advent of the jet fighter. The parachute might not have been packed properly or could have been damaged in air-to-air combat. It seems that collisions between parachuting airmen and other aircraft were virtually unknown, but on both sides there were the few renegade pilots who would shoot at an enemy pilot as he parachuted. Rescue launches and aircraft were also seen as fair game.

His next victim was on 8 October when he shot down another Fortress, bringing his total score of kills to eighteen. The following day, his flight attempted to intercept a formation of Fortresses that bombed Munster, but before they could reach the bombers, No. 5 Flight was in turn 'bounced' by Republic F-47 Thunderbolts. During the ensuing dogfight, Knoke noticed an Me110 twin-engined fighter fire four rockets at the bombers, blowing up two Fortresses in mid-air. The Thunderbolts turned their attention to the Me110, which unlike the Bf109G could not outmanoeuvre or outpace them. Knoke's fighters headed to the rescue of the Me110, with Knoke shooting down a Thunderbolt and another was shot down by one of his pilots. The Thunderbolts all turned on Knoke, who eventually escaped by making a spiralling corkscrew climb, knowing that the Thunderbolts could not follow this manoeuvre. He returned to the fray to help rescue the Me110, but his aircraft was badly damaged and spun out of control, falling more than 3,000 feet before he could recover. With his undercarriage gone, he had to make a crash-landing beside the runway, and, as he struggled out of his cockpit, an Fw190 landed, but an undercarriage leg broke and it overturned on the concrete and caught fire. The trapped pilot burnt to death before the helpless Knoke. This was followed by heavy bombing of the airfield.

'I have had enough for one day,' he conceded.

There can be no doubt that Knoke and his comrades fought as ferociously as the RAF had in the Battle of Britain and the Blitz. The intensity of the bombing was even greater as there was no let-up, with American day raids following British night raids. The decision to abandon heavy bomber development in Germany during the late 1930s also took its toll as the British and American bombers were heavier and carried a much greater warload. There was to be no German equivalent of the British 'earthquake' bombs, the 12,000lb 'Tallboy' and 22,000lb 'Grand Slam', against which few structures could survive. German industry managed to continue to supply replacement aircraft for most of 1944, but towards the end, production was badly affected, due in no small part to the shortage of rubber and ball bearings.

On the other hand, until the appearance of the Mustang, Thunderbolt and Lightning, the Germans did not have to contend with escort fighters, as the RAF's Spitfires would often provide an escort for the American bombers, but when heading for Germany, the bombers lost the Spitfire escort around Antwerp because of the aircraft's restricted range.

The *Luftwaffe* pilots were cunning as well as skilled. Although Knoke doesn't refer to this, one British account relates that when the first Thunderbolts appeared above the Fortresses, the *Luftwaffe* sent Fw190s above the bombers to tackle the Thunderbolts, realising that they could not engage in aerial combat without jettisoning their long-range tanks, which meant that they had to turn back, leaving the bombers without an escort.

Notes

1. Heinz Knoke, *I Flew for the Führer*, Bell & Hyman, London, 1953.
2. Heinz Knoke, *I Flew for the Führer*, Bell & Hyman, London, 1953.
3. Heinz Knoke, *I Flew for the Führer*, Bell & Hyman, London, 1953.
4. Heinz Knoke, *I Flew for the Führer*, Bell & Hyman, London, 1953.
5. Heinz Knoke, *I Flew for the Führer*, Bell & Hyman, London, 1953.
6. Heinz Knoke, *I Flew for the Führer*, Bell & Hyman, London, 1953.

Chapter 12

Towards Germany

In preparation for the invasion of France, which was seen by the Allies as *the* main invasion despite Churchill's advocacy of an advance through Italy and Austria into Germany, the main Allied air forces were restructured. The USAAF created the First Allied Tactical Air Force and the RAF created the Second Allied Tactical Air Force (2nd TAF).

The decision to create these tactical air forces was based on the hard-won experience gained in North Africa during 1942 and 1943. This was also a factor in creating two tactical air forces rather than just one as each would be tied to its related ground forces. While the RAF was the mainstay of 2nd TAF, this was an international organisation supporting primarily British and Canadian ground forces, but with British, Canadian, Australian and New Zealand units and also those of the 'free' forces consisting of personnel from the occupied countries of Europe, including units manned by personnel from Belgium, Czechoslovakia, France, the Netherlands, Norway and Poland. Both tactical air forces had their own fighters, fighter-bombers, medium bombers, reconnaissance aircraft and night fighters, with the bomber squadrons in the case of 2nd TAF coming from Bomber Command.

Just as the Desert Air Force had been highly mobile, so too, because of the short range of fighters and fighter-bombers, would be 2nd TAF. Essential to successful air-ground co-ordination was the ability to keep up with the advancing army, and 2nd TAF would have to move to improvised bases close to the front as soon as the Allied ground forces advanced. These bases were called 'Advanced Landing Grounds' (ALGs). During 1943 many ALGs were built throughout southern England, and fighter wings practised the technique of moving to them and back in late summer and early fall. Clearly, most of the workload fell upon ground personnel, and while sometimes the fighter and fighter-bomber squadrons would fly directly from one ALG to another, in other cases their sorties would begin at the first and end at the second ALG.

In effect, the tactical air forces became the air arms or corps of the respective Allied armies.

2nd TAF

The composition of 2nd TAF was mainly taken from RAF Fighter Command, which as mentioned earlier was split between 2nd TAF and the Air Defence of Great Britain (ADGB), but Bomber Command surrendered its medium and light bomber squadrons in its No. 2 Group, leaving its heavy bomber groups to continue the strategic offensive, mainly against Germany but also striking at vital targets in Italy and in places such as Romania with its oil production facilities. Four naval air squadrons were also included to ensure that there were sufficient fighters. There were also a number of Coastal Command units at the outset when the newly landed armies were at their most vulnerable and the flanks of the landing fleet, its supply train and the improvised ports were at risk of attack not just from the *Luftwaffe* but the *Kriegsmarine* as well.

The main units in 2nd TAF in June 1944 were:

No. 83 (Composite) Group

No. 15 Sector

- 122 Wing with No. 19 Squadron, Mustang III; No. 65 Squadron, Mustang III; No. 122 Squadron, Mustang III.
- 125 Wing with No. 132 Squadron, Spitfire IX; No. 453 (Australian) Squadron, Spitfire IX; No. 602 Squadron, Spitfire IX.
- 129 Wing with No. 184 Squadron, Typhoon Ib.

No. 17 (Canadian) Sector

- 126 (Canadian) Wing with No. 401 (Canadian) Squadron, Spitfire IX; No. 411 (Canadian) Squadron, Spitfire IX; No. 412 (Canadian) Squadron, Spitfire IX.
- 127 (Canadian) Wing with No. 403 (Canadian) Squadron, Spitfire IX; No. 416 (Canadian) Squadron, Spitfire IX; No. 421 (Canadian) Squadron, Spitfire IX.
- 144 (Canadian) Wing with No. 441 (Canadian) Squadron Spitfire IX; No. 442 (Canadian) Squadron, Spitfire IX; No. 443 (Canadian) Squadron, Spitfire IX.

No. 22 Sector

- 121 Wing with No. 174 Squadron, Typhoon Ib; No. 175 Squadron, Typhoon Ib; No. 245 Squadron, Typhoon Ib.
- 124 Wing with No. 181 Squadron, Typhoon Ib; No. 182 Squadron, Typhoon Ib; No. 247 Squadron, Typhoon Ib.
- 143 (RCAF) Wing (W/C M.T. Judd) with No. 438 (Canadian) Squadron, Typhoon Ib; No. 439 (Canadian) Squadron, Typhoon Ib; No. 440 (Canadian) Squadron, Typhoon Ib.
- 39 Recce Wing with No. 168 Squadron, Spitfire XIV; No. 400 (Canadian) Squadron, Mosquito XVII; No. 414 (Canadian) Squadron, Spitfire XIV; No. 430 (Canadian) Squadron, Spitfire XIV.

- Spotting Wing with Nos 652, 653, 658, 659 and 662 Squadrons, all with Auster AOP aircraft.
- 83 Group Reserve Squadrons in ADGB with No. 64 Squadron, Spitfire V; No. 234 Squadron, Spitfire V; No. 303 (Polish) Squadron, Spitfire V; No. 345 (French) Squadron, Spitfire Vb; No. 350 (Belgian) Squadron, Spitfire Vb; No. 402 (Canadian) Squadron, Spitfire V; No. 501 Squadron, Spitfire V; No. 611 Squadron, Spitfire V.

No. 84 Group

No. 18 Sector
- 131 (Polish) Wing with No. 302 (Polish) Squadron, Spitfire IX; No. 308 (Polish) Squadron, Spitfire IX; No. 317 (Polish) Squadron, Spitfire IX.
- 132 (Norwegian) Wing with No. 127 Squadron, Spitfire; No. 66 Squadron, Spitfire IX; No. 331 (Norwegian) Squadron, Spitfire IX; No. 332 (Norwegian) Squadron, Spitfire IX.
- 134 (Czech) Wing with No. 310 (Czech) Squadron, Spitfire Vc; No. 312 (Czech) Squadron, Spitfire IX.

No. 19 Sector
- No. 222 Squadron, Spitfire IX; No. 349 (Belgian) Squadron, Spitfire IX; No. 485 (New Zealand) Squadron, Spitfire IX.
- 145 (French) Wing with No. 340 (French) Squadron, Spitfire IX; No. 341 (French) Squadron, Spitfire IX.
- 133 (Polish) Wing with No. 129 Squadron, Mustang III; No. 306 (Polish) Squadron, Mustang III; No. 315 (Polish) Squadron, Mustang III.

No. 20 Sector
- 123 Wing with No. 198 Squadron, Typhoon Ib; No. 609 Squadron, Typhoon Ib.
- 136 Wing with No. 164 Squadron, Typhoon Ib; No. 183 Squadron, Typhoon Ib; No. 263 Squadron, Typhoon Ib.
- 146 Wing with No. 193 Squadron, Typhoon Ib; No. 197 Squadron, Typhoon Ib; No. 257 Squadron, Typhoon Ib; No. 266 Squadron, Typhoon Ib.
- 35 Recce Wing with No. 2 Squadron, Mustang I; No. 4 Squadron, Spitfire IX; No. 268 Squadron, Mustang I.
- 84 Group Reserve Squadrons in ADGB.
- 149 Wing with No. 33 Squadron, Spitfire IX; No. 74 Squadron, Spitfire IX.
- 233 Wing with No. 80 Squadron, Spitfire IX; No. 229 Squadron, Spitfire IX; No. 274 Squadron, Spitfire IX.
- No. 85 Group (night fighter and misc.).

- 141 Wing with No. 264 Squadron, Mosquito XIII; No. 322 (Dutch) Squadron, Spitfire IX; No. 410 (Canadian) Squadron, Mosquito VI.
- 142 Wing with No. 124 Squadron, Spitfire V.
- 147 Wing with No. 488 (New Zealand) Squadron, Mosquito VI; No. 604 Squadron, Mosquito XIII.
- 148 Wing with No. 29 Squadron, Mosquito VI; No. 91 Squadron, Spitfire V; No. 409 (Canadian) Squadron, Mosquito XIII.
- 150 Wing with No. 3 Squadron, Tempest V; No. 56 Squadron, Spitfire IX; No. 486 (New Zealand) Squadron, Tempest V. Reserves from ADGB.
- No. 406 (Canadian) Squadron, Beaufighter.
- No. 418 (Canadian) Squadron, Mosquito XIII.

No. 2 Group from Bomber Command
- 137 Wing with No. 88 Squadron, Boston III; No. 226 Squadron, Mitchell II; No. 342 (Lorraine) Squadron, Boston III.
- 138 Wing with No. 107 Squadron, Mosquito VI; No. 305 (Polish) Squadron, Mosquito VI; No. 613 Squadron, Mosquito VI.
- 139 Wing with No. 98 Squadron, Mitchell II; No. 180 Squadron, Mitchell II; No. 320 (Dutch) Squadron, Mitchell II.
- 140 Wing with No. 21 Squadron, Mosquito VI; No. 464 (Australian) Squadron, Mosquito VI; No. 487 (New Zealand) Squadron, Mosquito VI.

Headquarters Group
- 34 Wing with No. 16 Squadron, Spitfire IX PR; No. 69 Squadron, Wellington XIII; No. 140 Squadron, Mosquito.
- Naval Wing with Nos 808, 885, 886, 897 Naval Air Squadrons, all with Seafire III.
- Aerial Spotters in Nos 26 and 63 Squadrons, both with Spitfire V.

READY TO RETURN

Reflecting on the changes that would occur once the invasion started, Johnnie Johnson, returning to operations after a staff appointment, noted that the Big Wing formations were increasingly impractical and difficult to control as fighter speeds increased and could only be used for offensive operations, usually planned well in advance. The experience of the Desert Air Force showed that small manoeuvrable formations would be what was needed. In addition, once in France they would lack the cover and direction of the Chain Home radar network and be very much on their own, vulnerable to low-flying, hedge-hopping *Luftwaffe* attacks.

Johnson was by this time in command of a Canadian wing, and was prompted to reflect on the changes when asked by a young Canadian fighter pilot what it was like to be in a dogfight. He found himself quickly surrounded by young Canadian pilots and giving them a talk on how fighter tactics had developed. He recalled just how he had felt when he had arrived on his fighter squadron with little idea at all of tactics. His mentoring of the new pilots seemed to do the trick, as once based at Hurn, just outside Bournemouth, and conducting hit-and-run raids against enemy airfields, he found his new pilots acting like veterans after just three weeks.

Developments aimed at increasing the range of the Spitfire also meant that gradually their radius of operations increased, and they could actually reach the Rhine on what became known as 'Ranger' operations, which were better planned and more successful than the early Rhubarb operations in the wake of the Dunkirk evacuation ever could have been. They flew high across the Channel in good weather, often escorting a medium-bomber formation on the way, and then dived down to attack targets, often well inland as these were more lightly defended, especially away from airfields. This did not stop them leaving aircraft on an airfield near Paris as a line of blazing wrecks.

Not all of the action was air-to-ground. Approaching Brussels, Johnson was warned by one of his pilots that there was a twin-engined aircraft ahead. He noted that it was a Dornier Do217, and that the pilot who had given the warning had drawn alongside. For a moment, Johnson thought that the young Canadian was going to commit a breach of flying discipline, but when he remained level with his leader, Johnson gave him permission to attack the Dornier.

'It's yours, Wally. Let's see how you do it!'

He closed for the kill while the rest of us hung back to watch the duel. It was all over in a flash. There was no tearing pursuit. No twisting and weaving as the bomber tried to escape. It was a classic example of fine shooting with a master of the craft in the Spitfire. Wally nailed his victim with the first burst, and the Dornier pulled up steeply so that we saw it in plain view, hung for a moment in the air, and then fell on its side and crashed with a sheet of flame near the back gardens of a row of cottages.

'Well done, Wally,' I said. 'Re-form. There may be more about.'[1]

This was an easy kill for the young Canadian pilot. Much of the time, however, was spent gaining strafing practice at the cost of German road transport, and especially staff cars. This would stand them all in good stead as the front line advanced across Europe.

BACK ON FRENCH SOIL

Early on 8 June, just two days after the Normandy landings, Johnson was called by the AOC of No. 11 Group, telling him that the first airfield in Normandy was completed and would he send over a couple of good pilots to see if the landing strip was fully operational. He did as he was ordered and sent two pilots, who soon reported back that all was well. On reporting back to the AOC, he was told to take his wing from its base at Ford, in Sussex, to make a fighter sweep to the south of the beachhead, then land and refuel at St Croix-sur-Mer, the new airfield, then carry out a further sweep before returning to Ford.

This first operation was not as fruitful as Johnson had hoped, as poor weather with very low cloud prevented them reaching as far south as the river Loire, where the *Luftwaffe* had bases, and instead they landed at St Croix to refuel, after flying over it at 1,000 feet. The circuit was tight as the fighters had to avoid the barrage balloons floating over vulnerable troop and supply concentrations on the beaches. RAF servicing commandos were waiting, ready to guide the Spitfires off the dispersal pens, and had started refuelling the aircraft before the pilots could leave the cockpits. Within twenty minutes, the wing was ready to take off again.

The airfield commander arrived to warn them as they smoked that they should stay close to the landing strip as there were enemy snipers around as well as several minefields in the area. Everyone seemed to be jumpy because of this. That morning, a curious airman had wandered into an abandoned enemy strong point and found some discarded German uniforms. Thinking that it would be fun to wear one of these and show off to his comrades, he donned a uniform, and walked out shouting to attract their attention. The joke backfired horribly as the rest of the base's personnel did indeed mistake him for the real thing: he was shot dead.

When they returned to Ford, having had lunch at St Croix, the wing's ground crew and their equipment began the journey to Normandy, and, within a couple of days, the wing transferred to St Croix. The pilots packed their shaving gear, a spare shirt and a change of underwear into the cramped Spitfire cockpit before taking off for the thirty-minute flight. The arrangements for the transfer don't seem to have been too utilitarian, however, as on landing waiting to greet him was his Labrador, Sally. His batman, Corporal Fred Varley, had located a caravan for Johnson near the operations vehicles, and a cup of tea was waiting.

The base was also home to two army liaison officers, who were marking large-scale maps to show the friendly and enemy positions. These were hung on the sides of the briefing tent. Other intelligence reports were also being received, including several that showed that the anticipated *Luftwaffe* reinforcements had arrived at airfields to the south and south-east of St Croix. They were warned that the *Luftwaffe* command, *Jagdkorps* 2, had around 1,000 aircraft, of which 300 were fighters. Johnson was keen to ensure that the *Luftwaffe* positions were plotted on the maps, 'for we would pay them a social call at the very first opportunity.'

The base signals personnel had established good communications with 83 Group, who would provide air control. As the first wing to be based in Normandy, Johnson was pleased to see that the many exercises conducted in England had been worthwhile and the organisation was working efficiently.

Nevertheless, they were in a war zone and close to the front line. Varley warned Johnson that the evening barrage was very unpleasant and occurred just after dark when the *Luftwaffe* would send a few reconnaissance aircraft over, and every AA gun on the beachhead opened up. He rejected Varley's advice that the best place for his bed would be a narrow slit trench, and was later to regret it!

Johnson went to bed early after a long day and to prepare for what he hoped would be a busy and fruitful morrow. His slumbers were soon interrupted by the loud staccato clatter of a Bofors gun 20 yards from his caravan. He also heard the unsynchronised sound (both sides desynchronised their aircraft engines when over the other's territory to confuse sound detection devices that were still in use to augment radar, especially at AA positions) of enemy aircraft engines. On dressing and leaving his caravan, he saw fires to the south and that the *Luftwaffe* were mainly interested in the shipping lying off the coast. The naval AA gunners provided a dense AA fire over the shipping. Deciding that Varley was right he went to find him so that his bed could be moved to a more suitable position, but his batman had wisely gone to earth, taking Sally with him.

He spent the rest of the night in a sleeping bag under the caravan's rear axle, where he would be safe from the shrapnel falling from the skies, but got little sleep as the *Luftwaffe* kept sending the odd aircraft over, and there was no shortage of ammunition for the base's Bofors guns! When dawn broke, he went to the mess tent for a hot drink, wondering how his three squadron commanders were coping, but found them deep asleep in an underground shelter built by the Germans: he decided that he would join them in future!

The pattern of operations was that one of the three squadrons in the wing would be the readiness squadron each morning. The operations table at 83 Group was codenamed 'Kenway', and had the use of a mobile radar station. Once enemy air activity was detected, Kenway would telephone the base operations caravan, which would fire a Very light for the squadron to get airborne. Once airborne, they would receive their instructions from Kenway over the radio. On the first morning, Johnson was with one of his squadrons and its aircraft were divided into two flights, one led by the squadron commander and the other by the wing commander. Sitting in his cramped and uncomfortable cockpit, drowsy from lack of sleep, he was suddenly jerked alert by a red Very light being fired and immediately pressed the starter button. The Merlin roared into life, but his take-off was nearly a disaster as he raced the aircraft down the narrow taxiway and made the right turn onto the steel-planked runway too fast, and his starboard wingtip tilted down at a dangerous angle.

Once in the air, he contacted Kenway, using his call sign of 'Greycap'. They were told to investigate *Luftwaffe* air activity over Caen, but could not be given a height other than that the enemy were below 5,000 feet.

The weather was good with bright sunshine above scattered cloud, which lay between 5,000 and 6,000 feet. Johnson led the squadron below the cloud base and ordered the squadron leader to stay down-sun and as close to the cloud base as possible. Before he could drop down further, Johnson was alerted to a *Luftwaffe* formation heading towards them some 2,000 feet below. All in all there were about a dozen Fw190s and Bf109s, heading towards Caen. As the British formation dived down, the *Luftwaffe* scattered ready to fight, and Johnson noted that they were clearly led by an experienced fighter pilot.

Now twenty-four fighter aircraft twisted and jockeyed for an advantageous position. My number two called up:

'Greycap! Keep turning. There's a 190 behind!'

I kept turning and saw the ugly snout of the 190 over my shoulder. But he couldn't draw a bead on me and soon he was driven off by a Spitfire. I made a mental note to buy my number two a drink back at St Croix.

The enemy leader must have given the order to withdraw, for his aircraft dived towards the ground and set course for the south. Then I spotted four 190s flying in a wide, evenly spaced finger formation, but the starboard aircraft was lagging badly and, in this position, could not be covered by his colleagues.

'Red two. Cover my tail. I'm going to have a crack at the starboard 190.'

'O.K., Greycap. You're clear. Nothing behind.'[2]

By this time, Johnson was low, flying over the Normandy bocage with its high hedgerows, small fields and sunken roads. He started to close the gap between his Spitfire and the Fw190. He moved to one side rather than have a line astern shot and also gained some altitude to avoid high trees and allow himself to concentrate on the attack. His first burst hit the Fw190's engine cowling before the next burst hit the cockpit and the German crashed into the ground just feet beneath his aircraft. By this time, Johnson was over a heavily defended area and, as he climbed steeply away, his aircraft and his wingman found themselves amongst a high volume of light flak.

On returning to St Croix he learned that, in all, three aircraft had been shot down. Had not the Germans spotted them against the white cloud, they might have doubled this score. While this initial engagement had been without loss to the wing, later that day four aircraft were shot down, a complete section failing to return from a scramble. They had flown off late in the evening and in the failing light hadn't realised that the force of

Fw190s they engaged was far superior, so the Germans stayed to fight and shot down all four Spitfires. One of his pilots, Flight Lieutenant Don Walz, baled out as his fuel tanks exploded, but he was eventually helped back to Allied lines by the local people. The other three pilots were killed.

There were compensations. During a period of wet weather with low cloud, the pilots were introduced to the local mayor, who told them that the Germans had left behind a number of cavalry horses. On inspection, these animals proved to be sound and some of them were taken over, with the pilots enjoying the exercise and, on one occasion, Johnson turned up for a meeting with the army liaison officers at 83 Group on horseback, astonishing a cavalry officer!

LIFE IN NORMANDY

Naturally, living in hastily constructed landing strips, the normal comforts of a fixed air base at home were lacking. Unless a former German base was being used, accommodation was temporary, a mixture of caravans and tents, with a large tent used as the officers' mess. Food was cooked in field kitchens, with little provision for storage and preparation, and so everyone lived on tinned compo rations. The diet may have been adequate, but it was monotonous. Commanding a Canadian unit, with many of his personnel unused to the rationing and other supply difficulties with which their British counterparts were so familiar, especially when on leave, Johnson heard many complaints about the lack of fresh meat, milk, fresh bread (as opposed to the hard biscuits issued at meal times) and fruit juice, something that appeared on few British shopping lists at the time.

Salvation seemed to lie in an Avro Anson that arrived daily at St Croix from Tangmere carrying mail and newspapers as well as any spares that were urgently required. Johnson wrote to the landlord at The Unicorn, a public house in Chichester, close to Tangmere, explaining the situation and asking if he could arrange for fresh vegetables and bread, and perhaps meat, as well, which if delivered to Tangmere could be brought over to France in the Anson. Quite how the landlord, Arthur King, managed it we'll never know, but the following day the Anson arrived with a crate of tomatoes, loaves of new bread, fresh lobsters and a supply of stout. Interestingly, Johnson does not explain whether the bread was the much derided wartime utility loaf, which would have hardly have pleased his gourmet Canadians!

This lifeline, even better than expected, was maintained until Johnson's wing left the area close to the beachhead and moved inland, where they could source whatever they needed locally.

Meanwhile, they were visited by a party of journalists who had arrived to see his unit and he invited them to lunch. They were planning to drive to Bayeux, where they had been told a reasonable meal could be found, and no doubt had experienced 'canned hospitality' already, either with the

RAF or the Army. Expecting nothing exciting, they were impressed with the lobster and French wine set before them. Johnson told them of his arrangement with the landlord and a few days later the story appeared in a national newspaper. The landlord of The Unicorn was soon visited by a Customs & Excise official, who explained that he would need an export licence if his activities continued!

This was not the only attempt to improve their living conditions. One Spitfire, modified to carry a 500lb bomb under each wing, was given a further and strictly local modification so that it could carry a small barrel of beer instead.

Nevertheless, this was an aside; they were in France to fight, and that meant either destroying the *Luftwaffe*, often to prevent German formations reaching Allied troops, or attacking ground installations. It was a sign of the changing fortunes of war that the *Luftwaffe* units appeared in small formations, seldom more than twelve aircraft. This meant that many RAF wings no longer operated as a single formation but instead sent aircraft up in squadron strength. Johnson, in particular, was keen to increase his total score, even though he realised that this was a secondary consideration to leading his wing and ensuring that his pilots accounted for as many enemy aircraft as possible. His total at the time, June 1944, stood at twenty-nine aircraft.

As mentioned earlier, large formations were unwieldy and also conspicuous, which allowed the Germans to withdraw rather than fight as the supplies of new aircraft and new pilots began to dwindle. One advantage of sending up a squadron at a time was that Johnson was able to lead a single squadron once or twice a day, and so maintained contact with all his pilots rather than just the squadron commanders.

The weather was excellent on 23 June when Johnson joined one of his squadrons normally led by Squadron Leader Wally MacLeod. There was a lot of broken, fluffy white cumulous cloud at 6,000 feet, covering about half the sky. He took the squadron to just below the cloud base, where it would be safe from being 'jumped' from above. Flying past Alençon he spotted a formation of Fw190s also flying just below the cloud base and heading in the same direction as his squadron. There were just two options open to him. He could fly low and then attack the Fw190s from below, or he could climb and, staying on the same course as the Germans, wait until a gap appeared in the clouds above them and then attack. He chose the latter tactic. Flying above the clouds, he could see a gap about 5 miles ahead.

Fortunately, the German leader maintained his course and as they came to the gap in the clouds, Johnson could see at least twelve Fw190s below. He told Wally, leading blue section, to attack the German aircraft to port, and led red section to starboard in a fast dive on the Fw190s. Just as this happened, the Fw190s turned and passed under blue section. Wally fired and hit one of the Fw190s, which burst into flames, rolled over and dropped vertically out of the sky. The element of surprise was lost, but the Germans were confused by the sudden attack. As the Fw190s milled around, Johnson prepared to shoot at one of them, but before he could even press the firing button, cannon shells tore into the engine cowling and wing root, and the aircraft joined its companion in a dive to the fields below as a Spitfire climbed steeply past Johnson.

Wally had scored a double, shooting down an Fw190 as he dived, and then another as he pulled up and climbed back to rejoin his section. Back at base, after congratulating Wally on fine shooting, they checked his Spitfire to see how many rounds had been fired, and found that each cannon had fired just thirteen rounds out of a total magazine of 120 rounds per cannon.

Later, the *Luftwaffe* began to send over larger formations of as many as fifty aircraft in a complete change of tactics, but it was soon clear that the leaders could not control so many aircraft and the RAF continued to operate a squadron at a time.

UNFIT TO FLY

Initially, there was limited *Luftwaffe* action over Normandy as the Germans still regarded the invasion as a diversion and expected the main thrust to be across the Straits of Dover and into the Pas de Calais. Nevertheless, they soon realised as additional manpower and equipment flowed into Normandy that this was the invasion. Units were hastily assembled and sent to Normandy and the surrounding area. Some of these used a mixture of Bf109s and Fw190s, as aircraft were taken from depleted squadrons.

One of those unable to join them was Heinz Knoke, who had suffered a serious head injury in a fight with a Thunderbolt in late April. He had had to bale out yet again from his burning aircraft and the doctors discovered a fracture at the base of his skull. This was followed by a dangerous brain haemorrhage, and then a complete nervous breakdown so severe that for days he could not speak. On 10 June, hearing that his squadron had been moved to the invasion area, he telephoned the Second Fighter Division and asked to be returned to operational duties. Despite the growing shortage of experienced personnel, a general spoke to him.

'Knoke, your first duty is to get yourself fit,' he was told. 'You are not yet equal to going into the invasion sector. I am not going to let you commit suicide by sending you back on operations just now. You ought to think of your family.'

The general's judgement was confirmed by a medical at a *Luftwaffe* hospital, at which Knoke learned that he was 'totally unfit for flying duties'.

Despite earlier having been offered a place at a psychiatric hospital, which he immediately turned down, Knoke was by this time completely *compos mentis* and was watching the developing military situation with growing concern. He knew that the Russians were almost at Germany's eastern borders and that the troops on the Russian Front had been fighting without respite since the invasion in 1941, and reinforcements intended to strengthen the German resistance had had to be diverted to Normandy.

It was not until August that he returned to flying duties, after being given medical documents stating that he was still not fit for flying, but instead telephoning his division and declaring himself fit.

On 12 August his unit was transferred to Wiesbaden with seventy-four aircraft, but the squadron commander's aircraft caught fire and he was injured baling out, leaving Knoke in temporary command. The next day they were transferred to the Western Front, using a temporary airstrip on a rolled-down cornfield, where an *oberleutnant* was killed when his aircraft crashed into a telephone pole in the dark as they landed. That night, he was given command of the third squadron in the No. 1 Fighter Wing, III/JG 1.

His first operational sortie after his return to flying was on 14 August, when he took off with another pilot as his wingman. Emerging from cloud over Rennes, they found six Thunderbolts, and with his first burst of cannon fire, Knoke saw one of them explode in mid-air. They returned to the cloud and headed back to their base, only dropping below the cloud base once to find a convoy of jeeps with trailers, which both aircraft dived down to strafe. There were two more missions that afternoon, escorting fighter-bombers on strikes against US positions north of Rennes.

Knoke produced his twenty-eighth victory on 15 August, a day during which they flew six missions. This shows the intense pressure the *Luftwaffe* was under. Three or four missions a day would normally be regarded as stretching pilots and ground crew to the limit. The pace was a little easier the next day with just three missions, the first of which was prompted by an attack on the airfield by Spitfires, with the *Luftwaffe* taking off in hot pursuit and Knoke shooting down one of the British aircraft.

The pressure continued on 17 August. A reconnaissance aircraft appeared at 10.00, and an hour later eight fighter-bombers attacked the airfield, destroying one Bf109. Once again the Germans set off in hot pursuit, failing to catch the fighter-bombers, but Knoke managed to shoot down a lone Lightning. Returning from an attack on American tanks later that day, as they were about to land they saw the runway 'erupt in geysers of earth', and Knoke noticed the culprits – twelve Martin Marauder bombers in the sky overhead. Although almost out of fuel, they pursued the bombers and the squadron shot down four of them, one of which was credited to Knoke. Unable to land at their own airfield, they were diverted elsewhere, and then during the night moved again to Marolles, and again the next day to Vailly, east of Soissons. Despite this, on one sortie Knoke shot down another two fighters, in this case, both were Mustangs.

Knoke's optimism had gone by this time, whether because of the realisation that Germany has lost the war or because of not having recovered fully from his earlier wounds and illness, one cannot tell. The pressure did not help, nor did the lack of any mail from his family, although he counted this as a blessing as it stopped him being reminded of them. The oppressive summer heat added to his depression and he felt that 'every day I am dodging the strokes of the scythe . . . Death itself I do not fear; for it is quick . . . It is the awful waiting for the blow, and the uncertainty of when it will fall . . .'

The short summer nights were interrupted by a telephone call at 03.00 every day with orders from the wing headquarters for the day ahead. On 19 August, he was airborne four times, but with no possibility of attacking ground targets as ordered as his unit was always intercepted and heavily outnumbered by Allied fighters well before they reached the target area. Through what Knoke described as luck, on one sortie he shot down three Thunderbolts, but that was also the sortie that cost his squadron five of its aircraft, with their pilots.

In repeated attempts during another day, 27 August, in which six missions were flown in an attempt to stop the Allies crossing the Seine, the squadron lost twelve aircraft and started the following day with just four aircraft serviceable. Another two had badly twisted fuselages and could be flown, but Knoke refused to send any of his men on combat missions in 'such battered old crates'. For this, he was telephoned at 06.00 by the chief staff officer at headquarters, who had learned that the squadron had six aircraft rather than the four reported by Knoke.

'This morning you reported only four aircraft available for operations,' steamed the staff officer. 'I have just learned that you can still fly six. Are you crazy? Do you realise the seriousness of the situation? It is nothing but sabotage; and I am not going to tolerate it. Every one of your aircraft is to fly. That is an order!'

Furious at being reprimanded for the first time since he was a cadet, especially by what he considered to be a chair-borne strategist and a hero of the staff, he decided to take one of the battered aircraft himself and allocate the other to his wingman, a corporal. The squadron was due to take off at 08.00 and rendezvous with the other squadrons of the wing over Soissons, where Knoke was to take command of the entire formation. He had great difficulty getting his aircraft into the air, partly because of its condition and partly because of the soft earth runway, but his wingman, Corporal Doring, attempted to climb too soon, stalled and crashed into trees, being killed instantly. So much for the chief staff officer's orders!

Down to five aircraft, Knoke was then told that the rest of the wing's squadrons could not take off because their airfields were being strafed by Allied fighters. He proceeded to his target area, only to find more than sixty Mustangs and Thunderbolts. He turned off the radio as orders came through. His aircraft unable to climb above 10,000 feet, he realised that this must be its last flight. The ensuing air battle lasted just a few minutes, with another of his aircraft shot down in flames and the pilot unable to escape, then two more followed, although one of the pilots baled out. Knoke and his wingman were all that was left of the squadron, and he determined to sell his life as dearly as possible by ramming one of the American aircraft. Before he could do this, his aircraft, being battered by heavy fire, started to lose speed and he was unable to shake off a Mustang on his tail, but managed a burst of power and a climb and half-roll, which left the Mustang to shoot past him. This reversed the situation and he closed on the Mustang, guns blazing, determined to collide. There was a violent jolt and his starboard wing folded and broke off, he jettisoned the canopy and was thrown out of his seat and then out of his aircraft just as the Mustang and Bf109 exploded in a single ball of flame.

As he drifted down under his parachute, he saw another, that of his wingman. The squadron had been wiped out. A Mustang dived at Knoke, guns blazing and he covered his face with his hands, but the American missed. The same aircraft then turned on his wingman, who suddenly slumped lifeless.

Landing in a clearing, he did not know on which side of the front line he was, and as a precaution took off his rank badges and hid his German Gold Cross in his pocket. He was wearing an American leather flying jacket, a dark blue silk shirt and faded trousers with black walking shoes – hardly standard *Luftwaffe* uniform. His caution was soon rewarded as four French civilians approached, all armed: he had fallen into the arms of the resistance! He had schoolboy French, but on overhearing that they thought the parachutist was an American he decided not to disappoint them.

'Hello, boys!' said Knoke, as calmly as possible as he walked up to them, before asking in school French where he could find his comrades. They told him that an armoured unit with Sherman tanks was not far away, but to be careful as the area was still swarming with Germans. In fact, he had landed in the middle of the fighting. If this was not bad enough, the French resistance group seemed to want to stay with him, and one of them seemed suspicious over Knoke's claim to be American. As they prepared to cross a road with machine-gun fire all around them, Knoke suddenly realised that his 'minder' was convinced that he was German, and made a sudden dash into the forest, as the Frenchman opened fire with his Tommy gun. As he re-loaded, Knoke turned on him and shot him in the head with his service pistol, and then grabbed the re-loaded Tommy gun.

Fortunately for Knoke, shortly afterwards he ran into a German patrol from an armoured unit. He returned to his unit late that night, only to be telephoned shortly afterwards by his wing's commanding officer, telling him of an American breakthrough nearby, and that his squadron was to be evacuated immediately to a landing strip in Belgium.

GERMAN RESISTANCE FALLS APART

The move started on 29 August. There was no question of the pilots flying out in their aircraft – there weren't any left! They joined the ground crews and administrators in a forty-eight-hour struggle to reach Beaumont in Belgium. Attacked by the Allies by day and fighting off the resistance by night, Knoke had ordered brushes to be fitted to the wheels of all his vehicles, which spared them from being punctured by the nails spread across the roads by the Resistance, but could not protect them from the small contact mines. Hardly had they arrived then they were ordered to move on again to Manches, where an airstrip was being constructed by a thousand soldiers and the same number of Belgian labourers. Yet, by 10 September, after being transferred again to the Westerwald, Knoke could only fly with the headquarters flight of the wing, and was still waiting replacement aircraft and pilots to reform his own squadron. At a conference chaired by General Galland, in command of the *Luftwaffe's* fighters, he discovered that there was a possibility that his squadron could be disbanded. Aircraft production was finally being badly disrupted by Allied bombing and the fuel shortage was a serious concern.

The news that Himmler was being given command of all reserve forces dismayed him, but worse still was the discovery that Hitler had ordered the first jet fighters, Me262s, to be used as bombers for 'reprisal', or *Vergeltungswaffe*. *Luftwaffe* officers were even forbidden to discuss the possibility of using jet aircraft on fighter operations. By this time, from 27 July 1944, the RAF had already deployed its Gloster Meteor jet fighters operationally.

It was not until 2 October that Knoke learnt that his squadron was to be transferred to the 8th Fighter Division on the river Danube near Vienna, in Austria, where he would finally receive replacement aircraft and pilots. Over the next five days, he received a steady flow of new pilots, many of them returning after being wounded, others former bomber pilots whose units had been disbanded ... but still no aircraft! Early on 9 October, he was telephoned and ordered to transfer his squadron to Anklam, in the north of Germany, while he had to make his way by road in advance and report to a conference of fighter commanding officers organised by Goering.

Knoke was given thirty-six hours to make the journey, and took a driver and his adjutant. Leaving at 03.00, they loaded the car with cans of petrol as they were uncertain as to whether they could find fuel on the way. That afternoon, after a stop for coffee at an inn in Czechoslovakia, Knoke took a turn at driving. Just half a mile down the road, the car was shaken by an explosion and the steering failed, crashing them into the parapet of a bridge, with his adjutant thrown through the windscreen and breaking a leg. The driver collapsed after getting clear. A second explosion followed before a Volkswagen crashed into their car and then careered in flames down an embankment. Knoke struggled to get out of his car, with his left knee shattered and his right pelvis fractured. The driver of the other car was dead. They had to wait two hours to be rescued by the SS. The two cars had been wrecked by limpet mines attached by the Czech Resistance, doubtless during the coffee break.

They were taken to a *Luftwaffe* hospital in Prague, where Knoke had to insist that the surgeon did not amputate his left leg.

Over the next eight weeks, Knoke's left knee mended well, but his right leg was permanently crippled. In mid-December he noted that it was 2 inches shorter than his left leg. Even at this dire stage of the war for Germany, he was given radium bath treatment and convalescence in a resort in Austria. Keeping in touch with the news, he finally realised that Germany could no longer hope for victory. His regard for Hitler's military genius had already disappeared in the autumn. The only bright spot was that his wife managed to arrange for his transfer to a *Kriegsmarine* hospital near a house that she had managed to find. The transfer was fraught, and he endured several air raids and, unable to run to an air raid shelter, had to lie between the railway tracks. He finally arrived home at midnight on 23 December.

For Knoke, the air war was over. For his comrades, there was a last all-out effort on 1 January 1945, Operation *Bodenplatte* (base plate), when they strafed Allied airfields in France and Belgium, at a heavy cost of 500 *Luftwaffe* pilots killed. This was an act of desperation, with many of the pilots poorly trained and inexperienced, with aircraft crashing often due to navigational errors or because they were so battered that they should not have been in the air at all. Knoke spent the last weeks of the war as air liaison officer for part of the Wilhelmshaven fortifications, which was being defended by more than 40,000 naval personnel, few with land combat experience and without enough weapons to arm all of them. So bad was moral that the naval police (*Chainehunde*) were authorised to seek deserters and shoot or hang them on the spot. The Third Reich was falling apart and many servicemen wanted to be home to protect their families, especially from the rampaging Soviet armies.

Like many Germans at this time, Knoke was convinced that his country should make peace with the Western Powers, as the real enemy was Soviet Russia to the east. Like many Germans, he was also shocked at the revelations about atrocities in the occupied territories, especially in the east, and the genocide in the extermination camps.

Despite all of this, post-war Knoke entered politics and in 1951 was elected to the provincial legislature (*Länder*) of Lower Saxony as a member of the Socialist Reich Party, until that party was declared illegal by the Federal Republic's Supreme Court the following year.

BULGE AND *BODENPLATTE*

German aerial activity during the first half of December 1944 was limited, partly because of the poor weather, and partly because of harbouring resources and building up the *Luftwaffe*'s strength for the planned Operation *Bodenplatte*. The substantial force included some 3,000 German fighters, not all of which would be used against the Allied air forces as 500 would be deployed to the north and south of Germany to cut off crippled bombers heading for Sweden or Switzerland. The majority of the aircraft, around 2,000, would be sent against the USAAF in formations of around 60 aircraft, and be followed by another 500 aircraft. The timing of the operation was dictated by the weather, and the weather in early December was not encouraging for any kind of aerial campaign.

More often known as the 'Battle of the Bulge', the Germans also planned a massive ground attack through the Ardennes, the same area of wooded hills along which they had invaded France in 1940. After the failure of the Arnhem operation, the Allies had concentrated on shortening their lines of communication, taking the Belgian port of Antwerp, although this took from September until late November as, apart from taking the port, it had to be cleared of wrecks and mines. As in May 1940, the Ardennes was lightly defended in December 1944, while the relative lull in combat along the Western Front after Arnhem had enabled the German Army to re-equip and strengthen itself ready for the counteroffensive. Hitler wanted this to be a massive operation to drive a spearhead between the British and American forces and recapture Antwerp, while his generals, Rundstedt, Commander in Chief in the west, and Model, in command of Army Group B, simply wanted to ease the situation at Aachen. Hitler still believed that a negotiated peace could be had with the British and Americans, and saw the Ardennes offensive as buying time in the west while he prepared a counteroffensive in the east.

Operation *Bodenplatte* and the Ardennes offensive became intertwined when Galland, the architect of the air operation, was told to release a large part of his carefully assembled force to assist the ground offensive. Early on the morning of 16 December, three German armies totalling twenty-five divisions overwhelmed six American divisions, although the Americans managed to hold two important road junctions with that at Bastogne held throughout the campaign. Swift reinforcement followed, with British and American divisions fighting until the German advance was halted on 26 December near Dinant, close to the river Meuse. That coincided with improved weather and the Allied air forces were able to join the offensive and start to push the Germans back.

As the weather improved, Galland launched *Bodenplatte* on 1 January 1945, and once again achieved initial success before becoming overwhelmed by superior Allied air power and more experienced pilots, with the Germans losing around 500 pilots.

One of the great questions of the war years would have been what would have happened had it been possible to combine both operations. The poor flying weather would have meant that the ground offensive would have had to be delayed, and, despite the orders to Galland to join the operation, part of the logic for choosing 16 December as the start date was to take advantage of the lack of Allied air cover during bad weather. It seems reasonable to suggest that this would have made little difference other than prolonging the fight for a few more days. In fact, an idea of how poor the German fighter forces had become through the loss of so many experienced pilots was shown during several clashes between the *Luftwaffe* and the American 1st TAF during November, when the Germans were driven off, but suffered further heavy losses.

THE GERMAN JET FIGHTERS

After the debacle and, for the Germans, disappointment of *Bodenplatte*, the German fighter commanders had had enough of political interference and the growing criticism of their operations. Galland was officially suspended, although his successor did not arrive until January 1945. Meanwhile, a deputation of commanders led by Colonel Gunther Lutzow, highly decorated and holder of the Oak Leaves, sought a meeting with Hitler to protest at the defamation of their arm of the *Luftwaffe*. Hitler refused to see them, but the chief of the air staff, General Koller, arranged an audience with Goering.

Lutzow had come prepared with a list of demands. His first was that the authority exercised by the bomber command over the fighters must end. The second was that the Me262 must be reallocated from the bomber role to the fighter. The third was that the commander-in-chief must desist from his attacks on the fighting spirit and the insults to fighter pilots.

'It is mutiny,' screamed Goering. 'I shall have you shot!'

Lutzow wasn't shot but sent into exile in Italy and banned from returning to Germany.

Next, it was Galland's turn. Goering believed, wrongly, that Galland had been behind the delegation and their list of demands. Galland, as General der Jagdflieger, had not been allowed to fly, to his frustration, but he was also at one with Lutzow regarding using the Me262 as a fighter. Finally, on hearing of the row between Goering and the fighter commanders, Hitler yielded, and ordered Galland to lead a new formation of Me262s. As so often with Hitler, when he finally saw reason, it was too late. Goering had no option but to submit to the Führer's decision, but hoped to get his revenge by ordering Galland to take all the 'mutineers' with him. If this was meant as a punishment, Galland did not regard it as such as he was delighted to be in such good company and felt able to show what *Jagdverband* 44 could do with the Me262.

The new unit formed on 10 February 1945 at Brandenburg-Briest, and, after becoming familiar with the Me262, flew off to southern Germany to the bases at Lager Lechfeld and Munchen-Riem. Throughout March and April, as the Third Reich crumbled under the assault from east and west and from the air, *JV 44* was heavily engaged in operations against the USAAF's bombers, with its score soon rising rapidly as the jet fighter proved what it could do. Another unit, *JG 7*, was assigned to central Germany and the north.

As an example of what could be achieved, on 18 March, no less than 1,250 heavy bombers set off for Berlin on what was to be the capital's heaviest raid of the entire war. The weather was poor, but the German fighter controllers managed to assemble no less than thirty-seven Me262s of *JG 7* to confront the USAAF bomber formation, which was protected by fourteen P-51 Mustang fighter groups. For the loss of just two jets, *JG 7* accounted for nineteen definite victories plus two probables, according to German figures, but the USAAF reported the loss of twenty-four bombers and five fighters.

A single night fighter squadron was also formed with the Me262, 10/*NJG 11*. On the night of 30/31 March, *Oberleutnant* Welter shot down four Mosquitoes.

Other successes followed, although by this time the number of Allied aircraft was such that the relatively small band of jet fighters was making the merest dent in their strength. On 4 April, *JG 7* sent forty-nine Me262s against 150 bombers over Nordhausen, accounting for at least ten and possibly as many as fifteen aircraft. The following day, Galland led just five Me262s against a large bomber force that was heavily escorted, accounting for two of the aircraft without loss to his own force.

More was to come. On 7 April, in Operation *Wehrwolf*, the attack was directed not at the bombers but at their fighter escorts. With few losses to *JG 7*, that unit alone accounted for twenty-eight Mustangs. Yet, this achievement paled into insignificance compared with the fact that no less than 183 Bf109s and Fw190s were accounted for that day by the Mustangs, with more than half the German pilots killed.

On 10 April, retribution came. A total of 1,200 USAAF bombers attacked the fighter bases at Burg, Brandenburg-Briest, Oranienburg, Parchim and Rechlin-Larz, at a cost of just 10 bombers to the Me262s, who, unable to return to their bases, were forced to divert with at least one aircraft landing as far away as Prague.

That was the last major action for the Me262. A few isolated actions followed, but fuel, spares and pilots were all running short as the Third Reich collapsed.

Notes

1. 'Johnnie' Johnson, *Wing Leader*, Chatto & Windus, London, 1956.
2. 'Johnnie' Johnson, *Wing Leader*, Chatto & Windus, London, 1956.

Chapter 13

Into the Reich

Despite the experience gained by the Desert Air Force and in Italy, at times it was inevitable that the front line moved forward quicker than new airfields could be found or built. These were respites for the pilots of 2nd TAF, and Johnson's wing, which by this time consisted of no less than four Canadian squadrons, put the time to good use by 'training'. 'Training' meant brushing up on deflection shooting with shotguns, with the exercise officially intended to improve the air fighting skills of the pilots. In practice, finding the Normandy countryside overrun with game as the locals had not been allowed their customary shooting parties during the German occupation, this was a shooting party. On one occasion, they managed to bag fifty brace of grouse, which they had served at dinner a couple of days later accompanied by vintage champagne presented to the wing by a wealthy and grateful Frenchman, who had somehow managed to keep his cellar from the attentions of the Germans.

Nevertheless, by November, the *Luftwaffe* was regaining in strength and confidence, having earlier moved many of its units back to east of the Rhine. As mentioned in the previous chapter, the emphasis was put on fighter and fighter-bomber production at the expense of bombers and even night fighters. The idea was that the 'revenge weapons', such as the V-1 and V-2, would take over from the bombers. This also meant that the fighter squadrons were reinforced by many pilots trained to fly bombers. The irony of this situation was that what promised to be the most effective German fighter of the war, the Me262 jet, was prohibited by Hitler from being used in its intended role and instead forced to operate as a bomber.

Aircraft production in Germany enjoyed a last-minute spurt, almost a case of the light burning brightest before it went out. Apart from the attacks on the ball bearing and synthetic rubber plants, aircraft factories were notoriously hard to destroy as the jigs for building aircraft were light enough to be reassembled quickly. Even so, Albert Speer, in charge of armaments production, must have performed miracles to ensure that the regime lasted as long as it did under attack in the west, in the east and in Italy, and with its allies falling out of the war.

By this time, the 2nd TAF had been reinforced, and the structure of the Air Defence of Great Britain was no longer appropriate, so, on 15 October 1944, Fighter Command was resurrected.

ARNHEM

The revival of the *Luftwaffe* caused much anxiety to 2nd TAF when, on 17 September 1944, British paratroops and glider-borne air-landed troops took part in Operation Market Garden, the attempt to capture the bridge at Arnhem, in the Netherlands. This was an attempt to bridge the Rhine by taking the bridges over the Maas, the Waal and the Neder Rijn. Bad weather delayed the reinforcing airlift the following day, and while some of the paratroops had been landed 8 miles from their objective, there were also far stronger German armoured units than expected in the area. The operation that was meant to shorten the war and enable the Allies to 'leapfrog' closer to Germany was in trouble.

Units of 2nd TAF were moved forward to airfields in Belgium to provide standing air patrols over Arnhem, using Le Culot, a former *Luftwaffe* airfield south of Louvain. Patrols of twelve aircraft, a squadron at a time, were mounted so that there could be continuous cover over the battle zone. The role of the protecting Spitfires was hampered by continued bad weather, with heavy rain and unbroken layers of cloud. On one occasion, a squadron of Spitfires suddenly ran into a large formation of Bf109s, to the surprise of both sides, so that when the RAF squadron leader turned his squadron round to pursue the Germans, they had disappeared into cloud.

During the Arnhem campaign and afterwards, 2nd TAF was criticised for not providing enough close air support. The Spitfires were there to provide air cover, keeping enemy aircraft out of the sky, while close air support was the job of the Hawker Typhoons – fast aircraft usually armed with rockets or bombs, who had to target their weapons close to the British troops but without suffering a friendly fire incident. They not only had to be on the lookout for precise targets and cope with the weather, but their attacks faced intense light flak. They also did not want to be shot down by the troops at Arnhem, but the Normandy landings had been accompanied by a change to Allied aircraft markings, with clear broad black and white stripes painted on the wings and fuselages to prevent mistakes.

The Typhoons usually operated in 'cab ranks' of eight or more aircraft and these peeled off one at a time to attack enemy armour, self-propelled guns or troop carriers, trains and road transport, virtually acting as airborne artillery. Inevitably, there were heavy casualties. The German 88mm gun was especially lethal, indeed better than any Allied anti-aircraft weapon.

Between 17 and 25 September, the Typhoon units flew every day except one. The nearest Typhoon wing to Arnhem was based 40 miles away at Eindhoven, with other wings not much further away.

Nevertheless, on this one occasion there was a breakdown in the close liaison for which 2nd TAF had become famous. Its Commander in Chief, AM Sir Arthur Coningham, was in charge of operations in the field, but Operation Market Garden was being controlled from the other side of the Channel, in England. Little thought seemed to be given to close liaison on the ground and the use of 2nd TAF's fighter-bombers in close support of the Arnhem operation.

The problems started right from the beginning on 17 September, when 2nd TAF's fighters were banned from the Arnhem area because of fears that USAAF and RAF fighters might clash, even though they had already operated together for two years! The same happened during the seven resupply and reinforcement missions. Bad weather added to the un-certainty over the timetable for the resupply and reinforcement missions, and, to make matters worse, the troops at Arnhem were allocated a radio frequency already being used by a powerful British radio station, so vital messages from Arnhem to 2nd TAF were never received.

As the desperate situation over Arnhem became clear, Typhoons were sent on freelance armed reconnaissance missions similar to those that had wreaked such havoc on the Germans around Falaise. Unfortunately, the roads around Arnhem were thickly wooded and so, early in the autumn, the trees still had their leaves, so provided excellent concealment for the German armour closing in on the beleaguered British troops. There were no messages from radio vehicles at Arnhem and no coloured smoke fired from forward positions so that the Typhoons could locate targets.

In the end, just 2,000 of the 10,000 troops landed avoided capture or death.

The lessons were learnt quickly, and later, during the crossing of the Rhine, air cover was controlled by 2nd TAF's C-in-C.

'MISTLETOE'

Possibly one of the most unusual applications of a fighter was the device known as 'Mistletoe'. This was a composite aircraft consisting of a Bf109 bolted to an unmanned Ju88 bomber, loaded with high explosive. The Bf109 pilot took the aircraft as close as possible to the target, aimed it, released the bolts and the Ju88 continued on its own power to the target. This was used against the Allied airfields in Belgium in October 1944 as 2nd TAF continued its advance eastwards. Johnson's Canadian wing was on the receiving end of one of these aircraft, but it exploded causing no casualties.

Mistletoe and the glider bombers first used at Anzio were amongst the first stand-off weapons of warfare, just as the V-1 pre-dated the cruise missile and V-2 the ballistic missile. Examples of German ingenuity, these were available too little and too late to change the course of the war. It is also open to question whether the expenditure of increasingly scarce raw materials in these ways at this stage of the war could be justified.

THE END OF THE LUFTWAFFE

The *Luftwaffe* had been in the war since the invasion of Poland, giving it a couple of days longer than the RAF. It had also in many cases been fighting against air forces with inferior aircraft. There was no *Luftwaffe* equivalent of the Gloster Gladiator, for example; the Germans had learnt that lesson during the Spanish Civil War, which had been an invaluable training ground for the service. There was no *Luftwaffe* equivalent of the Boulton Paul Defiant, whose performance was crippled by its having a pilot and a rear gunner, who proved to be of little use once the German fighter pilots realised what was happening and who could, in any case, easily out-manoeuvre the Defiant.

Many of the *Luftwaffe*'s fighter pilots claimed more than 200 kills, with the lead taken by one Erich Hartmann, who was credited with 336 victories. Apart from the early superiority of the *Luftwaffe*, not least against the Poles and the Russians, both of whom deployed a substantial proportion of obsolete aircraft, one should also remember that in the melee and confusion of fighter warfare, fighter pilots tend to over-claim and sometimes more than one pilot had a hand in dealing with a single enemy aircraft.

By 1945, only a few of the German aces survived, and in part the success of Galland and the two Me262 fighter units was as much due to their having the cream of the surviving pilots as to the superiority of the aircraft. The number of *Luftwaffe* fighters shot down on 1 January and 7 April was due to the inexperience and over-hasty training of the German pilots as the war drew to a close.

One difference between the Allies and the Germans was that the latter had a formal points scheme for their fighter pilots. On the Western Front, shooting down a single-engined fighter earned one point, with two points for a twin-engined bomber and three points for a four-engined bomber. Senior formation leaders were also credited with extra points based on the total score of the pilots they led. At night, double points were awarded. Late in the war, a fighter pilot with twenty points on the Western Front was awarded the Knight's Cross of the Iron Cross, but his comrade on the Eastern Front had to achieve double this number of points to be awarded the same decoration. Many believe, rightly, that this says much about the different tempo of operations on the two fronts, even as the Western Allies pressed closer, but it also says something about the German leadership. There is only so much adulation that a totalitarian state can allow its heroes.

ACROSS THE RHINE – OPERATION VARSITY

All of the accumulated experience gained by the British and the Americans was put into the last major airborne operation of the war, the crossing of the Rhine, codenamed Operation Varsity. The scale of this operation was tremendous, and places in doubt Germany's ability at any time to have crossed the English Channel. The British 6th Airborne Division and the US 17th Airborne Division combined to form the 17th Airborne Corps. There were 1,696 transport aircraft towing 1,348 gliders, enabling 21,680 troops to be carried in a single lift, escorted by more than 1,000 fighter aircraft with another 2,000 to support the ground operations. The assault force approached its dropping and landing zones in broad daylight starting at 10.00 on 24 March, flying in three columns, each nine aircraft wide. It took up to two hours for this massive formation to pass any given point on the ground.

Conducting this type of operation in broad daylight ensured that accidents were kept to a minimum, but naturally exposed the assault force to the defences. No German fighters appeared during the fly-in, but almost 250 troop-carrying aircraft, including gliders, were shot down by AA fire, and half the surviving aircraft were damaged. Despite this, only thirty-five gliders failed to make the landing zone. The paratroops descended amidst a hail of small arms fire.

It was realised in advance that suppressing the AA fire would be important, and 2nd TAF sent its rocket-armed Typhoons on anti-flak patrols. The normal practice was for these units to fly in three sections each of two aircraft, 1,000 yards apart, so that when the AA fire opened up at the leading section, the next pair dived and made a rocket attack. Any guns firing at the second pair were picked off by the third pair. After the attack, the leading pair circled to see if any further action was needed, and then moved on to the next target.

While this was going on, 2nd TAF's Spitfires were engaged in fighter sweeps, mainly looking for *Luftwaffe* aircraft on the ground, but also free to attack any other worthwhile target of opportunity.

The flak-suppression Typhoons were in the air again while Varsity progressed, and, despite their earlier efforts, noted some flak exploding amongst the vulnerable paratroops.

Amongst those whose wings were moved to the first available airfield east of the Rhine was Johnnie Johnson, but without his Canadian squadrons as he was posted to 125 Wing, based at Eindhoven, in the Netherlands, and promoted to group captain. The congratulations on his promotion were overshadowed by a reminder that once the war ended he would revert to a less senior rank, a reminder too that the days of the war in Europe were numbered. As he arrived by road at his new base, he saw one of his squadrons return after the twelve aircraft had shot down seven Fw190s. His new command included two Canadian squadrons, Nos 41 and 130, as well as the Belgian squadron, No. 350. In his new rank, he had his own wing leader, but insisted on having his own Spitfire, the new 14, as he not only wanted to remain proficient but also felt that he needed to fly with the wing at least two or three times a week to boost morale and get to know his men.

A base was available, albeit with a grass strip, on 28 March. The strip, near Wesel, was waterlogged and unsuitable, so instead of moving into German territory for the first time, they were posted to Twente, still in the Netherlands but close to the German border. This was a former *Luftwaffe* base with a hard runway, but this had been bombed several times and, despite the damage being repaired, still seemed unusable, so, instead, Johnson's squadrons used the grass strip next to the runway.

Johnson's first landing was nearly his last, for as he reached the dispersal and one of the ground crew started to undo his safety harness, a Bf109 raced overhead.

> The Hun had seen us, and over the far side of the field began to turn for his strafing run. I tore a fingernail on the Sutton harness. Then I scrambled out of the cockpit with the parachute still strapped on, tumbled down the easy slope of the wing root, fell to the ground and grovelled under the belly of the Spitfire. We could hear the Messerschmitt boring in. What a bloody way to buy it, I thought. After five years and just being made a group captain!
>
> We heard two crumps in quick succession above the noise of the engine, then a large explosion when the Messerschmitt hit the deck. The two of us scrambled to our feet; on the far side of the field a column of dark, oily smoke rose into the calm spring air. The boy and I slapped the dirt from our uniforms and laughed together. I said: 'Fill her up, son. I want to take off in half an hour.'[1]

A jeep appeared and Johnson drove across the airfield to thank the RAF Regiment gun crew who had saved his life, promising them a crate of beer as soon as he could find one. He was puzzled when the young corporal in charge asked him to confirm that they had shot down a Bf109, and suggested that the wreckage was all the confirmation they needed. The corporal explained that no one would believe that they had shot down an enemy aircraft with just two rounds.

His unit remained at Twente for just a few days, partly because the grass strip proved to need constant rolling to remain usable, and of course because of the need to keep up with the advancing front. They were moved to Celle, a former *Luftwaffe* airfield north of Hanover. The airfield had been captured just two days earlier. After they landed, the airfield's Bofors guns opened up as four Fw190s raced across the airfield.

The next fortnight saw much air-to-air combat as the *Luftwaffe* was compressed into an ever tighter area and fewer airfields, mainly east of the Elbe, squeezed between the British and Americans on one side and the Russians on the other. Johnson's squadrons took off before first light every day to catch the *Luftwaffe* as its squadrons got ready, and the last patrol landed using a flare path. They destroyed Stuka dive-bombers on the ground, even found seaplanes on a lake and destroyed those as well. They couldn't catch the jets in the air, but found their base at Lubeck and ensured that they caught them taking off or landing.

Johnson was anxious to lead his squadrons in a flight over Berlin. They flew over roads to the west of the city, packed with refugees, and found the smoke over Berlin so dense that they had to descend to a lower altitude. To the east, fighting continued and they could see the flashes of the guns. He was alerted to a large formation of around fifty or more aircraft and, on asking whether they were German, was told that they were Russian Yak fighters. He ordered his pilots to maintain a tight formation, realising that if they were shot at, he would be for it. Some minutes followed with the Russian formation turning and turning again, while the British formation also turned and tried to draw alongside the Russians. At one stage, Johnson found himself flying a parallel course to the Russian fighter leader, and rocked his wings to show that he had no aggressive intentions, but got no response. The message had got through, however, as soon afterwards the Russian fighter leader led his somewhat ragged formation off to the east.

Not surprisingly, they were forbidden from flying over Berlin again because of the risk of an accidental clash between the Western Allies and the Russians. This was sound advice as Johnson and many others had not realised how tense the situation was on the ground as the wartime alliance began to crumble in the absence of a common foe.

Notes

1. 'Johnnie' Johnson, *Wing Leader*, Chatto & Windus, London, 1956

Chapter 14

What Might Have Been

The entire course of any major war is full of 'what ifs' and 'what might have been'. The Second World War was no exception.

In the late 1930s, decisions were taken by both sides that could have had a profound impact on the outcome of the war. Had not the British persisted with radar and created the Chain Home network, the Battle of Britain would have been more difficult to fight and could well have been lost. Had not the Germans abandoned their heavy bomber programme, the blitz against British cities would have been crippling. As it was, German bombs, seldom more than 2,000lbs, could, and did, penetrate even the deep-level Underground or 'tube' stations. Had they been able to drop the equivalent of the RAF's 4,000lb 'cookie' or 8,000lb 'double cookie', the death toll in Britain's major cities would have been far greater than it was and London's transport system would have been brought to a halt.

When the Germans did finally get a heavy bomber into the air, there were too few and it was too late.

To some extent, the RAF was lucky. It ignored the de Havilland Mosquito at first, when it could have had the aircraft almost a year earlier, with all of its potential as a night fighter and a truly fast light bomber capable of handling the warload of many a so-called medium bomber. It was also luck of a different kind for the RAF and USAAF that Hitler refused to allow the Me262 to operate in its designed role as a fighter. The losses amongst British and American bomber crews in 1944 would have been much higher.

What would have happened had the RAF lost the Battle of Britain?

To look for an answer we need to look at the Battle for Crete. Even before Greece fell, British forces had lost aerial supremacy in the eastern Mediterranean. The RAF and Fleet Air Arm could protect Alexandria and the Suez Canal and lacked the resources to do more. This was why the Germans were able to seize Crete, but the price was high, so high that Hitler refused to sanction any further parachute assaults for some time. Had the defenders not lost most of their communications equipment in the evacuation from Greece, the battle on the island might have turned out differently, despite Axis aerial superiority. Meanwhile, despite having limited air cover from a base in Greece and a large fleet carrier, the Mediterranean Fleet inflicted terrible damage on the invasion *caïques* (Greek fishing vessels used as invasion barges), with further heavy losses for the German assault force.

The point is that the Royal Navy never lost control of the seas in the eastern Mediterranean or the English Channel. Without air cover, the Royal Navy's losses would have been heavy, but the less forgiving seas of the English Channel would have made the planned invasion of England much more difficult than Crete. The Germans did not have landing craft in 1940; no country had them at that time. Instead, they were planning to use barges, which would have been towed and vulnerable.

Winston Churchill recognised this. A month after telling the British public that: 'We shall fight them on the beaches . . .' he sent a message to the Commander in Chief Home Forces saying: 'I find it hard to believe that the South Coast is in serious danger at the present time.'

No matter what Hitler believed, his senior naval officers would have agreed with Churchill's assessment. *Vizeadmiral* Kurt Assmann of the *Kriegsmarine*'s staff once remarked that 'we could not simply swim over.' Expanding on this, he continued to explain that the naval staff 'appreciated that air supremacy alone could not provide permanent security against vastly superior naval forces in the crossing area.'

Looking back with the benefit of hindsight, which always guarantees 20:20 vision, some historians have criticised Dowding for depending too much on air defence and not doing more to put Fighter Command on the offensive, with more sweeps and attacks against *Luftwaffe* bases in France. Yet, he had to husband his resources carefully, especially with regard to the supply of pilots. As we have seen earlier, such attacks were not always successful and did not always justify the losses that were suffered, not only in 1940–1941, but also in 1944–1945, even though, by the end, the aircraft were remarkably better, faster and better armed.

Losing the Battle of Britain would probably have resulted in a stalemate, with those on both sides who believed that a negotiated settlement was possible pressing their case. If this seems hard on such people, one must also recall that the Germans had won every time they had engaged in battle up to the Battle of Britain. This really is the victory that was achieved: the *Luftwaffe* and German military might as whole was no longer invincible, all conquering. Invasion of any part of Great Britain (the Channel Islands are British, but not part of the United Kingdom) would not have happened, but most of Europe would have been under the jackboot.

Without US support, occupied Europe would have remained occupied. At that time, many American politicians believed that that the UK was finished, and even after the Japanese attack on Pearl Harbor, there would have been little incentive for the US to come to Britain's aid. Instead, the war in the Far East would have had priority. That said, of course, one has to remember that Germany declared war on the United States in 1941, not the other way round.

In the UK, a state of siege could have prevailed with a hostile neighbour across the Channel and North Sea, little foreign currency and limited imports of food and fuel, unless, of course, we formally accepted German hegemony over Europe.

The other beneficiary of the Battle of Britain was the Soviet Union. With a negotiated peace in the West, Hitler could have devoted even greater resources to the invasion of Russia. With no pressure to overcome British and Greek resistance in the Balkans, Operation Barbarossa could have started earlier and reached its objectives. There would have been no British and perhaps no US aid for the Russians. No Hurricanes, no jeeps.

Such would have been the consequences of our defeat in the air.

Chronology

1939

January

17 Auxiliary Air Force Reserve established to enable ex-members of the Auxiliary Air Force to serve with AuxAF squadrons in an emergency.

February

17 RAF Reserve Command formed under AM C.L. Courtney.

April

27 RAF roundels on camouflaged surfaces changed to blue and red only.

July

1 Women's Auxiliary Air Force (WAAF) formed.

August

8–10 Last major peacetime British air defence exercise, lasting for three days and involving 1,300 aircraft. Ended with a civilian 'blackout' rehearsal.

26 RAF moved to Readiness State 'D', with aircraft dispersed on their airfields and personnel recalled.

28 WAAF mobilised.

September

1 Royal Proclamation activates the RAF Reserve and AuxAF.

2 First units of the Advanced Air Striking Force (AASF) moved to France, and, by 15 September, ten squadrons based in France.

3 United Kingdom declares war on Germany.

6 'Battle of Barking Creek': Technical fault on Chain Home station at Canewdon led to friendly aircraft being identified as an approaching air raid, while Hurricanes of No. 56 Squadron scrambled were in turn identified as hostile on their return. Further squadrons were scrambled and, in the confusion, a flight of Spitfires from No. 72 Squadron mistook two Hurricanes for Bf109s and shot both down.

9   The Air Component of the BEF starts to deploy to France, with two squadrons of Hurricanes, joined by another two within a week.

10   First awards gazetted with DFCs to Flying Officer A. McPherson, No. 139 Squadron, and Flight Lieutenant K.C. Doran, No. 110 Squadron.

20   Three *Luftwaffe* Bf109s of *Jagdgruppe* 153 attack three Battles of No. 88 Squadron, AASF, shooting two down west of Saarbrucken.

October

8   RAF scores its first enemy 'kill' of the war when one of three Hudsons attacks a Dornier Do18 of *Kurstenfligergruppe* 506, forcing it to land on the water, which was destroyed after its crew abandoned the aircraft.

16   First enemy aircraft shot down over the UK when Ju88 of *Kampfgeschwader* 30 intercepted by Spitfires of No. 602 Squadron, crashing in the Firth of Forth near Crail, in Fife, with the pilot the only survivor. A second aircraft was downed shortly afterwards by No. 603 Squadron.

17   *Luftwaffe* attacks naval base of Scapa Flow, but no casualties.

28   Spitfires of Nos 602 and 603 Squadrons shoot down He111 of *Stab/Kampfgeshwader* 26 near Haddington – the first enemy aircraft to be brought down on the mainland.

30   Hurricane of No. 1 Squadron shoots down Do17O reconnaissance aircraft over France.

November

18   First Spitfire photo-reconnaissance sortie by Flight Lieutenant M.V. Longbottom, flying from Seclin, in France.

December

8   British Air Forces in France (BAFF) formed to co-ordinate all RAF operations in France.

18   'Battle of the Heligoland Bight' and first use of air defence radar by Germany: RAF sends twenty-four Wellingtons of Nos 9, 37, 38 and 149 Squadrons on anti-shipping reconnaissance around Wilhelmshaven, with half shot down by *Luftwaffe* fighters guided by an experimental Freya early warning installation at Wangerooge.

29   Captured Bf109E flown from France to England for evaluation with a Hudson escort.

1940
January

1   RAF introduces coding on IFF to distinguish between commands. VHF R/T installations completed in eight fighter sectors.

February

22 British Army announces details of a scheme to allow army officers to become pilots in the RAF with the intent of filling fifty per cent of the pilot numbers of RAF Army Co-operation Squadrons. All were given temporary RAF commissions while surplus numbers were deployed to Bomber Command.

March

15 Air Ministry works unit landed in France to construct airfields, but the project is abandoned after three months due to the rapid German advance.

16 *Luftwaffe* attacks Scapa Flow, first British civilian casualty.

April

8 Civilian Repair Organisation (CRO) formed for the rapid repair of RAF aircraft to minimise use of RAF engineering resources. CRO repaired 80,666 aircraft before the end of the war.

9 Germany invades Denmark and Norway.
Bomber Command mounts attacks on enemy shipping and airfields.

10 Night Interception Unit formed with six Blenheims at RAF Tangmere, Sussex, to conduct trails using air interception (AI) radar. Later renamed Fighter Interception Unit.

11 Six Wellingtons escorted by a fighter escort of two Blenheims of No. 254 Squadron attack Stavanger Sola airfield. The first of sixteen raids over this airfield.

12 British forces start to land in Norway.
RAF Bomber Command abandons daylight bombing after unsustainable losses over Germany.

24 Eighteen Gladiators of No. 263 Squadron delivered to Norway aboard HMS *Glorious*, and are flown to frozen Lake Lesjaskog to support ground forces. The next day, ten were lost in a German air raid and the remaining aircraft withdrawn to Aandalsnes.

29 Empire Air Training Scheme starts in Canada, Australia and New Zealand.

May

2 Night Interception Committee decides to fit 100 Blenheim fighters with AI equipment as a priority.

10 Germany invades Belgium and the Netherlands in *Fall Gelb* (Operation Yellow).

12 Strike by No. 12 Squadron Battles against Maastricht bridges, leading to posthumous VCs to Flying officer D. Garland and Sergeant T. Gray.

14 German Army breaks through at Sedan.

Seventy-one Battles and Blenheims faced with heavy *Luftwaffe* fighter defences as they attempt to strike at pontoon bridges and troop columns, with forty-one aircraft shot down: a fifty-eight per cent loss rate.

16 ACM Sir Hugh Dowding, C-in-C Fighter Command, expresses concern over plans to reinforce fighters in France, pointing out that it had been determined that defence of the UK required fifty-two squadrons, but he had only thirty-six.

17 Eleven out of twelve Blenheims of No. 82 Squadron attacking a German armoured column shot down by German fighters, with the sole survivor damaged beyond repair.

21 No. 263 Squadron's Gladiators arrive in Norway aboard HMS *Furious* and fly to Bardufoss, near Narvik.

23 First air-to-air combat between Spitfires and Bf109s.

24 First EFTS RAF students commence training near Salisbury, Rhodesia (now Harare, Zimbabwe).

26 Eighteen No. 46 Squadron Hurricanes deployed to Bardufoss aboard HMS *Glorious*.
Operation Dynamo, the evacuation of the BEF and French forces from Dunkirk, begins, with air cover provided by some 200 Hurricanes and Spitfires based in south-east England flying 2,739 sorties.

27 Training Command divided into Flying Training Command and Technical Training Command, while Reserve Command disbanded.

29 No. 264 Defiants claim to have shot down seventeen Bf109s and a Ju87 over Dunkirk in the morning, followed in the afternoon by another eighteen Ju87s and a Ju88.
First fighter operations using VHF radio telephone conducted during air battle over Dunkirk.

June

1 Joint Air Training Plan in South Africa under the van Brookham agreement initiated.

3 No. 71 Wing, AASF, moved to two airfields near Marseilles, ready for Italy to enter the war.

4 Operation Dynamo completed, with 338,226 troops evacuated to the UK. Air-to-air combat costs the RAF 177 aircraft, including 106 fighters, while the *Luftwaffe* lost 132 aircraft.

8 Sinking of HMS *Glorious* with Hurricanes of No. 46 Squadron aboard by the battlecruisers *Scharnhorst* and *Gneisenau*. The 1,207 men lost include forty-one RAF ground crew and eighteen pilots.

10 Italy declares war on the UK and France.

11 Italian *Regia Aeronautica* attacks RAF Hal Far on Malta and the flying boat base at Kalafrana, with the three Sea Gladiators flown by RAF pilots damaging one Italian aircraft.

13 Gladiator of No. 94 Squadron shoots down the first Italian aircraft, an S81 bomber, off Aden.

14 First RAF success in North Africa when a Gladiator of No. 33 Squadron shoots down an Italian CR42 fighter near Bardia.

15 AASF evacuated from France.

16 Night Interception Committee forms a ground radio interception unit to investigate German navigation raids.

18 RAF Hurricane squadrons of the BEF's Air Component ordered back home from France. Operations in Belgium, the Netherlands and France cost the RAF 1,029 aircraft with 1,500 casualties.

21 First two Hurricanes land at RAF Ta Kali in Malta to reinforce the fighter flight, and were joined by a further six the next day, the survivors of twelve that had left the UK.
First RCAF unit, No. 1 Squadron with Canadian-built Hurricanes, arrives to join Fighter Command at RAF Middle Wallop. Later renumbered No. 401 (RCAF) Squadron.

22 First Italian aircraft shot down over Malta by a Sea Gladiator nicknamed *Faith*.

July

10 Battle of Britain starts with the *Kanalkampf* (Channel Battle), with attacks on coastal shipping and south coast ports.
First Czechoslovak squadron, No. 310, formed with Hurricanes at RAF Duxford.

14 Reception area for crated aircraft formed at Takoradi, Gold Coast (now Ghana), so that aircraft can be assembled before being ferried across Africa to Egypt.

16 German War Directive No. 16 issued for the invasion of Great Britain, *Seelowe* (Operation Sealion). The first priority is the reduction of the RAF so that it cannot attack the invasion fleet.

22 First AI night interception Do17 shot down by Blenheim of Fighter Interception Unit off Sussex coast.

August

1 Hitler's War Directive No. 17 specifically orders the *Luftwaffe* to destroy the RAF.

2 Operation Hurry sees twelve Hurricanes flown off HMS *Argus* to form No. 261 Squadron. Over the next twenty-six months, 346 Hurricanes and 396 Spitfires delivered to Malta by aircraft carriers, for the loss of 28 aircraft.

8 Second phase of the Battle of Britain with intense fighting over the English Channel off the Isle of Wight.

12 Battle of Britain reaches its peak with assault on radar sites and coastal fighter bases.
Chain Home radar station at Ventnor, Isle of Wight, damaged.

13 *Adler Tag* (Eagle Day) sees more than 1,500 *Luftwaffe* sorties against Fighter Command, which loses thirteen fighters for forty-seven German aircraft, but another forty-seven RAF fighters destroyed on the ground.

15 *Luftflotte* 5 in Norway and Denmark attacks targets in the north-east of England and in eastern Scotland, but without fighter escorts as Bf109 lacks the range. Heavy losses ensure that there are no further daylight raids against Scotland by the *Luftwaffe*.

16 Fighter Command's only VC is awarded to Flight Lieutenant Eric Brindlay of No. 249 Squadron, who shot down an enemy fighter near Southampton despite his aircraft being on fire and being badly burned.

17 Due to heavy casualties, fighter OTUs cut training period so that pilots join Hurricane and Spitfire squadrons with between ten and twenty hours advanced training.
Pilot Officer Billy Fiske flying with No. 601 Squadron becomes first US casualty when his Hurricane crash-lands in flames after combat over Bognor. He dies the next day.

18 Known as 'The Hardest Day' in the Battle of Britain with both the RAF and *Luftwaffe* suffering their highest losses. Three major attacks launched and three Fighter Command stations badly damaged but remained operational. *Luftwaffe* loses sixty-seven aircraft; the RAF thirty-one fighters.

20 Battle of Britain: Churchill tells the House of Commons that 'Never in the field of human conflict was so much owed by so many to so few.'

24 Battle of Britain changes to third phase with attacks on fighter stations near London, which also suffers a night attack.

September
7/8 Day and night *Luftwaffe* raids on London.

15 Now celebrated as 'Battle of Britain Day', the day when the *Luftwaffe* mounted its heaviest attack against London, with 1,020 sorties over England. Fighter Command mounted 705 sorties and the *Luftwaffe* lost fifty-six aircraft. While the battle lasted for another couple of weeks, the *Luftwaffe* realised that Fighter Command was unbeaten.

17 The first fully-effective radar-equipped aircraft, the Beaufighter, flies its first operational sortie with No. 29 Squadron.

19 First American 'Eagle' fighter squadron, No. 71, formed. Two further squadrons, Nos. 121 and 133 follow.

Takoradi-Khartoum-Egypt ferry route initiated when six Hurricanes flown to Abu Sueir, where they arrive on 26 September. At Takoradi, between 120 and 150 aircraft assembled each month.

October
1 Generally as the opening of the final phase of the Battle of Britain, daylight raids replaced by night attacks.

12 Hitler postpones Operation Sealion.

28 Italian forces based in Albania invade Greece. By late December, the RAF deploys three Blenheim squadrons and Nos 80 and 112 Squadrons equipped with Gladiators, which held their own against Italian aircraft.

31 Battle of Britain finally ended. Since 10 July, 544 RAF pilots and air gunners lost their lives. The *Luftwaffe* lost 1,733 aircraft with another 643 damaged.

November
14/15 *Luftwaffe* attacks Coventry.

19 No. 604 Squadron Beaufighter night fighter scores first AI radar-assisted success, shooting down a Ju88A near Chichester, West Sussex.

No. 80 Squadron Gladiators flying from Trikkala in Greece shoot down nine Italian fighters.

25 'Bomber' Harris appointed Deputy Chief of the Air Staff.

December
1 RAF Army Co-operation Command established.

12 Camouflage schemes standardised for British aircraft. Disruptive pattern of dark green and dark earth for temperate land, and dark slate-grey and dark sea-grey for temperate sea, on upper and side surfaces. Under-surfaces matt black for night-flying aircraft and dark eggshell blue for day-flying aircraft. Photographic reconnaissance aircraft given pink finish.

20 No. 66 Squadron Spitfires flew first 'Rhubarbs', fighter offensive sweeps, around Le Touquet.

1941

January
First mobile ground control interception (GCI) station sited at RAF Sopley, Hampshire. Four more were in position by the end of the month.

24 Secretary of State for Air approved the establishment of the Directorate of Sea Rescue Services, later known as Air Sea Rescue to differentiate itself from the Naval Sea Rescue Service, within Fighter Command.

February

6 Directorate of Sea Rescue Services becomes operational and until the end of the war rescues 5,772 RAF and USAF personnel in UK waters, and another 3,200 abroad, as well as 4,665 soldiers, sailors and merchant seamen.

28 RAF in Greece strengthened by arrival of No. 33 Squadron with Hurricanes, as well as two Blenheim squadrons and a Lysander squadron.

March

11 US Congress authorises the Lend-Lease Programme.

April

1 First edition of *Tee Emm*, aircrew training publication, issued, using the blunder-prone Pilot Officer Prune to show how not to do it!

3 Iraqi revolt led by pro-Axis Raschid Ali, backed by four generals, seizes power in Baghdad.

9 Observer Corps becomes Royal Observer Corps in recognition of its service during the Blitz.

10 WAAF is recognised as part of the armed forces.

24 Evacuation of Greece completed, with the last aircraft being seven Hurricanes withdrawn to Crete. The Greek campaign cost the RAF almost 200 aircraft.

28 US War Department confirms that approval given for six British Flying Training Schools (BFTS) in the US, under RAF control but financed and operated under Lend-Lease Act. Nearly 7,000 RAF pilots graduated under this scheme.

30 Iraqi forces surround RAF Habbaniya, a training station. Reinforcements sent while training aircraft modified as light bombers, giving four light bombing squadrons and a Gladiator fighter flight.
Defiant declared non-operational.

May

'Bomber' Harris headed an RAF delegation to Washington.

4 Iraqi rebellion finally broken and the Regent returned to power.

5 Merchant Ship Fighter Unit (MSFU) formed using Hurricanes and based at Liverpool.

6 Iraqi forces withdraw from area around Habbaniya.

10 ROC post in County Durham tracks unidentified aircraft as it crosses the coast. The aircraft, an Me110, crashes south of Glasgow and its sole occupant, Rudolph Hess, Deputy Führer, is captured.

13 *Luftwaffe* fighters arrive in Iraq to support rebellion, but suffer constant attack by RAF aircraft and provide little support.

15 First British jet-powered flight by Gloster E28/39 at RAF Cranwell lasts seventeen minutes.

19   Last airworthy aircraft on Crete evacuated to Egypt.

20   *Luftwaffe* launches airborne assault on Crete with paratroops and air-landed troops.

21   PRU Spitfire photographs German battleship *Bismarck* at anchor near Bergen, marking the start of the hunt for this ship and her eventual sinking.

31   Armistice signed in Iraq, *Luftwaffe* aircraft withdraw and rebellion ends after all nineteen aircraft deployed to the country destroyed along with transport aircraft.

June

1   Last Allied troops evacuated from Crete, but 226 RAF personnel left behind to become POWs.

7   First 550 RAF students begin flying training in the USA.

8   Start of offensive against Vichy French forces in Syria. Hurricanes of Nos 80 and 208 Squadrons and Tomahawks of No. 3 (RAAF) Squadron supported ground forces, and were joined by Blenheims within a few days.

14   Operation Battleaxe sees Commonwealth forces start to drive Axis forces out of Cyrenaica and relieve the siege of Tobruk, supported by No. 253 Wing Hurricanes, Blenheims and Tomahawks. Offensive fails and highlights need for improved air/ground co-operation.

27   British mission to the Soviet Union arrives in Moscow five days after the start of the German invasion, Operation Barbarossa.

July

8   Operational debut of B-17 when No. 90 Squadron attacks Wilhelmshaven.

13   First operational Mosquito delivered to No. 1 PRU at RAF Benson.

21   No. 331 Squadron formed with Norwegian personnel.

August

2   Desert camouflage introduced for aircraft in the Middle East and North Africa, consisting of a disruptive pattern of dark earth and middle stone.

9   Wing Commander Douglas Bader, leader of the Tangmere Wing, fails to return from a sweep over France. Became a POW.

12   Strong fighter escort as far as the Dutch Coast provided for Blenheims of 2 Group making daylight attack on power stations near Cologne.

21   RAF fighters change camouflage to disruptive pattern of ocean grey and dark green to mark the change from defensive operations over southern England to offensive sweeps over occupied France.

September

1 No. 151 Wing RAF, comprising Nos 81 and 134 Squadrons with Hurricanes, is shipped into Archangel with aircraft dismantled and crated.

11 No. 151 Wing is fully operational with aircraft assembled and air-tested in just ten days, based at Vaenga, near Murmansk. Additional aircraft arrived on 7 September aboard HMS *Argus*. Fighter protection for convoys continues to 10 October, destroying fifteen *Luftwaffe* aircraft, after which Russian pilots converted to the aircraft and these were handed over to the Red Navy's air arm.

October

No. 335 Squadron formed at Aqir, Egypt, with Greek personnel.

9 Air Force Headquarters Western Desert, the HQ for the Desert Air Force, DAF, established at Maaten Bagush, in Libya.

10 The first Greek squadron, No. 335 moved to Libya, equipped with Hurricanes.

November

7 First Free French unit, No. 340 Squadron, formed at RAF Turnhouse, Edinburgh.

10 In London, Churchill maintains that the RAF finally at least equals the *Luftwaffe* in 'size and number, not to mention quality . . .'

13 No. 350 Squadron formed with Belgian personnel at RAF Valley, Anglesey, using Spitfires.

16 Combined Army/Air Force Headquarters established ready for offensives in the Western Desert.

18 Operation Crusader begins as British Empire forces launch an offensive in the Western Desert, with sixteen fighter squadrons operating Hurricanes, Tomahawks and Beaufighters, eight bomber squadrons, and three tactical reconnaissance squadrons with Hurricanes and Bostons.

29 No. 151 Wing personnel return to the UK having converted Russian pilots to their Hurricanes.

December

8 Following Japanese landings in northern Malaya, RAF and RAAF squadrons mount attacks on enemy troop positions and airfields, but suffer heavy losses leaving the RAF badly depleted within twenty-four hours.

10 Brewster Buffalos of No. 453 Squadron scrambled to protect battleship HMS *Prince of Wales* and battle cruiser HMS *Renown* off the east coast of Malaya, but are too late and both ships are sunk.

11 Germany and Italy declare war on the United States.

13 First Mosquito night fighter squadron, No. 157, formed.

23 No. 67 Squadron Buffalos destroy six Japanese bombers and four fighters over Rangoon, but five Buffalos lost.

25 RAF fighters destroy eighteen Japanese bombers and six fighters over Burma, while No. 67 Squadron claims a further twelve aircraft over Rangoon.

1942
January
Washington Conference formulates strategy for an RAF–USAAF bombing campaign against Germany.

3 Fifty-one crated Hurricane fighters and twenty-four pilots arrive in Singapore with advance parties for Nos 17, 135, 136 and 232 Squadrons.

20 Singapore-based Hurricanes shoot down eight out of a force of twenty-seven Japanese bombers.

31 Air Ministry orders formation of three Servicing Commando Units (SCU) ready to occupy advance landing grounds and provide ground support for fighter squadrons.

February
1 Royal Air Force Regiment formed for the defence of airfields.

6 Japanese begin attacks on airfields at Palembang, Sumatra, with the RAF losing thirty Hurricanes over eight days, many of them on the ground on 7 February.

8 Japanese forces land on Singapore and capture RAF Tengah.

10 Singapore's Kallang airfield evacuated and No. 232 Squadron's surviving eight Hurricanes evacuated to Sumatra.

15 Singapore surrenders to Japanese forces.

17 Off Sumatra, six Japanese troopships sunk for the loss of seven British aircraft.

18 RAF aircraft in Sumatra, including eighteen Hurricanes, fall back on Java.

March
3 Surviving Allied aircraft leave Java except for a small force of RAF and Royal Netherlands East Indies Air Force fighters, which remain until 7 March.

7 Malta receives its first Spitfires with fifteen flown off USS *Wasp* to fly 400 miles to RAF Ta Kali, re-equipping No. 249 Squadron.

April
16 Malta awarded the George Cross.

23 Mosquito night fighter patrols begin, initially over East Anglia.

30 Blitz on Malta reaches its height, with forty-four RAF aircraft destroyed on the ground, eighty-two damaged and twenty-two shot down for the loss of forty-five enemy aircraft.

May

1 Racecourse at Gibraltar converted to an airfield and opened as RAF North Front.

9 Operation Bowery has sixty-four Spitfires flown off HMS *Eagle* and USS *Wasp* in the largest of twenty-five reinforcement operations since 2 August 1940. As the first aircraft landed at RAF Ta Kali, fresh pilots were waiting and many were airborne within fifteen minutes to provide cover for the remaining aircraft.

10 *Luftwaffe* mounts further heavy attacks against Malta with sixty-three aircraft lost or damaged to RAF fighters and AA fire.

25 Merchant Ship Fighting Unit (MSFU) scores first 'kill' after a Hurricane is catapulted from the merchant vessel *Empire Morn* on Convoy QP12 from Murmansk, shooting down a Ju88 220 miles east of Jan Mayen Island. The pilot, Flying Officer J.B. Kendall, bales out as he returns to his ship, but his parachute only partially opens and he dies of his injuries.

30 First operational sorties of Typhoon.

June

12 No. 236 Squadron Beaufighter flies at low level along the Champs Elysées in Paris to drop a large French tricolour over the Arc de Triomphe and strafes the Gestapo headquarters.

August

6 Eight Defiants flying in a fixed formation south of Portland use the RAF's first offensive radio counter-measure (RCM) radar jammer, Moonshine, to produce false returns on the enemy's early-warning radar.

17 US 8th Air Force attack on the railway junction at Rouen escorted by No. 11 Group Spitfires.

19 Seventy squadrons including Fighter Command units provide air support for Operation Jubilee, the amphibious operation to take temporary control of the port of Dieppe.

24 Flying a specially converted Spitfire Vc from Alexandria, Flying Officer G.W.H. Reynolds intercepted a Ju86P-2 high altitude reconnaissance aircraft at 42,000 feet and shot it down. He was awarded the DFC.

30 Battle of Alam el Haifa lasts a week but marks the first instance of improved air support for ground forces in the field.

September

29 Three RAF 'Eagle' Squadrons, Nos. 71, 121 and 133, manned by US citizens, transferred to US 8th Air Force at Bushey Hall, forming the First Fighter Group becoming Nos. 334, 335 and 336 Squadrons, equipped with Spitfires.

October

11 *Luftwaffe* resumes attacks on Malta, although in 2,400 sorties only two aircraft destroyed on the ground. In the air, the *Luftwaffe* lost forty-six aircraft and the RAF thirty.

19 Middle East Air Force squadrons mount all-out effort against Axis air and ground forces in the Western Desert to prepare for the British 8th Army to break out of El Alamein, which started on 23 October.

20 *Luftwaffe* attacks on Malta ease as units are transferred to North Africa to support the *Afrika Korps*.

24 Desert Air Force provides support for 8th Army at El Alamein.

25 Four *Luftwaffe* Fw190s attack the RAF Officers' Hospital in the former Palace Hotel, Torquay, killing nineteen patients and nurses, and wounding forty-five, on a 'tip-and-run' raid.

November

6 RAF ground crew complete the assembly of 122 crated Spitfires and Hurricanes at Gibraltar having taken nine days. The aircraft are needed for Operation Torch, the Allied invasion of North Africa.

7 650 aircraft parked at RAF North Front ready for the invasion.

8 Operation Torch begins just after midnight. Eighteen Hurricanes of No. 43 Squadron land at Maison Blanche at 10.00 to be met by Nos 3201 and 3202 Servicing Commando Units, in use for the first time, who refuel the aircraft so that they can undertake standing patrols.

12 No. 243 Wing Hurricanes based at LG 125, behind enemy lines, strafe retreating *Afrika Korps* units, destroying more than 300 vehicles and eleven aircraft on the ground, before withdrawing after four days.

1943
January

21 The Casablanca Directive defines primary objectives of the Allied bomber offensive.

30 RAF Mosquitoes of Nos 105 and 139 Squadrons bomb Berlin in daylight for the first time.

February

18 Mediterranean Air Command formed at Algiers, comprising Middle East Command, North West African Air Forces and RAF Malta.

25 RAF Bomber Command begins 'round-the-clock' bombing of targets in occupied Europe and Germany.

26 School of Air-Sea Rescue formed at RAF Squires Gate, Blackpool.

March

26 Battle of the Mareth Line: major air offensive with medium and light bombers supported by fighter-bombers and Hurricane tank-busters against the German line in southern Tunisia. The enemy was overwhelmed in 2¼ hours after the DAF made 412 sorties, with eleven pilots missing.

April

1 HM King George VI marks the RAF's twenty-fifth anniversary by awarding 'The Standard', a ceremonial flag, to twenty-five squadrons on completion of twenty-five years' unbroken service. Because of the drastic post-First World War cutbacks, the first presentation (to No. 1 Squadron) was not until 20 April 1953.

10 Twenty-four Ju52 transports shot down.

17 Final phase of DAF's air campaign in Tunisia begins.

18 RAF and USAAF fighters intercept eighty escorted Ju52 transports off Cape Bon, Tunisia, either shooting down or forcing down fifty-nine transports.

22 *Luftwaffe* sends the Me323 transports to reinforce troops in Tunisia, but twenty-one shot down as well as ten escorting fighters. Throughout the month, the Allies shot down 432 transports for the loss of thirty-five fighters.

May

1 Beaufighter of No. 600 Squadron, attached to No. 153 Squadron, on pre-dawn patrol south of Sardinia encounters force of Ju52 transports carrying reinforcements to Tunisia. Within ten minutes, five were shot down, for which the pilot and navigator were both awarded the DFM.

13 Axis forces in Tunisia surrender. Since 18 February, North West African Tactical Air Force units conducted 59,000 sorties, destroying 573 Axis aircraft, more than 500 vehicles and twenty-three ships in the heaviest air support for ground forces at the time.

June

1 Army Co-operation Command disbanded on the formation of the Tactical Air Force within Fighter Command.

10 Combined Chiefs of Staff issue the 'Pointblank' directive calling for the destruction of the *Luftwaffe*'s fighter force and aircraft manufacturing plants.

22 Beaufighters of Nos 143 and 236 Squadrons use 3-inch rocket projectiles for the first time, attacking a convoy off the Dutch coast.

24 RAF in India adopts blue-white roundels to avoid confusion with the red roundels on Japanese aircraft.

July

10 Operation Husky, the Allied invasion of Sicily.

13 No. 244 Wing Desert Air Force (Nos 92 and 145 Squadrons RAF and No. 1 Squadron SAAF) arrive at Pachino, Sicily, from Malta.

25 Spitfires of No. 322 Wing, DAF, encounter *Luftwaffe* attempt to reinforce Sicily and shoot down twenty-four Ju52 transports and four Bf109s.

28 *Empire Darwin* and *Empire Tide* steaming north from Gibraltar both launch their MSFU Hurricanes to counter three Fw200 Condors, shooting two down before the pilots baled out successfully to be picked up by the convoy. Both were awarded the DFC.

August

This is the month of the Quebec Conference, codenamed 'Quadrant', at which the Allies agree that the invasion of Normandy will take place in 1944.

September

2 British services adopt the term 'radar' in preference to RDF.

8 Armistice between Italy and the Allies publicly announced.

9 Operation Avalanche, the Allied landings at Salerno, the mainland of Italy.

14 No. 324 Wing Spitfires, FAA Seafires and USAAF Lightnings deployed ashore in Italy to provide land-based air cover over Salerno. 1st Tactical Air Force flies 700 sorties.

28 DAF HQ occupies airfields around Foggia, southern Italy, with operations beginning on 1 October.

October

25 First Typhoon rocket attack by No. 181 Squadron against power station near Caen, France, but three out of six aircraft shot down.

November

Allied Conference in Cairo, codenamed 'Sextant'.

8 Two No. 615 Squadron Spitfires score the aircraft's first kill over Burma when they shoot down a 'Dinah' reconnaissance aircraft over Chittagong.

15 Fighter Command dissolved and its units divided between 2nd Tactical Air Force and the Air Defence of Great Britain.

19/20 First operational use of 'Fido' at Graveley.

December

10 Mediterranean Air Command and North West Africa Air Force merged to form Anglo-American HQ Mediterranean Allied Air Forces.

1944

January

4 As the Germans take control of Italy, an air interdiction campaign begins against the roads and railways to support the Allied landings at Anzio.

22 Operation Shingle, the Allied landings at Anzio.

February

27 In the Mediterranean, priority given to air attacks on Italy.

April

5 Japanese forces completely surround Kohima, leaving the garrison to be supplied by air drops while Hurricane and Vengeance aircraft provide close support until the garrison is relieved on 20 April.

14 RAF Bomber Command and US 8th Air Force placed under Eisenhower's operational direction.

22 No. 352 Squadron formed with Yugoslav personnel at Benina, Libya.

May

10 Preparing for Operation Overlord, the Normandy landings, attacks concentrate on German communications and radar sites, mainly by Spitfires and Typhoons of Nos 83 and 84 Groups.

11 The Gustav line in Italy gives way and fighter-bombers provide ground support for the advancing Allied ground forces.

21 Bombers operating on the 'Transportation Plan' attacking German transport in France and Belgium are joined by fighters and fighter-bombers operating against locomotives and rolling stock, leaving the bombers to concentrate on bridges.

June

1 RAF Balkan Air Force formed to provide support for Yugoslav partisans, with Mustangs and Spitfires destroying 262 railway locomotives in the first month.

6 D-Day. Allied forces land in Normandy in Operation Overlord.

10 No. 124 Wing's Typhoons make a rocket attack on *Panzergruppe* West's HQ at Chateau-la-Caine, south-west of Caen, followed by medium bombers at 12,000 feet. HQ out of action until 28 June, with the chief of staff and many senior officers killed.

12 First V-1 lands in England.

14 A Mosquito VI of No. 605 Squadron destroys the RAF's first V-1.

22 In Burma, siege of Imphal lifted, after 15,000 sorties by RAF transport aircraft and 25,000 sorties by Hurricane and Vengeance aircraft in close support, under air superiority gained by five squadrons of Spitfires.

23 No. 91 Squadron Spitfire destroys V-1 by using its wing to tip up the flying bomb after running out of ammunition.

July

1 RAF reaches its peak personnel strength of 1,185,833, including 174,406 women.

12 First Meteor jet fighter delivered to No. 616 Squadron.

18 2nd Army begins breakout from Normandy beachhead with the heaviest air support given to any army at that time.

27 First operational Meteor sortie by No. 616 Squadron, with an F1 seeking V-1s.

August

4 No. 616 Squadron Meteor uses wing to knock a V-1 off course after its cannons jammed, leaving the V-1 to crash harmlessly near Tonbridge, Kent.

7 'Day of the Typhoon' as seventeen Typhoon squadrons operating from advanced landing grounds attack German column and tanks attempting to cut off US 30th Infantry Division. Relays of Typhoons make 458 sorties, firing 2,088 rockets and dropping 80 tons of bombs. Over the next four days, 2,193 sorties are flown, 9,580 rockets fired and 398 tons of bombs dropped.

14 Operation Dragoon, the invasion of the south of France begins. FAA aircraft and No. 225 Squadron Spitfires provide air cover and tactical reconnaissance.

18 In France, attacks by 2nd TAF reach a peak as German forces attempt to flee east from the Falais pocket.

29 Eighty-seven out of ninety-seven V-1s launched are destroyed, sixty-two by AA fire, nineteen by fighters and two by balloons, with four destroyed by a combination of balloons and guns.

September

1 V-1 launchings from sites of the Pas de Calais end.

4 Central Fighter Establishment at RAF Wittering authorised.

8 First V-2s land on London and Paris.

24 First RAF unit to return to Greece when Araxos airfield is taken is No. 32 Squadron with Spitfires.

27 Wing Commander J.E. 'Johnnie' Johnson, wing leader of No. 27 Spitfire Wing, shoots down Bf109 over Germany, his thirty-fourth confirmed victory plus another seven shared, making him officially the RAF's top-scoring fighter pilot. (It is believed that this score may have been exceeded by Squadron Leader M.T. Prattle of No. 33 Squadron, who shot down 'around fifty' enemy aircraft before losing his life in Greece in April 1941.)

October

1 Fighter Interception Unit and Air Fighting Development Unit absorbed into Central Fighter Establishment.

5   Five Spitfires of No. 401 (RCAF) Squadron combine to shoot down a Me262 near Nijmegen, the first jet fighter to be shot down.

15   Air Defence of Great Britain (ADGB) renamed RAF Fighter Command.

24   Five Typhoon squadrons of No. 146 Wing make precision attack on German 15th Army HQ at Dordrecht at lunchtime. Two generals, seventeen general staff officers and many others killed.

November

28   First jet fighter to succumb to ground fire was an Me262 shot down by Bofors Detachment B.11 of No. 2875 LAA Squadron RAF Regiment at Helmond, Netherlands.

December

16   Germans launch Ardennes offensive under bad weather that makes Allied air attack difficult until weather lifts on 23 December, after which Germans retreat.

29   Flight Lieutenant R.J. Audet flying a Spitfire IX of No. 411 (RCAF) Squadron becomes the first pilot to claim five victories in a single sortie. His first encounter with enemy aircraft meant that he became an ace, shooting down three Fw190s and two Bf109s near Osnabruck.

27   Fighter Leaders School absorbed into Central Fighter Establishment.

1945
January

1   Operation Baseplate (*Bodenplatte*) sees *Luftwaffe* send more than 800 fighters and fighter-bombers in low-level surprise attack on Allied airfields in Belgium and the Netherlands. Despite many attacks being ineffective, 224 Allied aircraft were destroyed, including 144 RAF, with another eighty-four damaged beyond repair. The *Luftwaffe* lost 500 pilots.

7   Except for night fighters and bombers and aircraft in the Far East, British military aircraft revert to red, white and blue roundels.

February

8   Prior to the Allied crossing of the Rhine, 2nd TAF fighter-bombers attack enemy HQ, trains and bridges as well as undertaking reconnaissance.

March

3   Operation Gisella, mounted by the *Luftwaffe* as some 200 night fighters conduct sorties over England to attack returning bombers, shooting down twenty bombers for the loss of three fighters.

21 Mustangs of No. 64 Squadron and 17 Mosquitoes of Nos 21, 464 and 467 Squadrons destroy Gestapo HQ in Copenhagen, but a Mosquito crashes on a school with heavy loss of life.

24 Operation Varsity, the Rhine Crossing, is given heavy support by 2nd TAF.

29 Last V-1 shot down near Sittingbourne. During the V-1 campaign, 3,957 were destroyed, with fighters accounting for 1,847, AA guns 1,866, balloons 232 and 12 the RN.

31 British Commonwealth Air Training Plan comes to an end.

April

24 First operation in mainland Europe by RAF jet aircraft when Meteors of No. 616 Squadron attack Nordholz airfield.

May

7 Germany surrenders, ending the war in Europe.

Bibliography

Ashworth, Chris, *Action Stations: Military Airfields of the South-West*, PSL, Wellingborough, 1983.

Ashworth, Chris, *Action Stations: Military Airfields of the Central South and South-East*, PSL, Wellingborough, 1990.

Barrymore Halpenny, Bruce, *Action Stations: Military Airfields of Lincolnshire and the East Midlands*, PSL, Wellingborough, 1981.

Barrymore Halpenny, Bruce, *Action Stations: Military Airfields of Yorkshire*, PSL, Wellingborough, 1982.

Barrymore Halpenny, Bruce, *Action Stations: Military Airfields of Greater London*, PSL, Wellingborough, 1984.

Bekker, Cajus, *The Luftwaffe War Diaries – The German Air Force in World War II*, Doubleday, New York, 1968.

Boiton, Theo, *Nachtjagd, Night Fighter versus Bomber War over the Third Reich, 1939–1945*, The Crowood Press, Ramsbury, 1997.

Bowyer, Michael J.F., *Action Stations: Military Airfields of East Anglia*, PSL, Wellingborough, 1979.

Bowyer, Michael J.F., *Action Stations: Military Airfields of the Cotswolds and the Central Midlands*, PSL, Wellingborough, 1983.

Bowyer, Michael J.F., *Action Stations: Cambridgeshire*, PSL, Wellingborough, 1987.

Bowyer, Michael J.F., *Action Stations: Oxfordshire*, PSL, Wellingborough, 1988.

Boyle, Andrew, *Trenchard: Man of Vision*, Collins, London, 1962.

Clarke, Ronald, *Rise of the Boffins*, Harrap, London, 1962.

Clarke, Ronald, *Battle for Britain*, Harrap, London 1965.

Collier, Basil, *History of Air Power*, Weidenfeld & Nicolson, London, 1974.

Douglas Hamilton, James, *The Air Battle for Malta*, Mainstream, Edinburgh, 1981.

Halley, James J., *The Squadrons of the Royal Air Force & Commonwealth, 1918–1988*, Air Britain, Tonbridge, 1988.

Johnson, Group Captain 'Johnnie', *Wing Leader*, Chatto & Windus, London, 1956.

Knoke, Heinz, *I Flew for the Fuhrer*, Bell & Hyman, London, 1953.

Lucas, Laddie, *Five Up*, Sidgwick & Jackson, London, 1978.

Piekalkiewicz, Janus, *The Air War: 1939–45*, Blandford, London, 1985.

Pitchfork, Air Cdre Graham, *The Royal Air Force Day by Day*, Sutton, Stroud, 2008.

Price, Alfred, *Battle Over The Reich*, Ian Allan, London, 1973.

Price, Alfred, *Blitz on Britain 1939–1945*, Ian Allan, London, 1977.

Renaut, Michael, *Terror by Night*, Kimber, London, 1982.

Richards, Denis and Saunders, Hilary, *The Royal Air Force 1939–45*, Vols 1–3, HMSO, London, 1974.

Shores, Christopher, *Fighters over Tunisia*, Spearman, London, 1975.

Shores, Christopher, *Malta: The Hurricane Years, 1940–44*, Grub Street, London, 1987.

Shores, Christopher, *Malta: The Spitfire Year, 1942*, Grub Street, London, 1991.

Shores, Christopher and Thomas, Chris, *2nd Tactical Air Force*, Vols 1–3, Classic (reprint), London, 2004.

Smith, David, *Britain's Military Airfields 1939–1945*, PSL, Wellingborough, 1989.

Smith, David, *Action Stations: Military Airfields of Wales and the North-West*, PSL, Wellingborough, 1981.

Smith, David, *Action Stations: Military Airfields of Scotland, the North-East and Northern Ireland*, PSL, Wellingborough, 1989.

Smithies, Edward, *War in the Air*, Viking, London, 1991.

Tams, F.A.B., *A Trenchard 'Brat'*, Pentland Press, Edinburgh, 2000.

Turner, John Frayne, *VCs of the Air*, Harrap, London, 1960.

Winfield, Dr Roland, *The Sky Shall Not Have Them*, Kimber, London, 1976.

Wragg, David, *Malta – The Last Great Siege*, Pen & Sword, Barnsley, 2003;

Wragg, David, *RAF Handbook 1939–1945*, Sutton, Stroud, 2007.

Index

213